2010

ECCE ROMANI III
A LATIN READING PROGRAM

FROM REPUBLIC TO EMPIRE
SECOND EDITION

Longman

Ecce Romani Student Book III
From Republic to Empire, second edition

Longman, 10 Bank Street, White Plains, N.Y. 10606

Associated companies:
Longman Group Ltd., London
Longman Cheshire Pty., Melbourne
Longman Paul Pty., Auckland
Copp Clark Pitman, Toronto

This edition of ECCE ROMANI is based on *Ecce Romani: A Latin Reading Course,* originally prepared by
The Scottish Classics Group © copyright The Scottish Classics Group 1971, 1982, and published in the United
Kingdom by Oliver and Boyd, a division of Longman Group. It is also based on the 1988 North American
edition. This edition has been prepared by American educators and authors
   Ronald B. Palma, Holland Hall School, Tulsa, Oklahoma
   David J. Perry, Rye High School, Rye, New York
   Revision Editor: Gilbert Lawall, University of Massachusetts, Amherst, Massachusetts

Photo and text credits appear on page 215.

Acknowledgments: The authors would like to thank the following individuals for their contributions to the
new edition:
   David J. Perry, for preparing the text on computer and for creating the initial arrangement of the text and
      graphics
   Professor James Ruebel, who assisted with the text of Asconius on pages 43, 45, 47, and 60
   Professor Gilbert Lawall, who improved the presentation of several items and helped make Book III
      consistent with other parts of the ECCE ROMANI program
   Professor Richard A. LaFleur, who helped refine many of the exercises
   Lyn McLean, Executive Editor, for her encouragement and support through all phases of the project
   Barbara Thayer, Project Editor, who helped in many ways, particularly with
      obtaining photographs
   All of the Longman staff who worked so hard to produce this new edition

Executive editor: Lyn McLean
Development editor: Barbara Thayer
Production editor: Janice L. Baillie
Production-editorial and design director: Helen B. Ambrosio
Production assistant: Karen Philippidis
Text design: Creatives NYC, Inc.
Cover design: Circa 86
Cover illustration: Yao Zen Liu
Photo research: Barbara Thayer

ISBN: 0-8013-1203-5 (case)
ISBN: 0-8013-1208-6 (pbk)

4 5 6 7 8 9 10 MV 04 03 02 01 00
9 10 11 12 13 14 MV 04 03 02 01 00 (HC)

CONTENTS

REFERENCE MATERIALS

MAPS AND PLANS

The illustrations in the panels above the table of contents illustrate the main themes of this book.

On pages iii, iv, and v is a relief from the Ara Pacis (see Chapter 63). It shows the procession that took place when construction of the altar was begun in 13 B.C. On page iv, the tall man in the center with his toga drawn over his head is Agrippa, Augustus' lieutenant and son-in-law, followed by his young son Gaius and his wife Julia, daughter of Augustus (in the background with her hand on Gaius' head). The next two are Livia, Augustus' second wife, and her son Tiberius, who became the second emperor of Rome.

Pages vi and vii feature two scenes from the column built by the emperor Trajan, under whom the Empire reached its greatest size, to commemorate his victories over the Dacians (see pages 119–120). The left-hand panel shows the emperor overseeing the construction of a fortified camp, while the right-hand one shows wounded Roman soldiers being cared for.

The typeface used in the large headings in this book is based on the lettering found on the base of Trajan's column. This inscription is considered one of the finest examples of classical Roman lettering.

LITERATURE AND POLITICS
100 B.C.—A.D. 100

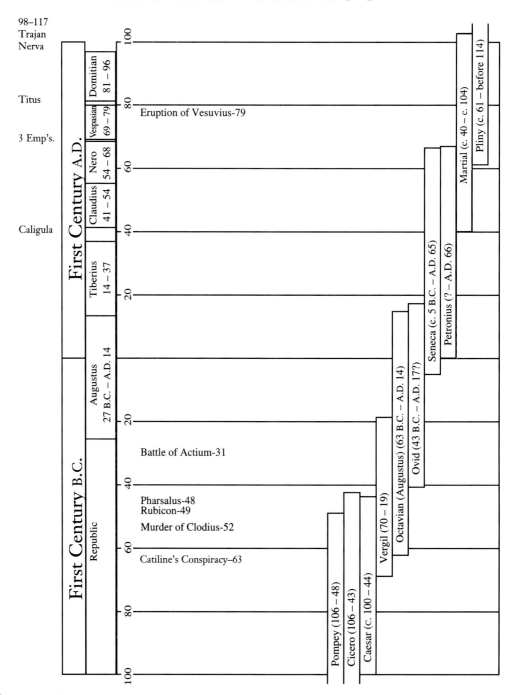

98–117
Trajan
Nerva

Titus

3 Emp's.

Caligula

First Century A.D.

Domitian 81 – 96

Vespasian 69 – 79

Nero 54 – 68

Claudius 41 – 54

Tiberius 14 – 37

Augustus 27 B.C. – A.D. 14

First Century B.C.

Republic

Eruption of Vesuvius-79

Battle of Actium-31

Pharsalus-48
Rubicon-49

Murder of Clodius-52

Catiline's Conspiracy–63

Martial (c. 40 – c. 104)

Pliny (c. 61 – before 114)

Seneca (c. 5 B.C. – A.D. 65)

Petronius (? – A.D. 66)

Octavian (Augustus) (63 B.C. – A.D. 14)

Ovid (43 B.C. – A.D. 17?)

Vergil (70 – 19)

Pompey (106 – 48)

Cicero (106 – 43)

Caesar (c. 100 – 44)

■■■■■ INTRODUCTION ■■■■■

You are about to begin Book III, the final book in the ECCE ROMANI series. This book marks an important point in your study of Latin, for you can now begin to read extensively in the works of ancient Roman authors.

ECCE ROMANI was designed to give you contact with ancient authors from the beginning of the course. In Book I this took the form of extracts in English translation, plus short Latin items such as graffiti and inscriptions. In Book II you read more original Latin, such as short poems of Catullus and Martial. You also read some material that was taken from ancient sources and adapted (that is, changed to use only grammar and vocabulary that you had learned), such as the stories of Pyramus and Thisbe and Androcles and the Lion. In addition, some of you may have used *The Romans Speak for Themselves*, two supplementary readers, which contain adapted selections from a variety of ancient authors. You may also have read the un-adapted extracts from Roman authors such as Ovid, Cicero, Pliny, and Aulus Gellius that appear in Language Activity Book II-B.

As you look back, you can see that you have had more and more contact with ancient authors as you have progressed through ECCE ROMANI. Book III is the culmination of this process; it contains only original Latin readings. Furthermore, the Latin texts in Book III are very close to what the authors originally wrote; the Latin has not been simplified in the way the story of Androcles was, although parts have been left out of some long stories.

In addition to containing only original Latin, Book III also continues your study of Roman history. This book opens with selections from a short account (*Breviarium*) of Roman history by the historian Eutropius, beginning with the year 64 B.C. There follow selections from the writings of Marcus Tullius Cicero and Gaius Julius Caesar, both of whom wrote during the second half of the first century B.C., and of the Emperor Augustus, who wrote an account of his own achievements (*Res gestae*) in A.D. 14. The book concludes with selections from Pliny and Petronius, two authors of the first century A.D.

The format of Book III is different from that of the previous books. Because the readings in this volume are unadapted, many new words occur in them. We have therefore arranged the readings on right-hand pages only, with running vocabulary lists and notes on the facing left-hand pages. Below each reading selection are comprehension questions in English. At the end of the book are charts of forms, a review of syntax, a Latin to English vocabulary, and an index.

The running vocabulary lists contain all words that were not presented in Books I and II. A few words that did occur in Books I and II, but were not used frequently, are printed in the lists with a bullet (•); the bullet is a reminder that you have seen the word before, although not a large number of times. New words that will occur again in this volume are marked with an asterisk (*). Words with bullets and asterisks should be thoroughly learned, since they are normally not given again in the running vocabularies.

In connection with Part I, you will review some important grammatical topics originally presented in Book II. Parts II–V present some additional grammatical material, but there is much less new grammar for you to learn in Book III than in the earlier books; most of your time will be spent reading original texts. We think you will enjoy this book!

PART I
THE END OF THE REPUBLIC AND THE ESTABLISHMENT OF THE PRINCIPATE

The essays on Roman history in Books I and II showed how Rome developed from a small city-state to the head of a vast empire and presented some information about the system of government the Romans used. In order to understand the Latin texts in this book, you need to review and expand your knowledge of these topics.

THE ROMAN POLITICAL SYSTEM

According to tradition, Rome was founded in 753 B.C. by Romulus, who was its first king. Six kings ruled after him; the last one, Tarquinius Superbus, was expelled in 509 B.C. A form of government known as the Republic was then established. Under this government, laws were passed by the Senate; the executive branch was headed by two officials known as consuls, who were elected annually for one-year terms. As time went on, additional offices were created to help the consuls: praetors, who served as judges; aediles, who supervised roads, sewers, water supplies, and food supplies; tribunes, who protected the common people against oppression by the nobility; and quaestors, who handled government finances.

An ambitious young aristocrat would often begin his career by serving as an army officer; he would then return to Rome and run for quaestor, the lowest office. He would advance as far as he could through the sequence of offices (quaestor, tribune, aedile, praetor, and consul), which was known as the **cursus honōrum**. With a combination of ability and luck, he would finally be elected consul. All these offices were for a term of one year, with no reelection.

This form of government worked well enough while Rome was a small state in central Italy. By the mid-second century B.C., however, Rome was a world power with a large empire, and her system of government was no longer adequate. Why did the system fail? It is hard to give a simple answer to this question, but we can say that this failure resulted from two factors, the nature of Roman politics itself and changes in the values of the Roman upper class.

Let us examine the first of these factors, the nature of Roman politics. The Romans did not have political parties in the sense that modern states do; rather, each individual strove to advance himself by acquiring as much prestige (**dignitās**) and influence (**auctōritās**) as he could. The individual achieved this prestige and influence by leading

an army, by being elected to higher and higher offices in the **cursus honōrum**, by becoming a member of the Senate, and by serving the state in other ways, such as governing a province. The individual aristocrat was helped in his quest for **dignitās** by his **amīcī**, people who did favors for him and whom he helped in return, and by his **clientēs**, people of lower social standing who depended on him and who supported him in his political campaigns. Roman politics was—to put it simplistically—the maneuvering by various groups of **amīcī** to advance their own cause. Eventually this maneuvering got out of hand and led to civil war.

The second factor is the value system of the Roman aristocracy. The early Romans had been a stern, almost puritanical people. The wealthy did not flaunt their wealth in luxurious living but rather considered self-sacrificing service to the state the highest activity. As time went on, Rome became a major power and was no longer threatened with destruction from external enemies; at the same time, the upper classes became richer and richer. Although they still kept service to the state as an ideal, in reality they devoted more and more effort to gratifying themselves. In Rome, however, this gratification came not only from wealth, but from prestige. By the first century B.C., some nobles were no longer willing to work within the traditional political system if it denied them the prestige and power they sought. Instead, they used force to seize power. The result was a gradual breakdown in law and order, leading ultimately to a series of civil wars and a reform of the government.

FROM MARIUS TO THE DEATH OF CAESAR

The first civil war sprang from the actions of Gaius Marius. Marius made himself a military dictator and held the consulship seven times between 107 and 86 B.C.; he also introduced the idea of a professional army, with soldiering as a career. This change caused soldiers to shift their allegiance from the state as a whole to their own general, who paid them and saw to it that they were well looked after. Then Cornelius Sulla, acting on behalf of the Senate, killed hundreds of Marius' supporters and reorganized the government so that the Senate would be more firmly in control (83–79 B.C.).

In 63 B.C., an ambitious aristocrat named Catiline, who had run unsuccessfully three times for the consulship, formed a conspiracy to seize control of Rome. He enlisted in his conspiracy both aristocrats who did not want to work through the system and poor people who felt they had nothing to lose. The conspiracy was suppressed by the consul of 63, Marcus Tullius Cicero.

Not long after, the general Gnaeus Pompeius (Pompey) returned victorious from the East. He asked the Senate to make permanent the arrangements he had made for the government of several provinces there and to grant land to his veterans. The Senate refused. Pompey therefore formed a private arrangement with Marcus Crassus, the wealthiest man in Rome, and Julius Caesar, an ambitious man who was not popular with the Senate and therefore stood little chance of becoming consul. This arrangement is known as the First Triumvirate. The three men together were influential enough to secure the election of Caesar as consul for 59. Pompey married Caesar's daughter Julia to strengthen the ties between them. When the Senate continued to balk at fulfilling Pompey's demands, the triumvirs used armed gangs to keep their opponents away from the voting. Milo and Clodius were two leaders of such gangs.

It was customary for ex-consuls and ex-praetors to go out as governors of provinces after their terms were over. Caesar manipulated the system of assignments so that he would receive the province of Gaul (**Gallia**). At this time the Romans controlled only a part of the Alps and the southern coast of France; the rest of France, Switzerland, and Belgium (all of which were included in the area called **Gallia**) were outside the Roman sphere. During his nine years as governor, Caesar conquered all the rest of Gaul; these conquests brought him not only a reputation as a skillful general, but also a large amount of money from the sale of slaves and other booty. He used this money to pay off the huge debts he had incurred while running for consul.

The Triumvirate continued to function while Caesar was in Gaul. In 56 the three men met, renewed their association, and decided that Pompey and Crassus should be consuls for the following year. Crassus became governor of Syria in 54, but he was soon killed in battle against the Parthians. Pompey remained in Rome, where disorder reigned due to the activities of such political hooligans as the rivals Milo and Clodius. The Senate finally gave Pompey extraordinary powers to end the political violence, which he did; Milo's bodyguards had murdered Clodius in January of 52, and Pompey had Milo tried for the murder and exiled. (You will read more about this murder trial in Chapters 58–59.)

Caesar was now approaching the end of his governorship of Gaul. You will read in the Latin texts in Chapter 55 how Caesar became sole ruler of the Roman world and how he died. You will then read how his nephew, Gaius Octavius, took over leadership of Caesar's followers and himself became sole ruler, under the name Augustus, from 27 B.C. onwards.

AUGUSTUS ESTABLISHES THE PRINCIPATE

Augustus recognized that there had to be a fundamental change in the structure of Roman government. Rule by one man seemed the only way to avoid the factional strife that had plagued Rome for the previous hundred years. Augustus set himself up as this one ruler under the title **princeps**, *first citizen*; this form of government is known as the Principate, or the Empire. In Part IV of this book you will read part of Augustus' own account of his principate, the *Res gestae*, and you will look more closely at Augustus and how he managed to make his one-man rule acceptable to the majority of citizens.

Under the Principate, the Senate and the old republican offices (consul, praetor, aedile, and the rest) continued seemingly unchanged, but real power was concentrated in the hands of the **princeps**. Some emperors got along well with the Senate and gave it a large share in the government; others distrusted it and ruled almost entirely through their own agents, who were often freedmen. But, for better or worse, it was under this form of government that the Roman world continued until the last emperor was killed by the advancing barbarians in A.D. 476.

EUTROPIUS THE HISTORIAN

We know very little about Eutropius, the historian whose work appears in Part I. He was born sometime around A.D. 340; he took part in the Persian campaign of the Emperor Julian in 363. He wrote a short handbook of Roman history in ten chapters, entitled *Breviarium ab urbe condita*. It covered Roman history from the foundation of the city by Romulus in 753 B.C. to the death of the Emperor Jovian in A.D. 364, and it was completed by 380. It has been admired since its completion as a straightforward, evenhanded account of Roman history.

Exercise 1

Answer the following questions based on the introduction to Part I:

1. What was the sequence of offices that made up the **cursus honōrum**? How long was each term of office? What were the duties of each office?
2. List as many events as you can (in chronological order) that show that the Roman government was not stable during the first century B.C.
3. Why was the government unstable during this period? Can you think of any similar situations in our own time?
4. How did Augustus try to solve this instability?
5. Historians often identify three periods of Roman history—the Monarchy, the Republic, and the Empire. Give dates for each and briefly describe the form of government in each period.

Exercise 2

By referring to the timeline on page viii, answer the following questions:

1. How old was Vergil when Caesar crossed the Rubicon?
2. How many years did the emperor Augustus live?
3. Who was older, Cicero or Pompey?
4. How old was Octavian when Caesar was assassinated?
5. How old was Pliny when Vesuvius erupted and destroyed Pompeii?
6. What emperor was born in Cicero's consulship?
7. By how many years did Cicero outlive Caesar?
8. What famous poet was born the year Cicero died?
9. When was Petronius born?
10. Who was older, Pliny or Martial? By how many years?
11. How old was Ovid at the time of the battle of Actium?
12. How old was Cicero at the time of Catiline's conspiracy?

1   **M. Tulliō . . . cōnsulibus**: ablative absolute, *during the consulship of M. Tullius Cicero the orator and C. Antonius* (63 B.C.). Since the consuls were elected annually, naming them identified the year. The other way of expressing the year was the **ab urbe conditā** method found in the next clause.

    C. Antōniō: this Gaius Antonius was the uncle of the famous Marc Antony.

  •**cōnsul, cōnsulis**, m., *consul* (one of two "co-presidents" of the Roman Republic).

  •**condō, condere, condidī, conditus**, *to establish, found.*

    ab urbe conditā: *from the founding of the city.* Rome was supposedly founded in 753 B.C.

    sexcentēsimus, -a, -um, *600th.*

2   **octōgēsimus, -a, -um**, *80th.*

  •**nōnus, -a, -um**, *ninth.*

    sexcentēsimō octōgēsimō nōnō: one of the problems with the **ab urbe conditā** system of dating was that not all Roman historians used the same method of calculating when Rome was founded. Eutropius' calculations result in dates that differ by two years from the standard ones (754 – 689 = 65, not 63).

  * **genus, generis**, n., *race, class, family.*

  •**ingenium, -ī**, n., *intelligence, ingenuity, character.*

3   **prāvus, -a, -um**, *depraved, corrupt.* The genitive phrase **ingeniī prāvissimī** goes with **vir**.

    ad dēlendam: *to destroy, for the purpose of destroying.*

  * **patria, -ae**, f., *country, fatherland.*

    coniūrō, -āre, -āvī, -ātūrus, *to plot, make a conspiracy.*

  * **clārus, -a, -um**, *well-known, distinguished.*

4   **urbe**: = **ex urbe**. The preposition is not used because it is already present in the compound verb **expulsus est**.

  * **socius, -ī**, m., *comrade, associate.*

    eius: = **Catilīnae**.

    dēprehendō, dēprehendere, dēprehendī, dēprehēnsus, *to seize, catch.*

  * **carcer, carceris**, m., *prison, cell.*

5   •**vincō, vincere, vīcī, victus**, *to conquer, overcome.*

  * **proelium, -ī**, n., *battle.*

  * **interficiō, interficere, interfēcī, interfectus**, *to kill*

Quō usque tandem abūtēre, Catilīna, patientiā nostrā? *For how long will you abuse our patience, Catiline?* (Cicero, *In Catilinam I.1*).

CHAPTER 55

THE LATE REPUBLIC

A. CICERO AND CAESAR

M. Tulliō Cicerōne ōrātōre et C. Antōniō cōnsulibus, annō ab urbe conditā sex- 1
centēsimō octōgēsimō nōnō, L. Sergius Catilīna, nōbilissimī generis vir, sed ingeniī 2
prāvissimī, ad dēlendam patriam coniūrāvit cum quibusdam clārīs quidem sed audācibus 3
virīs. Ā Cicerōne urbe expulsus est. Sociī eius dēprehēnsī in carcere strangulātī sunt. 4
Ab Antōniō, alterō cōnsule, Catilīna ipse victus proeliō est interfectus. 5

—Eutropius, *Breviarium* VI.15

1. When did these events take place? (1–2)
2. How is Catiline described? (2–3)
3. What kind of people were involved in Catiline's conspiracy? (3–4) The word
   audācibus is often translated as *bold*, but can also have a negative connotation such
   as *reckless*. Which meaning is more appropriate here? Why?
4. How did Cicero deal with the crisis brought on by Catiline? (4)
5. What finally happened to Catiline? (5)

"Cicero and Catiline in the Senate,"
19th century oil painting by Cesare Maccari
Palazzo Madama, Rome

6　**Annō . . . tertiō**: the date of Caesar's consulship is 59 B.C. As in line 2 above, Eutropius' calculations are two years off.

　　nōnāgēsimō: deduce from **octōgēsimō** (2).

7　•**imperō, -āre, -āvī, -ātus**, *to order, rule.*

　　quī posteā imperāvit: i.e., as dictator.

　　L. Bibulō: Eutropius has confused Lucius Bibulus with his father, Marcus Calpurnius Bibulus, who was Caesar's colleague as consul.

　　***dēcernō, dēcernere, dēcrēvī, dēcrētus**, *to decide, assign.*

　　　dēcrēta est: it was customary for a former consul to rule an area of the Empire as governor after his consulship was over.

　　***Gallia, -ae**, f., *Gaul.* Caesar was allotted *Transalpine Gaul* (what is now southeastern France) and *Cisalpine Gaul* (northern Italy.) He extended Roman control over all of Gaul, roughly what is now France, Belgium, and Switzerland.

　　Illyricum, -ī, n., *Illyricum* (modern Bosnia and Croatia; see the map on page 12).

　　***legiō, legiōnis**, f., *legion* (military unit of 3,000–5,000 men).

8　**Helvētiī, -ōrum**, m. pl., *the Helvetians* (a Gallic tribe).

　　***appellō, -āre, -āvī, -ātus**, *to call by name, name.*

　　vincendō: *by conquering.*

9　***usque ad** + acc., *as far as, up to.*

　　Ōceanum Britannicum: the English Channel.

　　•**prōcēdō, prōcēdere, prōcessī, prōcessūrus**, *to step forward, proceed, go.*

　　domō, domāre, domuī, domitus, *to tame, subdue, master.*

10　•**ferē**, adv., *almost, nearly.*

　　flūmen, flūminis, n., *river.*

　　Rhodanus, -ī, m., *the Rhone River.*

　　***Rhēnus, -ī**, m., *the Rhine River.*

11　**(quae) circuitū patet**: *which stretches in circumference*; **omnis Gallia** is the antecedent.

　　bis et triciēs centēna mīlia passuum: *3,200 miles*, literally, 2 (x 100) + 30 (x 100).

　　　mīlia passuum: a Roman mile was 1000 paces, **mīlle passūs**; *miles* is **mīlia passuum**. Notice that **mīlia**, *thousands*, is followed by the genitive.

12　***bellum īnferre**, idiom + dat., *to make war upon.*

　　eōs: = **Britannōs**.

13　***obses, obsidis**, m., *hostage.*

　　obsidibus acceptīs: ablative absolute. Among the tribes of Gaul and Germany, it was customary to exchange hostages to guarantee that a treaty would be observed. If one side broke the treaty, the other side would kill the hostages, who were usually sons of influential citizens.

　　stīpendiārius, -a, -um, *tributary, paying tribute.*

　　Galliae: dative with **imperāvit**, *he levied on Gaul.*

　　tribūtum, -ī, n., *tribute, tax.*

　　annuus, -a, -um, *annual, yearly.*

14　**stīpendium, -ī**, n., deduce from **stīpendiārius**, above.

　　quadringentiēs, adv., *400 times* (400 x 100,000 sesterces = 40,000,000 sesterces).

15　***aggredior, aggredī, aggressus sum**, *to attack.*

　　•**immānis, -is, -e**, *huge, immense, extensive.*

Annō urbis conditae sexcentēsimō nōnāgēsimō tertiō C. Iūlius Caesar, quī posteā imperāvit, cum L. Bibulō cōnsul est factus. Dēcrēta est eī Gallia et Illyricum cum legiōnibus decem. Is prīmus vīcit Helvētiōs, quī nunc Sēquanī appellantur, deinde vincendō per bella gravissima usque ad Ōceanum Britannicum prōcessit. Domuit autem annīs novem ferē omnem Galliam, quae inter Alpēs, flūmen Rhodanum, Rhēnum et Ōceanum est et circuitū patet ad bis et triciēs centēna mīlia passuum. Britannīs mox bellum intulit, quibus ante eum nē nōmen quidem Rōmānōrum cognitum erat, eōsque victōs, obsidibus acceptīs, stīpendiāriōs fēcit. Galliae autem tribūtī nōmine annuum imperāvit stīpendium quadringentiēs. Germānōsque trāns Rhēnum aggressus immānissimīs proeliīs vīcit.

—Eutropius, *Breviarium* VI.17

6. What did Caesar accomplish in the year 59 B.C.? (6)
7. To what area of the Roman Empire was Caesar assigned as governor after his consulship? (7) What did the fact that he was given ten legions imply about this area?
8. On the map on page 17, find the **Helvētiī**. (8) To what modern country is this area equivalent?
9. Describe the region conquered by Caesar during his governorship. (9–11)
10. Describe the relationship between Romans and Britons before Caesar's arrival. (11–12) What happened to the Britons while Caesar was governor of Gaul? (12–13)
11. Describe the financial arrangements Caesar made in Gaul. (13–14)
12. What happened to the Germans who lived across the Rhine? (14–15)

Cicero

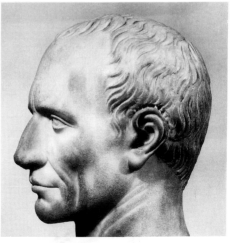

Caesar

1   •**hinc**, adv., *from here; next.*
    ***succēdō, succēdere, successī, successūrus**, *to follow, succeed.*
    exsecrandus, -a, -um, *accursed, detestable.*
    lacrimābilis, -is, -e, *lamentable, terrible.*
    quō: *through which, by means of which*; take with **mūtāta est** (line 2).
    •**praeter**, prep. + acc., *beyond.*
2   ***fortūna, -ae**, f., *fortune, luck.*
    ***mūtō, -āre, -āvī, -ātus**, *to change.* Eutropius means that the Roman state as a whole,
        which had been very successful in fighting foreign enemies, had a run of bad luck when
        its leaders became embroiled in civil war. The **calamitātēs**, deaths of individuals and
        destruction of property, are contrasted with the changed **fortūna** of the whole state.
3   **rediēns**: the present participle of **redīre**.
    ***cōnsulātus, -ūs**, m., *consulship.*
    dubietās, dubietātis, f., *doubt, hesitation.*
4   ***dēferō, dēferre, dētulī, dēlātus**, irreg., *to carry down; offer, confer.*
    Contrādictum est: an impersonal expression, *It was opposed, There was opposition.*
5   **iussusque**: supply **est**, *and he was ordered.* The Senate, at the urging of Pompey and Cato,
    took this vote on 1 January 49 B.C.
    dīmissīs: deduce from **dis-** + **mittō**. It was illegal for Caesar to bring his army out of his
    own province, the southern boundary of which was the Rubicon River.
    ***exercitus, -ūs**, m., *army.*
    ***iniūria, -ae**, f., *injustice, injury.* The "injustice" was from Caesar's point of view; there was
    no reason that Caesar had to be granted a second consulship.
6   **Arīminum, -ī**, n., *Ariminum* (a town near the Rubicon River in northern Italy, modern
    Rimini; see the map on page 12).
    adversum, prep. + acc., *against.*
      adversum . . . vēnit: on 10 January 49, Caesar led his troops across the Rubicon River,
        thereby making civil war inevitable. He spoke the famous words **Ālea iacta est** to
        describe the irrevocable decision he had just made.
7   ***senātus, -ūs**, m., *senate.*
    ***ūniversus, -a, -um**, *all, entire, whole.*
    nōbilitās, nōbilitātis, f., *aristocracy, senatorial class.*
8   **trānseō, trānsīre, trānsiī, trānsitūrus**, irreg., *to go across.*
    •**apud**, prep. + acc., *in, at.*
    Ēpīrus, -ī, m., *Epirus* (a province in northwest Greece).
    Macedonia, -ae, f., *Macedonia* (a province to the north of Greece).
    Achaea, -ae, f., *Achaea* (a province in Greece, on the Gulf of Corinth).
    ***dux, ducis**, m., *leader*
      Pompeiō duce: *under the leadership of Pompey.*
    •**contrā**, prep. + acc., *opposite, facing, against.*

B. CIVIL WAR: CAESAR VS. POMPEY

While Caesar was in Gaul, Pompey remained in Rome, and Crassus was sent in command of an army to fight the Parthians, a warlike people who lived on the eastern border of the Roman world. In 53 B.C., Crassus was killed in battle. His death brought an end to the First Triumvirate and paved the way for a showdown between Caesar and Pompey.

Hinc iam bellum cīvīle successit exsecrandum et lacrimābile, quō praeter ca- 1
lamitātēs, quae in proeliīs accidērunt, etiam populī Rōmānī fortūna mūtāta est. Caesar 2
enim rediēns ex Galliā victor coepit poscere alterum cōnsulātum atque ita, ut sine du- 3
bietāte aliquā eī dēferrētur. Contrādictum est ā Marcellō cōnsule, ā Bibulō, ā Pompeiō, 4
ā Catōne, iussusque dīmissīs exercitibus ad urbem redīre. Propter quam iniūriam ab 5
Arīminō, ubi mīlitēs congregātōs habēbat, adversum patriam cum exercitū vēnit. Cōn- 6
sulēs cum Pompeiō senātusque omnis atque ūniversa nōbilitās ex urbe fūgit et in Grae- 7
ciam trānsiit. Apud Ēpirum, Macedoniam, Achaeam Pompeiō duce senātus contrā 8
Caesarem bellum parāvit. 9

(continued)

1. What did Caesar do as he prepared to leave Gaul? (2–4)
2. Who opposed this action? (4–5)
3. What was Caesar ordered to do? (5)
4. What action did Caesar take in response? (5–6)
5. Who fled to Greece? (7–8)
6. What took place in Epirus, Macedonia, and Achaea? (8–9) Find these provinces on the map, page 12.

Cato the Younger, one of Caesar's staunchest opponents (above: 5)

10   *vacuus, -a, -um, *empty.*

    dictātor, dictātōris, m., *dictator.* The dictator was originally a special official, appointed in emergencies to rule with absolute power for six months.

    Hispānia, -ae, f., *Spain.* The plural is used here because Spain was divided into two provinces.

    *petiit: = petīvit. Eutropius prefers this alternate perfect form of **petere**.

11   **validus, -a, -um**, *healthy, strong, powerful.*

    •**tribus**: ablative of **trēs**.

12   **in Graeciam trānsiit**: in November 49 B.C.

13   *dīmicō, -āre, -āvī, -ātūrus, *to fight, struggle.*

    Prīmō proeliō: when Caesar first landed in Greece, his troops fought with Pompey's near the town of Dyrrachium.

    *fugō, -āre, -āvī, -ātus, *to put to flight.*

    •**ēvādō, ēvādere, ēvāsī, ēvāsus**, *to escape.*

    *quia, conj., *because.*

    interveniō, intervenīre, intervēnī, interventūrus, *to come between, intervene.*

14   **nec**: = **nōn**.

    scīre: *to know how* when followed by an infinitive.

15   **sē**: Caesar. Caesar is saying that only on this particular day of the battle did Pompey have a chance for victory.

Italy and Greece Showing Civil War Sites

Caesar vacuam urbem ingressus dictātōrem sē fēcit. Inde Hispāniās petiit. Ibi Pompeiī exercitūs validissimōs et fortissimōs cum tribus ducibus, L. Afrāniō, M. Petreiō, M. Varrōne, superāvit. Inde regressus in Graeciam trānsiit, adversum Pompeium dīmicāvit. Prīmō proeliō victus est et fugātus, ēvāsit tamen, quia nocte interveniente Pompeius sequī nōluit, dīxitque Caesar nec Pompeium scīre vincere et illō tantum diē sē potuisse superārī.

—Eutropius, *Breviarium* VI.19–20

7. What did Caesar do after he entered Rome? (10)
8. Whose armies did Caesar defeat in Spain? How are these armies described? (10–12)
9. Where did Caesar finally fight against Pompey? (12–13)
10. What was the outcome of the first battle? Why? (13–14)
11. What comment did Caesar make about Pompey? (14–15)

This medieval illustration of Caesar crossing the Rubicon combines elements from the accounts of two Roman writers. The poet Lucan described how, on the night before crossing the Rubicon, Caesar dreamed that the spirit of Rome begged his army to remain on the north bank. According to Suetonius, an unearthly being sat on the riverbank playing a reed pipe while Caesar's army drew near. As the army reached the river, this being seized a trumpet from a soldier, blew a loud blast, and then crossed the river. Interpreting this as a favorable omen, Caesar told his men to follow.

Musée Condé, Chantilly, France

BUILDING THE MEANING
Participles (Review)

A participle is a verbal adjective—that is, an adjective formed from a verb. You have already learned the three Latin participles: present active, perfect passive, and future active. Use the chart on page 186 to review the formation of participles. You will recall that participles can be translated in many different ways, and that the literal translation is not always the best:

> Caesar **rediēns** ex Galliā victor coepit poscere alterum cōnsulātum.
> *Caesar, **returning** victorious from Gaul, began to demand a second consulship.* (literal)
> *Caesar, **who was returning** victorious. . . .*
> *Caesar, **while/as he was returning** victorious. . . .*
> *Caesar, **since he was returning** victorious. . . .*
> *Caesar **returned** victorious from Gaul **and** began to demand. . . .*

As the example above shows, the action of a present participle always takes place at the same time as the action of the main verb. Therefore, **rediēns** is translated as *was returning* or *returned*, because the main verb **coepit** is in a past tense. Conjunctions such as *while* and *as* can only be used for translating present participles.

> Eōs **victōs** stīpendiāriōs fēcit.
> *He made them, **having been conquered**, subject to tribute.*
> *He made them subject to tribute **after/when he had conquered** them.*
> *He made those **whom he had conquered** subject to tribute.*
> *He **conquered** them **and** made them subject to tribute.*

The action of a perfect passive participle always is thought of as having taken place prior to the action of the main verb. Therefore **victōs** is translated by an English pluperfect *had conquered* in the second and third translations above. The conjunction *after* can only be used for translating perfect participles.

The perfect participle of a deponent verb is active in meaning; like the perfect passive participle, it usually describes an action as having taken place before the action of the main verb:

> Caesar vacuam urbem **ingressus** dictātōrem sē fēcit.
> *Caesar, **having entered** the empty city, made himself dictator.*

The action of a future participle is thought of as taking place after the action of the main verb. It can be translated with the words *about to* or *going to* or *intending to*:

> Caesar, contrā Pompeium **pugnātūrus**, cōpiās parāvit.
> *Caesar, **about to fight** against Pompey, prepared his troops.*
> *Caesar, **who was going** to fight against Pompey, . . .*
> *Since Caesar **was intending** to fight against Pompey, he. . . .*

Exercise 55a

Reread Readings A and B and find five perfect participles and one present participle. Tell what word each participle modifies; then translate the sentence containing the participle in at least two ways.

Exercise 55b

Read aloud and translate; give at least two translations for the participles:

1. Catilīna, patriam dēlēre volēns, cum aliīs coniūrāvit.
2. Cōnsul Cicerō Catilīnam reī pūblicae nocitūrum urbe expulit.
3. Catilīna, Rōmā expulsus, ad exercitum suum processit.
4. Multī hominēs Cicerōnem contrā Catilīnam in Forō loquentem audīvērunt.
5. C. Iūlius Caesar in Galliam itūrus mīlitēs cōnscrīpsit.
6. Gallōs prō lībertāte pugnantēs vīcit Caesar.
7. Magnus numerus Gallōrum contrā Caesarem pugnantium occīsus est.
8. Caesar Gallīs victīs tribūtum annuum imperāvit.
9. Etiam Germānōs trāns Rhēnum habitantēs Caesar aggressus est.
10. Pompeius et multī senātōrēs, contrā Caesarem pugnātūrī, in Graeciam trānsiērunt.

> **rēs pūblica, reī pūblicae**, f., *state, government*
> **cōnscrībō, cōnscrībere, cōnscrīpsī, cōnscrīptus**, *to enlist, recruit*
> **Gallī, -ōrum**, m. pl., *the Gauls, people of Gaul*

Ablative Absolute (Review)

Observe the following examples:

1a. **Galliā omnīnō occupātā**, Caesar Rōmam rediit.
   Gaul having been completely conquered, *Caesar returned to Rome.* (literal)
   When Gaul had been completely conquered, *Caesar returned to Rome.*
   When/after he had completely conquered Gaul, *Caesar returned to Rome.*

1b. **Catilīnā contrā rem pūblicam coniūrante**, Cicerō senātum convocāvit.
   Because Catiline was plotting against the government, *Cicero summoned the Senate.*
   ***When Catiline was plotting.* . . .**

2. **Pompeiō duce** senātus bellum contrā Caesarem parāvit.
   With Pompey as leader, *the Senate organized a campaign against Caesar.*
   When Pompey was their leader, *the Senate.* . . .
   Under the leadership of Pompey, *the Senate.* . . .

3. **Caesare superbō**, senātōrēs coniūrāvērunt.
   Caesar being arrogant, *the senators made a conspiracy.*
   Because Caesar was arrogant, *the senators.* . . .

An ablative absolute can consist of a noun plus a participle (examples 1a and 1b), two nouns (example 2), or a noun plus an adjective (example 3); in each case, both words are in the ablative case. In types 2 and 3, supply the verb *to be* in English. It is often best to translate the ablative absolute as a subordinate clause in English. The subordinating conjunctions *when/after, since/because, while, if,* and *although* can be used.

Notice that the rules given on page 14 about the time relationships of participles apply also to ablatives absolute. Thus, in example 1a the perfect passive participle **occupātā** is translated as *had been conquered*, since it expresses time prior to that of the main verb **rediit**. In example 1b, the present participle **coniūrante** is translated as *was plotting*, since it expresses an action going on at the same time as that of the main verb **convocāvit**.

Exercise 55c
Reread Passages 55 A and B and find four ablatives absolute. Decide whether each one is type 1, type 2, or type 3, and translate.

Exercise 55d
Read aloud and translate; give at least two translations for the ablatives absolute:

1. Cicerōne cōnsule, Catilīna victus interfectusque est.
2. Catilīnā mortuō, rēs pūblica tūta esse vidēbātur.
3. Caesare in Galliā bellum gerente, Pompeius Rōmae mānsit.
4. Tōtā Galliā victā, Caesar alterum cōnsulātum cupīvit.
5. Caesare alterum cōnsulātum poscente, bellum cīvīle factum est.
6. Caesar, respōnsō senātūs acceptō, Rōmam cum exercitū profectus est.
7. Caesare in Italiam regressō, senātus ad Graeciam fūgit.
8. Senātōribus cum Pompeiō ad Graeciam fugientibus, Caesar sē dictātōrem fēcit.
9. Senātū absente, Caesar sē dictātōrem fēcit.
10. Exercitū Pompeiī in Hispāniā superātō, Caesar in Graeciam trānsiit.
11. Prīmō proeliō factō, Caesar ēvāsit quod Pompeius nocte sequī nōlēbat.
12. Pompeiō nocte sequī nōlente, Caesar effūgit.
13. Caesare et Pompeiō in Graeciā pugnantibus, cīvēs in urbe nesciēbant quis victor futūrus esset.

bellum gerere, *to wage war*

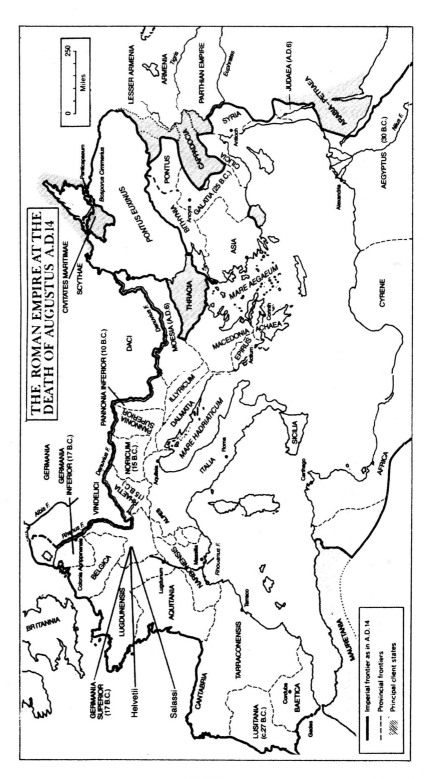

THE ROMAN EMPIRE AT THE DEATH OF AUGUSTUS A.D.14

250

0   Miles

BRITANNIA

GERMANIA

GERMANIA INFERIOR (17 B.C.)

Albis F.

Colonia Agrippinensis

BELGICA

Rhenus F.

GERMANIA SUPERIOR (17 B.C.)

VINDELICI

Helvetii

Salassi

LUGDUNENSIS

Lugdunum

AQUITANIA

NARBONENSIS

Tarraco

CANTABRIA

TARRACONENSIS

LUSITANIA (c.27 B.C.)

Corduba

BAETICA

Gades

Rhodanus F.

Massilia

ALPES

RHAETIA (15 B.C.)

NORICUM (15 B.C.)

Aquileia

PANNONIA SUPERIOR

PANNONIA INFERIOR (10 B.C.)

Danuvius F.

Danuvius F.

DACI

MOESIA (A.D.6)

ILLYRICUM

DALMATIA

MARE HADRIATICUM

ITALIA

Roma

SICILIA

Carthago

AFRICA

MAURETANIA

CIVITATES MARITIMAE

SCYTHAE

Panticapaeum

Bosporus Cimmerius

PONTUS EUXINUS

THRACIA

MARE AEGAEUM

MACEDONIA

EPIRUS

Actium

ACHAEA

Corinth

CYRENE

LESSER ARMENIA

ARMENIA

Tigris

PARTHIAN EMPIRE

Euphrates

JUDAEA (A.D.6)

ARABIA PETRAEA

CAPPADOCIA

PONTUS

BITHYNIA

GALATIA (25 B.C.)

Ancyra

ASIA

SYRIA

Antioch

CILICIA

AEGYPTUS (30 B.C.)

Alexandria

Nilus F.

Imperial frontier as in A.D.14
Provincial frontiers
Principal client states

1   **Thessalia, -ae**, f., *Thessaly* (a province in northern Greece).

    Palaeopharsālus, -ī, m., *Old Pharsalus* (a town in Thessaly, usually referred to simply as Pharsalus; see the map on page 12).

    prōdūcō, prōdūcere, prōdūxī, prōductus, *to lead forward.*

    utrimque, adv., *on both sides.*

    *__cōpia, -ae__, f., *abundance, supply:* pl., *troops.*

    dīmicāvērunt: the battle took place in June of 48 B.C.

2   *__aciēs, aciēī__, f., *line of battle.*

    *__quadrāgintā__, forty

    *__pedes, peditis__, m., *foot soldier, infantryman.*

    *__eques, equitis__, m., *horse soldier, cavalryman.*

3   *__cornū, cornūs__, n., *horn, wing* (of an army).

    sexcentī, -ae, -a, *600.*

    •**quīngentī, -ae, -a**, *500.*

    *__Oriēns, Orientis__, m., *the East.*

    auxilia: here *auxiliary troops,* soldiers recruited from various provinces to assist the Roman legions. In line 11 below it means *reinforcements.*

4   **innumerus, -a, -um**, *uncountable, innumerable.*

    praetōrius, -ī, m., *one holding the rank of praetor, an ex-praetor.*

    *__cōnsulāris, cōnsulāris__, gen. pl., **cōnsulārium**, m., *one holding the rank of consul, an ex-consul.*

5   **nōn integra trīgintā mīlia**: *not a complete 30,000,* i.e., *less than 30,000.*

7   •**adhūc**, adv., *up to this time.*

    in ūnum: = **in ūnum locum.**

    meliōribus ducibus: *with better generals,* an ablative of description.

8   **convēnerant**: deduce from **con- + venīre.**

    *__orbis, orbis__, gen. pl., **orbium**, m., *circle.* **orbis terrārum**: *the world.*

    facile subāctūrae . . . dūcerentur: *(who) would easily subdue the whole world, if they were led. . . .*

9   **Pugnātum . . . est**: an impersonal use of the verb, *It was fought, They fought.*

    contentiō, contentiōnis, f., *strife, struggle.*

    victus: = **victus est.**

    ad postrēmum: *in the end.*

10 **castra, castrōrum**, n. pl., *camp.*

    *__dīripiō, dīripere, dīripuī, dīreptus__, *to plunder, ransack.*

    Alexandria, -ae, f., *Alexandria* (the capital of Egypt, founded by Alexander the Great; see the map on page 17).

    tūtor, tūtōris, m., *guardian, protector.*

11 **datus fuerat**: = **datus erat. cui . . . datus fuerat**: *to whom he had been assigned as a protector.*

    iuvenīlis, -is, -e, *young, youthful.*

    *__aetās, aetātis__, f., *age.* Do not confuse with **aestās**, *summer.*

12 **amīcitia, -ae**, f., *friendship.*

13 **fundō, fundere, fūdī, fūsus**, *to pour out, shower, shed.*

    *__intueor, intuērī, intuitus sum__, *to gaze at, look upon, contemplate.*

    gener, generī, m., *son-in-law.* Pompey was Caesar's son-in-law because he had married Caesar's daughter Julia in 59 B.C. to cement the First Triumvirate.

14 *__quondam__, adv., *once, formerly.*

C. CAESAR VS. POMPEY, CONTINUED

Deinde in Thessaliā apud Palaeopharsālum prōductīs utrimque ingentibus cōpiīs 1
dīmicāvērunt. Pompeiī aciēs habuit quadrāgintā mīlia peditum, equitēs in sinistrō 2
cornū sexcentōs, in dextrō quīngentōs, praetereā tōtīus Orientis auxilia, tōtam nōbili- 3
tātem, innumerōs senātōrēs, praetōriōs, cōnsulārēs et quī magnōrum iam bellōrum vic- 4
tōrēs fuissent. Caesar in aciē suā habuit peditum nōn integra trīgintā mīlia, equitēs 5
mīlle. 6

Numquam adhūc Rōmānae cōpiae in ūnum neque maiōrēs neque meliōribus 7
ducibus convēnerant, tōtum terrārum orbem facile subāctūrae, sī contrā barbarōs dū- 8
cerentur. Pugnātum tum est ingentī contentiōne, victusque ad postrēmum Pompeius et 9
castra eius dīrepta sunt. Ipse fugātus Alexandriam petiit, ut ā rēge Aegyptī, cui tūtor ā 10
senātū datus fuerat propter iuvenīlem eius aetātem, acciperet auxilia. Quī fortūnam ma- 11
gis quam amīcitiam secūtus occīdit Pompeium, caput eius et ānulum Caesarī mīsit. 12
Quō cōnspectō Caesar etiam lacrimās fūdisse dīcitur, tantī virī intuēns caput et generī 13
quondam suī. 14

—Eutropius, *Breviarium* VI.20–21

1. Describe Pompey's army as completely as you can. (1–5)
2. How many foot soldiers and how many cavalry did Caesar have? (5–6)
3. In what way were these armies unique? (7–8)
4. What could they have done if they had fought against foreigners? (8–9)
5. What was the outcome of the battle? (9–10)
6. What was Pompey's relationship with the king of Egypt? (10–11)
7. What did Pompey expect to get in Egypt? (10–11)
8. What did King Ptolemy do? Why? (11–12)
9. How did Caesar react to this event? Why? (13–14)

After defeating Pompey at Pharsalus, Caesar went to Egypt. There he defeated King Ptolemy and installed Ptolemy's younger sister, Cleopatra, as queen. He then consolidated his power over the Roman world by defeating an army led by a group of senators in North Africa (46 B.C.) and by defeating the forces led by Pompey's two sons in Spain (45 B.C.).

1 orbem: = orbem terrārum.
   •compōnō, compōnere, composuī, compositus, *to compose, settle, complete.*
   agere: *to behave, to act.*
   īnsolentius: *rather arrogantly.*
2 *cōnsuētūdō, cōnsuētūdinis, f., *custom, practice.*
   *lībertās, lībertātis, f., *freedom, liberty.*
   *ergō, adv., *therefore.*
   *honor, honōris, m., *honor, mark of honor; position, political office.*
3 *voluntās, voluntātis, f., *will, wish.*
   *praestō, praestāre, praestitī, praestitus, *to bestow.*
   dēferō, dēferre, dētulī, dēlātus, irreg., *to award.*
   adsurgō, adsurgere, adsurrēxī, adsurrēctūrus, *to stand up.*
4 rēgius, -a, -um, *royal, kingly, typical of a king.*
   coniūrātum est: an impersonal use of the verb, *it was conspired, a conspiracy was made.*
   in: *against* (the normal translation when followed by a word referring to a person).
   sexāgintā, *sixty.*
5 *amplius, adv., *more.*
   equitibus: originally this word denoted those who could afford to keep horses and thus serve in the cavalry—citizens of some wealth, though not as wealthy as senators. By the first century B.C., the word came to refer to the wealthy class of businessmen. They could not enter politics, but they exercised considerable influence due to their wealth.
   *praecipuus, -a, -um, *notable, outstanding, remarkable.*
   coniūrātus, -ī, m., *conspirator.*
7 Cūriam: the original Curia had been burned in 52 B.C. by a mob. The Senate actually met in the Theater of Pompey on this occasion.
8 cōnfodiō, cōnfodere, cōnfōdī, cōnfossus, *to stab.*
9 ferē: Caesar was killed on the Ides of March, 44 B.C. Since Rome was supposedly founded on 21 April, 753 B.C., this date was "almost" the 709th year.
   reparāta sunt: deduce from re- + parō.
10 percussor, percussōris, m., *assassin.*
   cōnsul partium Caesaris: *the consul from Caesar's faction.*
11 turbō, -āre, -āvī, -ātus, *to disturb, upset, throw into confusion.*
   *rēs pūblica, reī pūblicae, f., *state, government.*
12 *iūdicō, -āre, -āvī, -ātus, *to judge.*
   missī: = missī sunt. Eutropius often leaves out forms of esse.
   ad eum persequendum: *to pursue him.*
13 annōs decem et octō nātus: *18 years old* (literally, *born for 18 years*).
14 *nepōs, nepōtis, m., *nephew, grandson*; Octavian was actually Caesar's grandnephew.
   ille: = Julius Caesar.
   *testāmentum, -ī, n., *will.*
   hērēs, hērēdis, m., *heir.*
     hērēdem: *as his heir.*
15 *potior, potīrī, potītus sum + abl. or gen., *to get control of, get possession of.*
     rērum potītus (est): *got control of affairs*, i.e., became emperor.
16 ēvenit, ēvenīre, ēvēnit, *it turns out.*
   victōrēs: translate this noun as an adjective, *victorious.*

D. THE DEATH OF CAESAR AND THE RISE OF OCTAVIAN

Inde Caesar bellīs cīvīlibus per tōtum orbem compositīs Rōmam rediit. Agere īnso- 1
lentius coepit et contrā cōnsuētūdinem Rōmānae lībertātis. Cum ergō et honōrēs ex 2
suā voluntāte praestāret, quī ā populō anteā dēferēbantur, nec senātuī ad sē venientī ad- 3
surgeret aliaque rēgia ac paene tyrannica faceret, coniūrātum est in eum ā sexāgintā vel 4
amplius senātōribus equitibusque Rōmānīs. Praecipuī fuērunt inter coniūrātōs duo 5
Brūtī ex eō genere Brūtī, quī prīmus Rōmae cōnsul fuerat et rēgēs expulerat, et C. Cas- 6
sius et Servīlius Casca. Ergō Caesar, cum senātūs diē inter cēterōs vēnisset ad Cūriam, 7
tribus et vīgintī vulneribus cōnfossus est. 8

Annō urbis septingentēsimō ferē ac nōnō interfectō Caesare cīvīlia bella reparāta 9
sunt. Percussōribus enim Caesaris senātus favēbat. Antōnius cōnsul partium Caesaris 10
cīvīlibus bellīs opprimere eōs cōnābātur. Ergō turbātā rē pūblicā multa Antōnius sce- 11
lera committēns ā senātū hostis iūdicātus est. Missī ad eum persequendum duo cōn- 12
sulēs, Pānsa et Hirtius, et Octāviānus adulēscēns annōs decem et octō nātus, Caesaris 13
nepōs, quem ille testāmentō hērēdem relīquerat et nōmen suum ferre iusserat. Hic est, 14
quī posteā Augustus est dictus et rērum potītus. Quī profectī contrā Antōnium trēs 15
ducēs vīcērunt eum. Ēvēnit tamen ut victōrēs cōnsulēs ambō morerentur. Quārē trēs 16
exercitūs ūnī Caesarī Augustō pāruērunt. 17

—Eutropius, *Breviarium* VI.25–VII.1

1. How did Caesar behave after he returned to Rome? (1–2)
2. Give two examples of this behavior. (2–4)
3. How did the senators and knights respond? (4–5)
4. Who was the ancestor of the two Bruti mentioned in this paragraph? (5–6)
5. What happened to Caesar after he entered the Senate meeting? (7–8)
6. In what year did civil war break out again? (9)
7. Whose side was the Senate on? (10)
8. What did Antony want to do? (10–11)
9. Why was Antony condemned by the Senate? (11–12)
10. Who was sent to crush Antony's army? (12–14)
11. Who won the battle? (15–16)
12. How did Octavian come to command three armies? (16–17)

FORMS
Infinitives (Review)

You have learned five infinitive forms. Here are all the infinitives of the verb **vidēre**:

	Active	Passive
Present	**vidēre** *to see*	**vidērī** *to be seen*
Perfect	**vīdisse** *to have seen*	**vīsus esse** *to have been seen*
Future	**vīsūrus esse** *to be about to see*	

The present active infinitive is the second principal part of the verb. The present passive infinitive is usually formed by changing the final -**e** of the present active infinitive to -**ī**. In verbs of the 3rd conjugation, however, you must drop the whole -**ere** ending: **dūcere** becomes **dūcī**, and **cōnspicere** becomes **cōnspicī**. The other infinitives are formed the same way for all verbs (see chart on page 188). The future infinitive of **esse** has two forms: **futūrus esse** or **fore**. Deponent verbs have only three infinitives; the infinitives of **loquor** are **loquī, locūtus esse,** and **locūtūrus esse**. The present and perfect infinitives of deponents follow the regular rule for such verbs—they have a passive form but are translated actively. The future infinitive of deponents has an active form as well as an active meaning.

Exercise 55e
Form all possible infinitives of the following verbs: **dīmicō, cognōscō, dēleō, aggredior, interficiō, audiō, cōnor,** and **sum**.

BUILDING THE MEANING
Indirect Statement (Review)

You have learned that a verb of thinking, saying, or feeling is often followed by a noun in the accusative and verb in the infinitive. This construction is called *indirect statement*:

Caesar est dictātor arrogāns. (direct)
Caesar is an arrogant dictator.

Senātus crēdit **Caesarem esse** dictātōrem arrogantem. (indirect)
The Senate believes (that) **Caesar is** *an arrogant dictator.*

The subject of the direct statement (**Caesar**) becomes accusative, and the verb (**est**) becomes an infinitive. Any word that agrees with the "subject accusative" also becomes accusative (**dictātōrem arrogantem**). The word *that* can be left out of the English translation; it is helpful, however, to include it as a reminder that you are dealing with an indirect statement.

In indirect statement, the present infinitive always shows an action going on at the *same time* as the action of the main verb; the perfect infinitive shows an action completed *prior to* the action of the main verb; and the future infinitive shows an action that will take place *after* the action of the main verb. These rules are similar to the rules about the time relationships of participles given on page 14. Notice how the translation of the indirect statements in the following examples changes when the tense of the main verb changes:

Senātus crēdit Caesarem rēgnāre velle.
The Senate believes that Caesar wants to rule.

Senātus crēdēbat Caesarem rēgnāre velle.
The Senate believed that Caesar wanted to rule.

Cicerō scit coniūrātiōnem fierī.
Cicero knows that a conspiracy is being made.

Cicerō sciēbat coniūrātiōnem fierī.
Cicero knew that a conspiracy was being made.

Nūntius dīcit exercit**ūs** Pompeiī superāt**ōs** esse.
The messenger says that the armies of Pompey have been defeated.

Nūntius dīxit exercit**ūs** Pompeiī superāt**ōs** esse.
The messenger said that the armies of Pompey had been defeated.

Caesar scit senātōr**ēs** sē aggressūr**ōs** esse.
Caesar knows that the senators will attack him.

Caesar sciēbat senātōr**ēs** sē aggressūr**ōs** esse.
Caesar knew that the senators would attack him.

Finally, notice two points:

1. If a perfect passive infinitive or a future infinitive is used, the ending on the participle must agree in gender, number, and case with the subject of the infinitive; the boldface endings in the last two examples show this.
2. The pronoun **sē** in indirect statement refers to the subject of the main verb (see the last example).

Exercise 55f

Read aloud and translate:

1. Caesar alterum cōnsulātum cupiēbat, sed intellēxit Pompeium sē nōn adiūtūrum esse.
2. Caesar sciēbat senātum Pompeiō magis quam sibi favēre.
3. Eutropius dīcit exercitūs apud Pharsālum fuisse maximōs.
4. Cīvēs Rōmānī audīvērunt Pompeium fugātum et castra eius dīrepta esse.
5. Pompeius crēdēbat rēgem Ptolemaeum sibi amīcum fore et auxilia datūrum esse; ergō Alexandriam iit.
6. Cōnstat Caesarem, caput Pompeiī intuentem, lacrimāvisse.
7. Eutropius dīcit Caesarem in Cūriā occīsum esse, sed scīmus rē vērā dictātōrem in theātrō Pompeiī mortuum esse.
8. Dīcitur sexāgintā senātōrēs contrā Caesarem coniūrāvisse.
9. Caesare mortuō, Antōnius nōn crēdēbat adulēscentem Octāvium posse imperāre.
10. Omnēs sciunt Octāvium testāmentō Caesaris adoptātum esse.

Praestat enim nēminī imperāre quam alicui servīre: sine illō enim vīvere honestē licet, cum hōc vīvendī nūlla condiciō est. *For it is better to give orders to no one than to be a slave to anyone: for without the former it is possible to live honorably, with the latter there is no way of living.*

(M. Junius Brutus, fragment of *De dictatura Pompei*)

The coin on the left was issued by Caesar and clearly shows his autocratic position: **CAESAR DICT(ATOR) PERPETVO**, *Caesar, Dictator for Life*, a title he assumed in 45 B.C. The coin on the right was issued by the Republican forces in Greece during the civil war to commemorate Caesar's murder. It shows two daggers and the cap that was awarded to slaves when they were given their freedom; it reads **EID(IBUS) MART(IIS).**

POLITICAL JOKES ABOUT CAESAR

The Romans, like many other people, frequently made fun of their politicians, either because they resented things the politicians had done or because politicians were generally easy targets for jokes. The Roman historian Suetonius, who wrote biographies of the first twelve Caesars (Julius Caesar to Domitian) preserved the following political jokes. Translate them.

1. During his consulship in 59 B.C., Caesar became notorious for his high-handed disregard of his colleague Bibulus (and Bibulus later opposed Caesar's attempts to become sole ruler of Rome; cf. Reading 55B). Remember that the standard way of designating a year was by the names of its consuls; 59 should have been **C. Iūliō Caesare et M. Calpurniō Bibulō cōnsulibus** (ablative absolute), but contemporaries jokingly referred to it as "the consulship of Julius and Caesar." An anonymous humorist expressed the idea thus:

   > Nōn Bibulō quiddam nūper sed Caesare factum est:
   > nam Bibulō fierī cōnsule nīl meminī.

   Nōn . . . quiddam: *not a thing*
   Bibulō . . . Caesare: supply **cōnsule** with each name
   meminī, *I remember*

2. Caesar's policy of admitting many provincials to the Roman Senate was unpopular:

   > Gallōs Caesar in triumphum dūcit—īdem in Cūriam;
   > Gallī brācās dēposuērunt, lātum clāvum sūmpsērunt.

   īdem, *the same (man)*
   brācae, -ārum, f. pl., *trousers* (regarded by Romans as outlandish and effeminate)
   lātum clāvum, the *broad (purple) stripe* of the senatorial toga

3. A mock public "announcement" on the same subject:

   > Bonum factum: nē quis senātōrī novō Cūriam mōnstrāre velit!

   factum, -ī, n., *deed, action*
   Bonum factum: a phrase used at the beginning of official decrees
   Nē quis . . . mōnstrāre velit: *Let no one point out . . . !*

4. These lines are directed against Caesar's arrogant behavior during his dictatorship:

   > Brūtus, quia rēgēs ēiēcit, cōnsul prīmus factus est;
   > Hic, quia cōnsulēs ēiēcit, rēx postrēmō factus est.

   Brūtus: the legendary first consul of Rome, who drove out the Etruscan kings
   ēiēcit: from ē + iacere
   Hic: = **Caesar**

1   *āmittō, āmittere, āmīsī, āmissus, *to lose.*

    cōnfugiō, cōnfugere, cōnfūgī, *to flee for refuge.*

      cōnfūgit ad Lepidum: in Gallia Narbonensis, on the southern coast of Gaul.

    Caesarī: *under Caesar, Caesar's.*

    magister equitum: a Roman dictator appointed a second-in-command who was known as
      magister equitum, *commander of the cavalry,* although he was not limited to that role by
      Caesar's time.

2   *suscipiō, suscipere, suscēpī, susceptus, *to undertake, support, receive* (under one's protection).

3   opera, -ae, f., *work, effort.*

    operam dare, *to pay attention, make efforts.*

    Caesar: this refers to Octavian. Gaius Octavius was Julius Caesar's grandnephew, whom he
      adopted in his will. The young man's name was then changed to Gaius Julius Caesar
      Octavianus, and it was as "Caesar" that he was known. When Eutropius uses **Caesar** in the
      following passages, it usually refers to Octavian (an exception is found in line 8, where it
      refers to Julius Caesar).

    *vindicō, -āre, -āvī, -ātus, *to avenge, get revenge for.*

4   adoptō, -āre, -āvī, -ātus, *to adopt.*

    extorqueō, extorquēre, extorsī, extorsus, *to wrench, wrest, extort.*

5   vīcēsimus, -a, -um, *twentieth.*

    vīcēsimō annō: *in his 20th year.*

    prōscrībō, prōscrībere, prōscrīpsī, prōscrīptus, *to outlaw.* Proscription was a practice in
      which the leaders of the winning side in a civil war would post a list of their enemies from
      the losing side; these men would be killed and their property confiscated.

    cum Antōniō . . . coepit: this is the Second Triumvirate, which lasted from 43 to 33 B.C.

6   Cicerō ōrātor occīsus est: on 7 December 43 B.C.

Julius Caesar
Sard oval intaglio set in gold ring.
Portrait head of Julius Caesar wearing
laurel wreath tied with fillet.
Museum of Fine Arts, Boston

THE FALL OF THE REPUBLIC

A. REPUBLICANS VS. CAESARIANS

Fugātus Antōnius, āmissō exercitū, cōnfūgit ad Lepidum, quī Caesarī magister 1
equitum fuerat et tum mīlitum cōpiās grandēs habēbat, ā quō susceptus est. Mox, 2
Lepidō operam dante, Caesar pācem cum Antōniō fēcit et quasi vindicātūrus patris suī 3
mortem, ā quō per testāmentum fuerat adoptātus, Rōmam cum exercitū profectus ex- 4
torsit ut sibi vīcēsimō annō cōnsulātus darētur. Senātum prōscrīpsit, cum Antōniō ac 5
Lepidō rem pūblicam armīs tenēre coepit. Per hōs etiam Cicerō ōrātor occīsus est 6
multīque aliī nōbilēs. 7

(continued)

1. To whom did Antony flee? (1) Describe this man's position. (1–2)
2. How did Octavian make peace with Antony? (2–3)
3. What unusual privilege did Octavian extort from the Senate? (4–5) Why did he ask for this? (3–4)
4. Name the members of the Second Triumvirate. (5–6)
5. Who was killed during the proscriptions? (6–7)

Mark Antony

8   **interfector, interfectōris**, m., *killer, murderer.*

9   **Macedonia, -ae**, f., *Macedonia* (a province to the north of Greece).

10   **remānserat**: deduce from **re- + manēre**.
    ad dēfendendam Italiam: *to defend Italy.*

11   **Philippī, Philippōrum**, m. pl., *Philippi* (a town). The battle of Philippi took place in 42 B.C.

12   **pereō, perīre, periī, peritūrus**, irreg., *to die, perish.*

13   **secundō**: = **secundō proeliō**.
    cum illīs: = **cum Brūtō et Cassiō**.
    bellum gerere, idiom, *to wage war.*

14   **interfēcērunt**: the subject is *they*, Octavian and Antony.
    dīvidō, dīvidere, dīvīsī, dīvīsus, *to divide.*

15   **Asia, -ae**, f., *Asia* (a Roman province containing what is now the southwestern part of Turkey).
    Pontus, -ī, m., *Pontus* (a Roman province containing the northeastern part of Turkey, along the Black Sea).
    L. Antōnius: the younger brother of Marc Antony. He opposed Octavian's distribution of land to soldiers, presumably to weaken Octavian's position while strengthening that of his brother.

16   •**commoveō, commovēre, commōvī, commōtus**, *to stir up, start.*

17   **Perusia, -ae**, f., *Perusia* (a town, modern Perugia, north of Rome).
    Tuscia, -ae, f., *Etruria* (the part of Italy north of Rome).
    cīvitās, cīvitātis, f., *citizenship; state, government; city* (in this context).
    victus et captus est: in 40 B.C.

This coin, issued in 39 B.C., celebrates the reconciliation of Octavian and Antony. It shows Antony on one side and on the reverse Octavia, Octavian's sister, whom Antony married to cement the alliance between the two men. He later divorced her and married Cleopatra (cf. B:5–6, page 31).

Intereā Brūtus et Cassius, interfectōrēs Caesaris, ingēns bellum mōvērunt. Erant 8
enim per Macedoniam et Orientem multī exercitūs, quōs occupāverant. Profectī sunt 9
igitur contrā eōs Caesar Octāviānus Augustus et M. Antōnius; remānserat enim ad 10
dēfendendam Italiam Lepidus. Apud Philippōs, Macedoniae urbem, contrā eōs pug- 11
nāvērunt. Prīmō proeliō victī sunt Antōnius et Caesar, periit tamen dux nōbilitātis 12
Cassius; secundō Brūtum et īnfīnītam nōbilitātem, quae cum illīs bellum gesserat, vic- 13
tam interfēcērunt. Ac sīc inter eōs dīvīsa est rēs pūblica, ut Augustus Hispāniās, Galliās 14
et Italiam tenēret, Antōnius Asiam, Pontum, Orientem. Sed in Italiā L. Antōnius 15
cōnsul bellum cīvīle commōvit, frāter eius, quī cum Caesare contrā Brūtum et Cassium 16
dīmicāverat. Is apud Perusiam, Tusciae cīvitātem, victus et captus est, neque occīsus. 17

—Eutropius, *Breviarium* VII.2–3

6. What were Brutus and Cassius doing? (8–9)
7. Who went to oppose them? Who stayed in Italy? (9–11)
8. Where did the battle take place? (11–12)
9. What was the result of the first battle? Of the second? (12–14)
10. How was the Roman world divided up after the battle? (14–15)
11. What was L. Antonius doing in Italy? (15–16)
12. What eventually happened to L. Antonius? (17)

The Forum of Augustus, with the temple of Mars Ultor. At the battle of Philippi
(above: 11–14), Octavian vowed to build a temple to Mars if he were victorious. He
fulfilled this vow many years later when he made the temple of Mars Ultor (Mars the
Avenger) the centerpiece of the new forum he constructed to the north of the original
Forum Romanum (see also the plan on page 120).

1   **M. Agrippa**: Agrippa was one of Octavian's closest friends and one of his generals.
  Aquitānia, -ae, f., *Aquitania (a province corresponding to southwestern France)*.
  rem . . . gessit: *he managed the situation*.
  prōsperē, adv., *prosperously, successfully*.
2   **irrumpō, irrumpere, irrūpī, irruptus**, *to break in*.
  Persās: *Persians* really means *Parthians*. Ventidius' victory occurred in 39 B.C.
4   **prīmus**: *he was the first to*. . . .
  *****iūstus, -a, -um**, *fair, just, well-deserved*.
  *****triumphus, -ī**, m., *triumph, victory parade*.
     triumphum agere: *to celebrate a triumph*. The victorious general entered Rome and
       marched through the city with his captives to the temple of Jupiter on the Capitoline.
       Bassus' triumph is described as **iūstissimus** because he was the first Roman general to win
       a decisive victory over the Parthians.
5   **repudiō, -āre, -āvī, -ātus**, *to reject, divorce*. Antony had married Octavian's sister Octavia to
     strengthen the alliance between himself and Octavian.
6   **dūxit uxōrem**: *he took as his wife*, a variation on the more common **dūxit in mātrimōnium**.
     This took place in 37 B.C.
7   *****famēs, famis**, f., *hunger, starvation*. Note the unusual long *e* on the ablative **famē**.
  pestilentia, -ae, f., *disease, plague*.
  labōrāvit: *suffered from*.
8   **īnstō, īnstāre, īnstitī** + dat., *to pursue closely, press hard upon*.
  prō victō: *as the defeated one*.
  recēdō, recēdere, recessī, recessūrus, *to go back, go away, retreat*.
10   **cupiditās, cupiditātis**, f., *greed, lust* (for power).
  muliebris, -is, -e, *of a woman, womanly*.
  in urbe: when Romans used **urbs** without specifying any other city, they meant Rome.
  *****rēgnō, -āre, -āvī, -ātus**, *to rule*.
  Victus est . . . apud Actium: in 31 B.C.
11   **clārus, -a, -um**, *important*.
  illūstris, -is, -e, *famous*.
12   **dēspērō, -āre, -āvī, -ātus**, *to give up hope, despair (of)*.
  trānseō, trānsīre, trānsiī, trānsitūrus, irreg., *to go across; to desert*.
  interimō, interimere, interēmī, interēmptus, *to kill*.
13   **aspis, aspidis**, f., *asp (a poisonous snake)*.
  *****admittō, admittere, admīsī, admissus**, *to let in, allow to reach*.
  *****venēnum, -ī**, n., *poison*.
  Cleopatra . . . exstīncta est: 30 B.C.
  Aegyptus . . . adiecta est: note the feminine gender.
14   *****imperium, -ī**, n., *power; empire*.
  *****adiciō, adicere, adiēcī, adiectus**, *to add*.
  praepōnō, praepōnere, praeposuī, praepositus + dat., *to put in charge of*.
  C. Cornēlius Gallus: this man was a long-time associate and friend of Octavian; he had
     helped defeat Antony's forces in Egypt and was later made the first Roman governor of
     Egypt.
15   *****iūdex, iūdicis**, m., *judge, magistrate; governor*.

B. ANTONY VS. OCTAVIAN

Eō tempore M. Agrippa in Aquitāniā rem prōsperē gessit et L. Ventidius Bassus ir- 1
rumpentēs in Syriam Persās tribus proeliīs vīcit. Pacorum, rēgis Orōdis fīlium, inter- 2
fēcit eō ipsō diē quō ōlim Orōdēs, Persārum rēx, per ducem Surēnam Crassum oc- 3
cīderat. Hic prīmus dē Parthīs iūstissimum triumphum Rōmae ēgit. 4

Antōnius, quī Asiam et Orientem tenēbat, repudiātā sorōre Caesaris Augustī Oc- 5
tāviānī, Cleopatram, rēgīnam Aegyptī, dūxit uxōrem. Contrā Persās etiam ipse pugnā- 6
vit. Prīmīs eōs proeliīs vīcit, regrediēns tamen famē et pestilentiā labōrāvit et, cum 7
īnstārent Parthī fugientī, ipse prō victō recessit. 8

Hic quoque ingēns bellum cīvīle commōvit cōgente uxōre Cleopatrā, rēgīnā 9
Aegyptī, dum cupiditāte muliebrī optat etiam in urbe rēgnāre. Victus est ab Augustō 10
nāvālī pugnā clārā et illūstrī apud Actium, quī locus in Ēpīrō est, ex quā fūgit in Ae- 11
gyptum et dēspērātīs rēbus, cum omnēs ad Augustum trānsīrent, ipse sē interēmit. 12
Cleopatra sibi aspidem admīsit et venēnō eius exstīncta est. Aegyptus per Octāviānum 13
Augustum imperiō Rōmānō adiecta est praepositusque eī C. Cornēlius Gallus. Hunc 14
prīmum Aegyptus Rōmānum iūdicem habuit. 15

—Eutropius, *Breviarium* VII.5–7

1. Describe Ventidius Bassus' campaign against the Persians. (1–4)
2. Whom did Antony divorce? Whom did he then marry? (5–6)
3. What happened to Antony as he was returning from his campaign against the Persians? (7–8)
4. Why, according to Eutropius, did Antony engage in a civil war? (9–10)
5. Who defeated Antony? How and where? (10–11)
6. Why did Antony commit suicide? (12)
7. What happened to Cleopatra? (13)
8. What arrangements were made for the government of Egypt? (13–15)

This coin shows King Orodes I of Parthia (above: 2–4)

Antony held the king of Armenia partially responsible for his defeat in Parthia (above: 7–8). He therefore seized Armenia in 34 B.C. This coin, depicting Antony, commemorates the event: **ANTONI(us) · ARMENIA · DEVICTA**, *After the conquest of Armenia.* On the reverse is Cleopatra, with the title **REGINA · REGVM**, *Queen of Kings.*

FORMS
The Subjunctive Mood (Review)

You have learned that Latin has three moods, the indicative, subjunctive, and imperative. Using the charts on pages 181–182, review the formation of the tenses of the subjunctive of regular and deponent verbs. Also review the subjunctive of the irregular verbs on page 185.

Exercise 56a
Give the requested forms of the following verbs in the present, imperfect, perfect, and pluperfect subjunctive. Use the active voice for numbers 1–7, the passive for 8–12.

1. āmittō *(3rd sing.)*
2. vindicō *(1st pl.)*
3. possum *(3rd pl.)*
4. impediō *(2nd sing.)*
5. commoveō *(1st sing.)*
6. volō *(2nd pl.)*
7. suscipiō *(3rd pl.)*
8. cōnor *(1st sing.)*
9. ferō *(3rd sing.)*
10. cōgō *(1st pl.)*
11. iubeō *(2nd pl.)*
12. regredior *(3rd pl.)*

BUILDING THE MEANING
Sequence of Tenses (Review)

As you learned in Book II-B, the subjunctive is most often used in various types of subordinate clauses. The tense of the subjunctive used is determined by the sequence of tenses.

SEQUENCE OF TENSES		
	Main Clause Indicative	**Subordinate Clause** Tense of Subjunctive *Time of Action* *Relative to Main Clause*
Primary ***Sequence***	Present Future Future Perfect	Present = *Same time or after* Perfect = *Time before*
Secondary ***Sequence***	Imperfect Perfect Pluperfect	Imperfect = *Same time or after* Pluperfect = *Time before*

The following examples illustrate sequence of tenses:

Octāviānus intellegit cūr Antōnius sē **impediat**.
*Octavian understands why Antony **is hindering** him.*
(primary sequence; same time)

Octāviānus intellegit cūr Antōnius sē **impedīverit**.
*Octavian understands why Antony **hindered** him.*
(primary sequence, time before)

Octāviānus intellegēbat cūr Antōnius sē **impedīret**.
*Octavian understood why Antony **was hindering** him.*
(secondary sequence, same time)

Octāviānus intellegēbat cūr Antōnius sē **impedīvisset**.
*Octavian understood why Antony **had hindered** him.*
(secondary sequence, time before)

Exercise 56b

Select the correct form to complete the sentence, read aloud, and translate:

1. Cum Lepidus operam (det, daret, dederit), Antōnius et Octāvius inter sē pācem fēcērunt.
2. Omnēs sciunt cūr Antōnius in Aegyptum (fūgisset, fugeret, fūgerit).
3. Antōnius volēbat scīre quot mīlitēs Octāvius (habēret, habeat, habuerit).
4. Cum Antōnius apud Actium (victus sit, victus esset, vincātur), multī ē mīlitibus ad Octāvium trānsiērunt.
5. Scīmus quōmodo Cleopatra (mortua sit, mortua esset, morerētur).
6. Magister nōs docuit quis (esset, fuerit, sit) prīmus iūdex Rōmānus in Aegyptō.
7. Octāvius, cum Aegyptum imperiō Rōmānō (adiēcisset, adiēcerit, adiciat), Rōmam rediit.
8. Omnēs sciunt ubi Cleopatra sē (interfēcisset, interficeret, interfēcerit).

A coin of Augustus, with the legend **AEGYPTO CAPTA**, *After the capture of Egypt.* The head is that of Augustus; the crocodile symbolizes the Nile and Egypt.

1 **Rōmam rediit**: 29 B.C.
   duodecimus, -a, -um: deduce from **duo + decem**.
2 **quam**: = **postquam,** *after.*
   Ex eō: *From that time.*
3 ***obtineō, obtinēre, obtinuī, obtentus**, *to hold, possess.*
4 ***initium, -ī**, n., *beginning.*
   ***prīncipātus, -ūs**, m., *leadership, principate* (period of an emperor's rule).
   obeō, obīre, obiī, obitūrus, irreg., *to die.*
   obiit: A.D. 14.
5 **morte commūnī**: i.e., Augustus died a natural death; he was not killed in battle or murdered by political enemies.
   in campō Mārtiō: the Campus Martius was a flat area to the northwest of the original
   city of Rome, first used for military training (hence the name). Later it became the site
   of many monumental buildings.
6 **immeritō**, adv., *unfairly, undeservedly.*
   ex maximā parte: *for the most part.*
7 ***ūllus, -a, -um**, *any, anyone.*
   eō: ablative of comparison, *than he.*
   moderātior: Augustus did not engage in proscriptions or other acts of revenge against
   those who had opposed him in the civil war.
8 **quibus**: *in which* (ablative of time when).
   cīvīlissimē: *like an ordinary citizen.*
9 **līberālis, -is, -e**, *generous.*
   fīdus, -a, -um, *loyal, faithful.*
   ēvehō, ēvehere, ēvexī, ēvectus, *to raise up, carry up.*
   honōribus: remember that **honor** may mean *political office.*
   ***aequō, -āre, -āvī, -ātus**, *to make equal.*
10 **fastīgium, -ī**, n., *height, high point; greatness.*
11 **rēs Rōmāna**: *the Roman state.*
   ***flōreō, flōrēre, flōruī**, *to bloom, flourish, prosper.*
12 **invictus**: deduce from **in- + vincō**.
13 ***penitus**, adv., *thoroughly, completely.*
   subigō, subigere, subēgī, subāctus, *to turn up, tame, conquer, subdue.*
14 **omnēs . . . cīvitātēs**: a group of cities in the Crimea, which had previously been controlled by Mithridates, King of Pontus. **Bosporus** was not a city, as Eutropius states;
   the word refers rather to the whole kingdom, whose capital was Panticapaeum.
   maritimus, -a, -um, *coastal, on the shore.*
   in hīs: *among them.*

THE PRINCIPATE OF AUGUSTUS

A. AUGUSTUS AS EMPEROR

Ita bellīs per tōtum orbem cōnfectīs Octāviānus Augustus Rōmam rediit, duo- 1
decimō annō quam cōnsul fuerat. Ex eō rem pūblicam per quadrāgintā et quattuor an- 2
nōs sōlus obtinuit. Ante enim duodecim annīs cum Antōniō et Lepidō tenuerat. Ita ab 3
initiō prīncipātūs eius ūsque ad fīnem quīnquāgintā et sex annī fuērunt. Obiit autem 4
septuāgēsimō sextō annō morte commūnī in oppidō Campāniae Ātellā. Rōmae in 5
campō Mārtiō sepultus est, vir quī nōn immeritō ex maximā parte deō similis est 6
putātus. Neque enim facile ūllus eō aut in bellīs fēlīcior fuit aut in pāce moderātior. 7
Quadrāgintā et quattuor annīs, quibus sōlus gessit imperium, cīvīlissimē vīxit, in cūnc- 8
tōs līberālissimus, in amīcōs fidissimus, quōs tantīs ēvexit honōribus ut paene aequāret 9
fastīgiō suō. 10

Nūllō tempore ante eum magis rēs Rōmāna flōruit. Nam exceptīs cīvīlibus bellīs, in 11
quibus invictus fuit, Rōmānō adiēcit imperiō Aegyptum, Cantabriam, Dalmatiam saepe 12
ante victam sed penitus tum subāctam, Pannoniam, Aquitāniam, Illyricum, Raetiam, 13
Vindelicōs et Salassōs in Alpibus, omnēs Pontī maritimās cīvitātēs, in hīs nōbilissimās 14
Bosporum et Panticapaeum. Vīcit autem multīs proeliīs Dācōs. 15

—Eutropius, *Breviarium* VII.8–9

1. When did Augustus return to Rome? (1–2)
2. How long did he rule the Roman world altogether? (2–4)
3. At what age and where did Augustus die? (4–5)
4. To whom was Augustus considered similar? (6)
5. How did Augustus behave during his principate? (7–10)
6. What was the general condition of the Roman empire during Augustus' reign? (11)
7. On the map on page 17 find all the places cited in the last paragraph. (12–15)
8. What is Eutropius' attitude toward Augustus? Cite Latin phrases to support your answer. Why do you think he might have felt this way?

1 ***caedō, caedere, cecīdī, caesus**, *to cut down, wipe out, kill.*
 ipsōs: *them*, whole tribes of Germans, as opposed to their soldiers who were killed.
 Albis, Albis, m., *the Elbe River.*
 fluvius, -ī, m., *river.*
 summōvit: deduce from **sub- + moveō.**
2 **barbaricō**: *foreign territory.*
 ultrā, prep. + acc., *beyond.*
 prīvignus, -ī, m., *stepson.* Drusus and Tiberius were sons of Augustus' second wife, Livia.
3 ***sīcut**, conj., *just as.*
 Pannonicus, -a, -um, *Pannonian* (Pannonia was an area that included what is now Austria and Hungary).
4 **trānstulit**: deduce from **trāns + ferō.**
 *rīpa, -ae, f., *bank* (of a river).
5 **collocō, -āre, -āvī, -ātus**, *to locate, settle.*
 quod nūllī anteā: *a thing which [they had done] for no one previously.* Note that **nūllī** is dative singular.
 Persae: this means the Parthians.
6 ***signum, -ī**, n., *sign, signal; standard* (a military term). Each legion had its own **signa**, symbols mounted on poles. Soldiers knew where to move by following the **signum** of their own regiment. To lose the **signa** to the enemy was an enormous disgrace.
7 **Scythae, -ārum**, m. pl., *Scythians* (a people living in what is now southern Russia).
 Indī, -ōrum, m. pl., *Indians.*
 incognitus, -a, -um, *unknown.*
 •**mūnus, mūneris**, n., *duty, obligation; gift.*
8 **Galatia, -ae**, f., *Galatia* (a province in central Asia Minor).
 cum: *although.*
9 **prōpraetōre**: it was customary for a praetor or consul to go out as governor of a province after his term of office was over. As governor he was referred to as **prōpraetōre** or **prōcōnsule.**
 Tantō . . . amōre . . . fuit: *He was so beloved* (literally, *He was of such love*). A noun in the ablative, modified by an adjective, is used to describe a personal quality or characteristic and is called the *ablative of description.*
10 **cīvitātēs**: = **urbēs.**
11 **obsequor, obsequī, obsecūtus sum** + dat., *to obey, yield to; to gratify, honor.*
12 **habitus, -ūs**, m., *dress, clothing.*
 togātus, -a, -um, *wearing a toga.*
 *scīlicet, adv., *of course, obviously.*
13 **dīvus, -a, -um**, *divine, deified.* Some Roman emperors were declared to be gods by the Senate after their death as a mark of respect; this had been done to Julius Caesar, who was then known as **Dīvus Iūlius.**

B. MORE OF AUGUSTUS' ACHIEVEMENTS

Germānōrum ingentēs cōpiās cecīdit, ipsōs quoque trāns Albim fluvium summōvit, 1
quī in barbaricō longē ultrā Rhēnum est. Hoc tamen bellum per Drūsum, prīvignum 2
suum, administrāvit, sīcut per Tiberium, prīvignum alterum, bellum Pannonicum. 3
Quō bellō quadrāgintā captīvōrum mīlia ex Germāniā trānstulit et suprā rīpam Rhēnī in 4
Galliā collocāvit. Armeniam ā Parthīs recēpit. Obsidēs, quod nūllī anteā, Persae eī dē- 5
dērunt. Reddidērunt etiam signa Rōmāna, quae Crassō victō adēmerant. 6

Scythae et Indī, quibus anteā Rōmānōrum nōmen incognitum fuerat, mūnera et 7
lēgātōs ad eum mīsērunt. Galatia quoque sub hōc prōvincia facta est, cum anteā rēg- 8
num fuisset, prīmusque eam M. Lollius prōpraetōre administrāvit. Tantō autem amōre 9
etiam apud barbarōs fuit ut rēgēs populī Rōmānī amīcī in honōrem eius conderent cīvi- 10
tātēs, quās Caesareās nōminārent. Multī autem rēgēs ex rēgnīs suīs vēnērunt ut eī ob- 11
sequerentur, et habitū Rōmānō, togātī scīlicet, ad vehiculum vel equum ipsīus cucur- 12
rērunt. Moriēns Dīvus appellātus est. 13

—Eutropius, *Breviarium* VII.9–10

1. How did Augustus deal with the Germans? (1–2)
2. Who conducted the campaign against the Germans for Augustus? (2–3)
3. What was done with the German captives? How many were there? (4–5)
4. Name two things that the Persians did as signs of respect for Augustus. (5–6)
5. What did the Scythians and Indians do during Augustus' reign? (7–8) Locate Scythia on the map on page 17.
6. What did friendly foreign kings do to honor Augustus? (9–11)
7. Why did foreign kings come to Rome? What did they do there? (11–13)
8. How did the Senate honor Augustus after his death? (13)

A coin of Augustus showing a kneeling Parthian returning the standards
taken from Crassus (above: 6). The legend (partly missing from this copy
of the coin) reads **CAESAR [AVGVSTVS SIG]N(īs) RECEPT(īs)**.

BUILDING THE MEANING
The Subjunctive in Subordinate Clauses (Review)

You have already met in Book II several types of subordinate clauses that use the subjunctive mood:

1. Indirect Questions:

   Senātōrēs rogābant **cūr** Caesar tyrannica **faceret.**
   *The Senators kept asking **why** Caesar **was acting** like a tyrant (doing tyrannical things).*

2. Circumstantial Clauses:

   Caesar, **cum** senātūs diē **vēnisset** ad Cūriam, cōnfossus est. (cf. 55D:7–8)
   ***When** Caesar **had arrived** at the Senate House on the day of a Senate meeting, he was stabbed.*

3. Causal Clauses:

   Senātōrēs, **cum** rēgnum Caesaris nōn iam ferre **possent,** coniūrāvērunt.
   *The senators made a conspiracy **because** they **could** no longer endure Caesar's rule.*

4. Result Clauses:

   Tantō amōre apud barbarōs fuit **ut** rēgēs amīcī in honōrem eius **conderent** cīvitātēs. (cf. 57B:9–11)
   *He (Augustus) was **so** beloved among foreigners **that** friendly kings **founded** cities in his honor.*

5. Indirect Commands:

   Rēgēs barbarī Augustum **ōrābant ut** sibi auxilium **daret.**
   *Foreign kings **kept asking** Augustus **to help** them.*

6. Purpose Clauses:

   Multī rēgēs ex rēgnīs suīs vēnērunt **ut** eī **obsequerentur.** (cf. 57B:11–12)
   *Many kings came from their realms **to honor** him.*

Remember that negative purpose clauses and negative indirect commands use **nē,** while negative result clauses use **ut . . . nōn.**

All these constructions follow the rules for sequence of tenses given on pages 32–33. Notice that indirect commands and purpose clauses always use either present or imperfect subjunctive, since the action in such constructions always takes place *after* that of the main verb. The other constructions can use any tense of the subjunctive, as the sense requires. In result clauses, sometimes the perfect subjunctive is found in secondary sequence instead of the imperfect, which seems contrary to the rule. The perfect is used in such clauses to stress the finality or completeness (**perfectum** = *completed*) of the action:

Senātōrēs quīdam Caesarī **adeō** invidēbant **ut** eum **occīderint.**
*Some senators hated Caesar **so much that** they **killed him.***

Exercise 57a
Read aloud and translate; identify the type of subjunctive clause in each sentence:

1. Cum Augustus mortuus esset, senātus eum Dīvum appellāvit.
2. Augustus multa bella gessit, ut esset pāx per tōtum orbem.
3. Tantus prīnceps fuit Augustus ut Eutropius in Breviāriō suō magnopere eum laudāret.
4. Omnēs sciunt cūr populus Rōmānus Augustum amāverit.
5. Senātus Octāviānō, cum rērum potītus esset, titulum Augustum dedit.
6. Multī rēgēs Rōmam vēnērunt ut Augustum honōrārent.
7. Iūlius Caesar erat tam arrogāns ut senātōrēs eum occīderint.
8. Prīnceps ōrat ut senātus sē adiuvet.
9. Nesciō quot bella Augustus gesserit.
10. Augustus ita sē gessit ut nēmō eum occīdere vellet.

      titulus, -ī, m., *title*   **sē gerere,** *to conduct oneself, behave*

Exercise 57b
Choose the correct form of the subjunctive. Be sure to follow the rules for sequence of tenses (review pages 32–33, if necessary).

1. Antōnius, cum tōtum orbem regere (vellet, velit, volēbat), bellum contrā Octāviānum commōvit.
2. Omnēs sciunt cūr Antōnius bellum (commōvit, commovēret, commōverit).
3. Antōnius contrā Persās bellum gessit nē in Syriōs iterum (irrumpant, irrūperint, irrumperent).
4. Ībunt ad Actium Cleopatra et Antōnius ut Octāviānum (vincant, vincerent, vincent).
5. Cum (victī sint, victī essent, victī erant), Antōnius et Cleopatra sē interfēcērunt.
6. Aegyptus erat prōvincia tam magna ut Augustus amīcum C. Cornēlium Gallum iūdicem (fēcerit, fēcit, faciat).
7. Cleopatra adeō Antōnium amābat ut cum eō morī (velit, volēbat, vellet).

REVIEW XIII: Chapters 55–57

Exercise XIIIa: Chronology
List the following events in correct chronological order:

1. battle of Actium
2. death of Julius Caesar
3. Octavian sole ruler of Rome
4. Antony marries Cleopatra
5. defeat of Pompey by Caesar
6. Second Triumvirate
7. Caesar's conquest of Gaul
8. defeat of Antony by Octavian and Senatorial forces
9. death of Cicero
10. reconciliation of Antony and Octavian
11. First Triumvirate
12. death of Pompey
13. Cicero's consulship

Exercise XIIIb: Important Events
Answer the following questions. Base your answers on the Readings in Part I (including the introduction to Part I, pages 2–4) as well as on any class discussion or individual research you have done:

1. What ability was responsible for Marcus Tullius Cicero's rise to prominence? Why was his election as consul particularly noteworthy? What difficult situation did Cicero have to deal with as consul, and what was the outcome?
2. Who were the members of the First Triumvirate? Why did they join together? Were they successful in meeting their goals?
3. What effects did Caesar's conquest of Gaul have upon Caesar personally and upon the Roman state?
4. Describe the steps that led Caesar to become sole ruler of Rome, beginning with his crossing of the Rubicon River.
5. Why was Caesar murdered? When and how was this done?
6. How was Octavian related to Caesar? With whom did he ally himself immediately after Caesar's death? What was the result?
7. Who brought about the reconciliation between Antony and Octavian? What were the results for the political situation in Rome?
8. What happened to the senatorial faction that assassinated Julius Caesar?
9. Describe the civil war between Antony and Octavian. How did it begin, and what were the results? What happened to Antony, to Cleopatra, and to Egypt?
10. How long did Octavian (Augustus) rule the Roman world? How did most Romans feel about him? What happened to the Roman empire during his rule?
11. What indications were there that Augustus was feared and respected by foreign powers? What special honor was given to Augustus upon his death?

PART II

POLITICAL VIOLENCE IN THE LATE REPUBLIC

In Part I, you learned that the last century B.C., a period known as the late Republic, was a time of political turmoil. It was characterized by the ascendancy of certain individuals who used military power and political intrigue to challenge control of the government by the senatorial class, which had ruled Rome since 509 B.C.

At the center of events during the late Republic was Marcus Tullius Cicero (106–43 B.C.), orator and statesman, philosopher and writer, who had risen to a position of political prestige through his brilliance as a lawyer, rather than by right of birth or wealth. He had served as consul in 63, during which time he discovered and suppressed Catiline's conspiracy to overthrow the government. As champion of the Senate and a political idealist, Cicero was often confused by the perplexities of politics and became the pawn of men with more powerful ambitions: first, Caesar and Pompey, and then, Antony and Octavian.

The events of 53–52 B.C. serve to illustrate the political forces and public personalities of the late Republic. During the previous decade, political gangs, led by P. Clodius Pulcher, agent of Caesar, and T. Annius Milo, henchman of the senatorial faction, opposed each other and disrupted the normal constitutional processes of state. Milo and Clodius themselves became political candidates for the elections of 53; the subsequent postponement of these elections due to violence eventually led to the murder of Clodius by Milo. During this crisis, the Senate turned to Pompey while Caesar was fighting in Gaul, and this set up a confrontation between Pompey and Caesar that was to lead to civil war (49–45 B.C.), about which you will read in Part III. In 52, Cicero delivered a courtroom speech of defense on behalf of his friend Milo, a speech that has been preserved and is titled *Pro Milone (For Milo)*. The commentary on this speech by Q. Asconius Pedianus, a scholar of the first century A.D., who consulted official records of the trial, gives us a unique perspective on the volatile politics of the late Republic.

Ō tempora, Ō mōrēs! *O the times, O the character (of men)!* (Cicero, *In Catilinam* I.1)

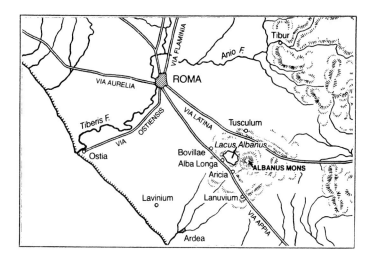

Central Italy

1   **A.d xiii Kal. Febr.**: = 18 January because, prior to Caesar's reform of the calendar in 46 B.C., January had 29 days, not 31.

    Lānuvium: home town of Milo, southeast of Rome along the Appian Way.

    *mūnicipium, -ī, n., *town.*

    dictātor: Milo was chief magistrate, or dictator, of Lanuvium.

2   **flāmen, flāminis**, m., *priest.*

      ad flāminem prōdendum: *for the purpose of appointing a priest.*

    •posterus, -a, -um, *next, following.*

    circā, prep. + acc., *around, about.*

3   **paulō**, *a little.*

    ultrā, prep. + acc., *beyond.*

    Bovillās . . . Arīciā: Bovillae was a small town south of Rome. Aricia, a bit further south, was the first way station (stopping point) on the Appian Way. See the map above.

    alloquor, alloquī, allocūtus sum, *to address, speak to.*

    decuriō, decuriōnis, m., *town councilman.*

4   ***vehō, vehere, vexī, vectus**, *to carry, convey;* (passive) *to ride.*

    trīgintā ferē: *about 30.*

    expedītus, -a, -um, *lightly-armed.*

    *mōs, mōris, m., *custom, habit.*

    iter facientibus: *for travelers,* literally, *for those making a journey.*

5   **gladiīs cīnctī**: *armed with swords.*

    •comes, comitis, m., *companion, comrade.*

6   **•eques, equitis**, m., *knight, member of the equestrian order.*

    *plēbs, plēbis, f., *plebeians, common people.*

7   **L. Sullae dictātōris**: L. Cornelius Sulla (138–78 B.C.) was a military dictator and champion of the Senate.

    *familiāris, familiāris, gen. pl., **familiārium**, m./f., *close friend.*

8   ***agmen, agminis**, n., *column, line.*

9   **eī**: = **gladiātōrēs.**

    in ultimō agmine: *at the rear of the column.* The two parties were passing one another, going in opposite directions.

    •euntēs: present participle of **eō, īre.**

    rixa, -ae, f., *skirmish.* **rixam committere**, *to begin a fight.*

CHAPTER
58

A POLITICAL MURDER (ASCONIUS' ACCOUNT)

The political struggles of 53 B.C. reached a climax in January of 52, when a brawl along the Appian Way between Clodius and Milo led to the death of Clodius. The account provided below is that produced by Asconius as part of his commentary on Cicero's speech of defense Pro Milone. *While preparing this commentary, Asconius consulted transcripts from the Senate and other documentation independent of Milo's testimony. As you read this and the selections from Cicero's speech in the next chapter, compare the two versions of what happened and consider the reasons for the differences between them.*

A. CLODIUS AND MILO ON THE APPIAN WAY

A.d. xiii Kal. Febr. Milō Lānuvium, ex quō erat mūnicipiō et ubi tum dictātor, pro- 1
fectus est ad flāminem prōdendum posterā diē. Occurrit eī circā hōram nōnam Clōdius 2
paulō ultrā Bovillās, rediēns ab Arīciā; erat autem allocūtus decuriōnēs Arīcinōrum. 3
Vehēbātur Clōdius equō; servī trīgintā ferē expedītī, ut illō tempore mōs erat iter fa- 4
cientibus, gladiīs cīnctī sequēbantur. Erant cum Clōdiō praetereā trēs comitēs eius, ex 5
quibus eques Rōmānus ūnus, duo dē plēbe nōtī hominēs. Milō raedā vehēbātur cum 6
uxōre Faustā, fīliā L. Sullae dictātōris, et M. Fufiō familiārī suō. Sequēbātur eōs mag- 7
num servōrum agmen, inter quōs gladiātōrēs quoque erant, ex quibus duo nōtī, Euda- 8
mus et Birria. Eī in ultimō agmine tardius euntēs cum servīs P. Clōdiī rixam com- 9
mīsērunt. 10

1. When and where did the events of the narrative take place? (1–3)
2. Why was Milo on the Appian Way? Why was Clodius? (1–4)
3. Describe the respective traveling styles of Clodius and Milo. (4–9)
4. Who began the skirmish? (9–10)

11 •**tumultus, -ūs**, m., *uproar, commotion.*
   *respiciō, respicere, respexī, respectus, *to look back.*
   minitābundus, -a, -um, *menacing.*
   umerus, -ī, m., *(upper) arm.*
12 **rumpia, -ae,** f., *pike, spear.*
   trāiciō, trāicere, trāiēcī, trāiectus, *to throw through, pierce.*
   •**orior, orīrī, ortus sum,** *to arise.*
   •**pugna, -ae,** f., *pitched battle* (as opposed to **rixa,** line 9).
13 **proximus, -a, -um,** *nearest.*
   Bovillānus, -a, -um, *belonging to Bovillae.*
     in Bovillānō: = *in the vicinity of Bovillae;* a noun such as **agrō** is understood.
   *dēferō, dēferre, dētulī, dēlātus, irreg., *to carry down.*
   Milō . . . exturbārī tabernā iussit: the complexity of this sentence may reveal the difficulty
     in Milo's mind of making the decision to do away with Clodius.
   vulnerātum: = **vulnerātum esse.**
14 **cum . . . intellegeret:** a **cum** causal clause, as is **(cum) . . . esset habitūrus** (14–15).
   sibi perīculōsius illud . . . futūrum (esse): *that that would be more dangerous for him.* **sibi:** =
     Milo. **illud:** = the wounding of Clodius.
   vīvō eō . . . occīsō (eō): ablatives absolute. **eō:** = Clodius.
15 **solācium, -ī,** n., *relief, consolation.*
   etiam sī subeunda esset poena: *even if he had to undergo punishment.*
   exturbō, -āre, -āvī, -ātus, *to force out.*
     exturbārī tabernā iussit: *ordered (him) to be dragged from the tavern.*
16 •**lateō, latēre, latuī,** *to lie in hiding.*
   •**cōnficiō, cōnficere, cōnfēcī, cōnfectus,** *to finish (off).*
     cōnfectus: = **cōnfectus est.**
   cadāver, cadāveris, n., *corpse, body.*
     Cadāver: object of **sustulit** and **iussit.**
17 •**graviter,** adv., *seriously.*
   saucius, -a, -um, *wounded, hurt.*
18 **rūs, rūris,** n., *country.*
   *revertor, revertī, reversus sum, *to turn back, return.*
   •**tollō, tollere, sustulī, sublātus,** *to lift, raise.*
19 **ipse:** = Sextus Teidius.
   eōdem, *to the same (place).*
   sē recipere, idiom, *to return, go back,* literally, *to take oneself back.*

B. THE MURDER OF CLODIUS

Ad quem tumultum cum respexisset Clōdius minitābundus, umerum eius Birria 11
rumpiā trāiēcit. Inde cum orta esset pugna, plūrēs Milōniānī accurrērunt. Clōdius vul- 12
nerātus in tabernam proximam in Bovillānō dēlātus est. Milō, ut cognōvit vulnerātum 13
Clōdium, cum sibi perīculōsius illud etiam vīvō eō futūrum intellegeret, occīsō autem 14
magnum solācium esset habitūrus etiam sī subeunda esset poena, exturbārī tabernā 15
iussit. Atque ita Clōdius latēns extractus est multīsque vulneribus cōnfectus. Cadāver 16
eius in viā relictum, quia servī Clōdiī aut occīsī erant aut graviter sauciī latēbant, Sex. 17
Teidius senātor, quī forte ex rūre in urbem revertēbātur, sustulit et lectīcā suā Rōmam 18
ferrī iussit; ipse rūrsus eōdem unde erat regressus sē recēpit. 19

5. Describe how the skirmish escalated into a pitched battle. (11–12)
6. Where was Clodius taken? (12–13)
7. Explain Milo's reasoning in deciding to kill Clodius. (13–16)
8. Describe the immediate circumstances of Clodius' death. (16)
9. What happened to the body at first? Finally? (16–19)
10. Why do you think that Teidius did not accompany the corpse? (19)
11. Imagine that you are traveling along the Appian Way on 18 January. Write a description or dramatic account of the events as you witness them.

Tombstone found at Gloucester, England

20 •**perferō, perferre, pertulī, perlātus**, irreg., *to deliver, bring in.*
   ante prīmam noctis hōram: about 5 P.M.
   īnfimus, -a, -um, *lowest, most vile.*
21 **lūctus, -ūs**, m., *mourning.*
   circumstō, circumstāre, circumstetī, *to stand around, surround.*
   •**augeō, augēre, auxī, auctus**, *to increase, magnify.*
22 *invidia, -ae**, f., *ill-will, hatred.*
      factī invidiam: *anger at the deed*; the objective genitive **factī** denotes the object of the anger,
         the killing of Clodius.
   effūsus, -a, -um, *effusive, unrestrained.*
23 •**ostendō, ostendere, ostendī, ostentus**, *to show, point out.*
   Maior: take with **multitūdō**.
   •**īdem, eadem, idem**, *the same.*
   cōnfluō, cōnfluere, cōnflūxī, *to flow together.*
24 **Eīs . . . hortantibus**: ablative absolute.
   *vulgus, -ī**, n., *rabble, mob.* Note the gender.
   imperītus, -a, -um, *ignorant.*
25 **calcō, -āre, -āvī, -ātus**, *to trample, crush with the feet.*
26 **rostra, -ōrum**, n. pl., *rostra* (**rostra** literally = *beaks of ships*, which decorated the speaker's
      platform in the Forum and gave it its name).
   prō contiōne: *before a public meeting.* A **contiō** was an open public meeting, usually rowdy
      and boisterous, where the issues involved in an upcoming vote for a law or magistrate were
      discussed. **Contiō** is a contraction of **conventiō**, *a coming together.*
   (T. Munātius) Plancus et (Q.) Pompeius (Rufus): tribunes who supported Milo's political
      opponents and who contributed to the general civil disorder of this period. Milo was run-
      ning for the consulship.
   competītor, competītōris, m., *political rival, fellow candidate.*
27 *studeō, studēre, studuī** + dat., *to be eager for, support.*
   Milōnī: *toward Milo*, dative of reference.
   duce Sex. Clōdiō scrība: ablative absolute.
   scrība, -ae, m., *scribe, clerk.* Sextus Clodius was an agent and probably a freedman of
      P. Clodius.
28 **cremō, -āre, -āvī, -ātus**, *to burn.*
   subsellium, -ī, n., *bench.*
   tribūnal, tribūnālis, n., *platform.*
   cōdicibus librāriōrum: *secretary's ledgers.*
29 **ignis, ignis**, gen. pl., **ignium**, m., *fire.*
   quō igne: ablative of cause, equivalent to **propter** + acc.
   *flagrō, -āre, -āvī**, *to burn, blaze up.*
   *item**, adv., *likewise, in the same way.*
   Porcia Basilica: this basilica, or public courthouse, the earliest in Rome, was built by Marcus
      Porcius Cato in 184 B.C. See the plan on page 47 (opposite).
30 •**iungō, iungere, iūnxī, iūnctus**, *to join, connect.*
   ambūrō, ambūrere, ambussī, ambustus, *to scorch, burn.*

C. THE BURNING OF THE SENATE HOUSE

Perlātum est corpus Clōdiī ante prīmam noctis hōram, īnfimaeque plēbis et servōrum maxima multitūdō magnō lūctū corpus in ātriō domūs positum circumstetit. Au-
gēbat autem factī invidiam uxor Clōdiī Fulvia, quae cum effūsā lamentātiōne vulnera
eius ostendēbat. Maior posterā diē lūce prīmā multitūdō eiusdem generis cōnflūxit,
complūrēsque nōtī hominēs vīsī sunt. Eīsque hortantibus vulgus imperītum corpus nū-
dum ac calcātum, sīcut in lectō erat positum, ut vulnera vidērī possent in Forum dētulit
et in rostrīs posuit. Ibi prō contiōne Plancus et Pompeius, quī competītōribus Milōnis
studēbant, invidiam Milōnī fēcērunt. Populus, duce Sex. Clōdiō scrībā, corpus P. Clōdiī in Cūriam intulit cremāvitque subselliīs et tribūnālibus et mēnsīs et cōdicibus librāriōrum, quō igne et ipsa quoque Cūria flagrāvit, et item Porcia Basilica, quae erat eī
iūncta, ambusta est.

—Asconius, *Oratio in Milonianum Ciceronis* (extracts)

12. Who came to mourn Clodius? (20–21)
13. Cite the Latin that describes the manner in which the news of Clodius' death was
    received in Rome. (20–21)
14. How did Fulvia magnify the outrage against her husband's death? (22–23)
15. What happened, of note, on the following day? (23–24)
16. How did the mob treat the body of Clodius? Why do you think they did these
    things? (24–26)
17. How did Milo's political rivals attempt to subvert his candidacy? (26–27)
18. Describe what finally happened to the body of Clodius. (27–29)
19. What consequences did this act have for the city of Rome? (29–30)
20. What have these readings revealed to you about political life during the late
    Republic?

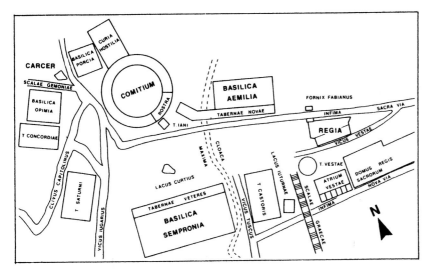

The **Forum
Rōmānum** in
Cicero's time

Building the Meaning
The Gerund or Verbal Noun

Look at the following sentence:

> Inde cum orta esset pugna, servī **adiuvandī** causā ad Milōnem accurrērunt.
> *Then, when an all-out battle had begun, slaves ran toward Milo for the sake **of helping out**.*

In this sentence, **adiuvandī** is a *gerund* or *verbal noun*, corresponding to the English verbal noun ending in *-ing*. The Latin gerund is active in meaning, *helping*, and is formed by adding **-nd-** to the present stem of the verb. The same endings are used as those of 2nd declension neuter singular nouns. There is no nominative case. Here are the forms:

	1st	2nd	3rd	3rd *-iō*	4th
Gen.	para**ndī**	habe**ndī**	mitte**ndī**	iacie**ndī**	audie**ndī**
Dat.	para**ndō**	habe**ndō**	mitte**ndō**	iacie**ndō**	audie**ndō**
Acc.	para**ndum**	habe**ndum**	mitte**ndum**	iacie**ndum**	audie**ndum**
Abl.	para**ndō**	habe**ndō**	mitte**ndō**	iacie**ndō**	audie**ndō**

Note: the gerunds of **īre** are **eundī, eundō, eundum, eundō**.

Here are some examples of how the gerund is used in Latin and translated into English. Note how the gerund can function in any of the usual constructions of nouns in the various cases:

1. In the genitive case the gerund is used with **causā** or **grātiā** to express purpose:

   > Cōnsul creātus est **gubernandī causā**.
   > *The consul was elected **for the sake of governing**.*

2. In the genitive case the gerund is also used with special adjectives:

   > Cōnsul erat **cupidus gubernandī**.
   > *The consul was **desirous of governing**.*

3. The dative case of the gerund is used when the gerund serves as the indirect object:

   > Cōnsul multum temporis **gubernandō** dabat.
   > *The consul was giving much time **to governing**.*

4. In the dative case the gerund is also used with special adjectives:

   > Cōnsul vidēbātur esse **idōneus gubernandō**.
   > *The consul seemed **fit for governing**.*

5. In the accusative case the gerund is found with **ad**, showing purpose:

> Cōnsul creātus est **ad gubernandum**.
> *The consul was elected **for the purpose of governing (to govern)**.*

6. The ablative case of the gerund is used in prepositional phrases with **dē**, **ex**, and **in**:

> Cōnsul multa cōnsilia capiēbat **dē gubernandō**.
> *The consul was making many plans **concerning governing**.*

7. The ablative case of the gerund may also serve as an ablative of means:

> Cōnsul reī pūblicae serviēbat bene **gubernandō**.
> *The consul was serving the state **by governing** well.*

Exercise 58a
Read aloud and translate:

1. Gladiātōrēs Milōnis cupidī pugnandī erant.
2. Gladiātōribus vīsīs, servī Clōdiī celeriter adiuvandī grātiā accurrērunt.
3. Servī Clōdiī ad resistendum celeriter concurrērunt.
4. Familiārēs Clōdiī in tabernā proximā latendī causā manēbant.
5. Gladiātōrēs, cum senātōrem appropinquantem cōnspexissent, fīnem pugnandī fēcērunt.
6. Complūrēs equitēs in Milōnem dīcendō tumultum in Forō faciēbant.
7. Putāsne Milōnem virum idōneum gubernandō fuisse?
8. Cicerō scrīpsit hominem ad duās rēs esse nātum, ad intellegendum et ad agendum.

Exercise 58b
Complete each of the following sentences with the correct form of the gerund and then translate the sentence. The infinitive is provided.

1. Fulvia, uxor Clōdiī, omnia parāverat ad _____. (proficīscī)
2. Clōdius spērābat sē ipsum ē perīculō ēripere posse _____. (fugere)
3. Nōnne sunt omnēs gladiātōrēs cupidī _____? (vincere)
4. Novī magistrātūs ā populō Rōmānō creābuntur ad _____. (gubernāre)
5. Ōrātor in rostra ascendit _____ causā. (loquī)

> **modus operandi**, *method of operation*
> **modus vivendi**, *way of living*
> **onus probandi**, *burden of proof*

Politics in the Late Republic

A candidate for political office, when canvassing for votes in the Forum, an activity called **ambitiō**, wore a toga of bright white rubbed with chalk (**toga candida**) as a symbol of his purity and fitness for office. The candidate was accompanied by a slave (**nōmenclātor**), who reminded him of voters' names, and by a crowd of partisans (**sectātōrēs**), mostly freedmen clients, whose task it was to secure votes through promises and even bribery.

In 64 B.C., Cicero's brother Quintus wrote a campaign handbook titled *De consulatu*, to assist his elder brother's election bid for the consulship of 63. This political pamphlet lists some things for a candidate to consider during a campaign:

Take care to have followers at your heels daily, of every kind, class, and age; because from their number people can figure out how much power and support you are going to have at the polls.

You particularly need to use flattery. No matter how vicious and vile it is on the other days of a man's life, when he runs for office it is indispensable.

Getting votes among the rank and file requires calling everyone by his name. Make it clear you know people's names; practice, get better at it day to day. Nothing seems to me better for popularity and gaining favor.

If you make a promise, the matter is not fixed. It's for a future day, and it affects only a few people. But if you say no, you are sure to alienate people right away, and a lot of them.

But, of all the forces at work in determining the outcome of an election, it was usually the character of the candidate himself that was the most influential factor.

When Scipio Nasica was seeking the office of curule aedile and, in the custom of a campaigner, had firmly grasped the hand of a certain man worn leathery with farm work, to get a laugh he asked the man whether or not he usually walked on his hands. This comment, when heard by bystanders and passed around, was the source of Scipio's downfall; for all the country voters thought he was laughing at poverty.

—Valerius Maximus, VII.5.2

Virtūs, probitās, integritās in candidātō, nōn linguae volūbilitās, nōn ars, nōn scientia requīrī solet. *Moral courage, honesty, and integrity are usually sought in candidates, not a glib tongue, skill, or knowledge.* (Cicero, *Pro Plancio*, 62)

Ō flexanima atque omnium rēgīna rērum ōrātiō! *O Eloquence who moves men's minds, queen of all things!* (Marcus Pacuvius, *Hermiona*)

These figures represent typical oratorical gestures and postures of the first centuries B.C. and A.D. The **āctiō**, or delivery of a speech, involved theatrics such as running about, stamping of feet, getting on one's knees, waving of arms, and a wide range of voices and expressions to play on the audience's emotions.

ORATORY IN REPUBLICAN POLITICS

Skill in public speaking, or rhetoric, was a requirement for political success in Rome, for all public offices required speechmaking and the ability to persuade. By Cicero's time, a Roman youth who had completed literary and linguistic studies with a **grammaticus** would finish his education by studying with a **rhētor**, an instructor in public speaking who taught skills in debate and in advocating a particular course of action. The preparation of a speech included gathering of material and its proper arrangement, selection of appropriate language, memorization, and delivery. A good speech had a certain structure to it, including a beginning (**exōrdium**), designed to win the favorable attention of the audience; the body (consisting of **partītiō**, "outline"; **cōnfirmātiō**, "positive arguments"; and **refūtātiō**, "rebuttal"); and the conclusion (**perōrātiō**), designed to summarize the arguments and appeal to the jurors' emotions. In *De oratore*, Cicero wrote:

> Eloquence requires many things: a wide knowledge of very many subjects (verbal fluency without this being worthless and even ridiculous), a style, too, carefully formed not merely by selection, but by arrangement of words, and a thorough familiarity with all the feelings which nature has given to men, because the whole force and art of the orator must be put forth in allaying or exciting the emotions of the audience.

The imperial writer Tacitus in his *Dialogus de oratoribus* reflects nostalgically on the "Golden Age" of Roman oratory during the final years of the Republic:

> The more influence a man could wield by his powers of speech, the more readily did he attain to high office, the farther did he, when in office, outstrip his colleagues, the more did he gain favor with the great, authority with the Senate, and name and fame with the common people.

1   **cum scīret Clōdius**: *since Clodius knew*, a **cum** causal clause.
    sollemnis, -is, -e, *customary, traditional.*
    lēgitimus, -a, -um, *legal, proper.*
2   **Milōnī esse**: *Milo had (to make)*, literally, *there was for Milo*, dative of possession.
      esse: following **scīret** in indirect statement, the subject of which is **iter**.
    ad flāminem prōdendum: note that the very same phrase appears in Asconius, page 43,
      line 2.
3   **ipse**: = Clodius.
4   •**prīdiē**, adv., *on the day before.*
    ut . . . collocāret: purpose clause.
    •**fundus, -ī**, m., *farm, estate.*
    quod rē intellēctum est: *as subsequent events proved*, literally, *which was learned from the event.*
    Milōnī: *for Milo*, dative of reference.
    īnsidiae, -ārum, f. pl., *ambush.*
    *****collocō, -āre, -āvī, -ātus**, *to arrange, set up.*
5   **ita profectus est**: i.e., Clodius' departure was so timed. **Ita** anticipates the result clause
      ut . . . relinqueret (5–6).
    contiōnem: the antecedent of the following relative pronouns **quā, quae**, and **quam**.
    turbulentus, -a, -um, *rowdy, boisterous.*
    eius: i.e., of Clodius.
    •**furor, furōris**, m., *rage, madness.* Cicero means that Clodius had the ability to whip
      crowds into a frenzy through his oratory.
    •**dēsīderō, -āre, -āvī, -ātus**, to long for, miss.
6   **nisi . . . voluisset . . . numquam relīquisset**: *unless he had wished, . . . he never would have left.*
    *****obeō, obīre, obiī** or **obīvī, obitūrus**, irreg., *to go to, appear at.*
    *****facinus, facinoris**, n., *villainy, crime, foul deed.*

      Silent legēs inter arma. *Amid arms, laws grow silent.* (Cicero, *Pro Milone* 11)

A POLITICAL MURDER
(CICERO'S ACCOUNT)

The court trial of Milo began on 4 April 52 B.C., and for the next three days the testimony of various witnesses was heard in the open Forum. On 8 April, the final day of the trial, the Forum was under armed guard as the prosecution delivered its summation within the prescribed two hours. Cicero, in his summation, tried to disprove the prosecution's contention that Milo had murdered Clodius with premeditation by attempting to prove, rather, that Clodius had deliberately ambushed Milo. Despite the presence of soldiers, Clodius' supporters were so intimidating that Cicero was prevented from completing his speech.

A. THE SETTING OF THE MURDER

    Interim cum scīret Clōdius (neque enim erat difficile scīre) iter sollemne, lēgiti- 1
mum, necessārium ante diem trēdecimam Kalendās Februāriās Milōnī esse Lānuvium 2
ad flāminem prōdendum, quod erat dictātor Lānuviī Milō, Rōmā subitō ipse profectus 3
prīdiē est, ut ante suum fundum (quod rē intellēctum est) Milōnī īnsidiās collocāret; 4
atque ita profectus est, ut contiōnem turbulentam, in quā eius furor dēsīderātus est, 5
quae illō ipsō diē habita est, relinqueret, quam, nisi obīre facinoris locum tempusque 6
voluisset, numquam relīquisset. 7

1. According to Cicero, why was Milo on the Appian Way? Does this agree with Asconius' account? (1–3; Chapter 58:1–2)
2. Where does Cicero say the confrontation took place? (4)
3. What claim does Cicero make regarding the nature of Clodius' confrontation with Milo? (4)
4. Describe the circumstances of Clodius' departure from Rome. (5–6)
5. According to Cicero, why might these circumstances be regarded as suspicious? (6–7)
6. What Latin words does Cicero use to suggest Clodius' violent tendencies?
7. Summarize Cicero's arguments for claiming that Clodius' meeting with Milo on the Appian Way was premeditated.

8   **cum . . . fuisset**: **cum** causal clause.

    eō diē: i.e., 18 January.

    *****quoad**, adv., *until.*

9   **calceus, -ī**, m., *shoe.* Senators wore special red leather half-boots.

    •**mūtō, -āre, -āvī, -ātus**, *to change.*

    •**paulisper**, adv., *for a little while*; take with **commorātus est**.

    ut fit: *as usual.*

    commoror, -ārī, -ātus sum, *to wait.*

10   **dein**: = **deinde**, adv., *then, next.*

    profectus: = **profectus est**.

    id temporis: *at that point in time.*

    cum iam Clōdius . . . redīre potuisset: *when Clodius could have already returned*, a thought
        completed by the simple condition **sī . . . ventūrus erat**, *if he was going to come (back).*

11   **obviam fit** + dat.: *(he) encounters, (he) meets.*

    expedītus, -a, -um, *lightly-armed.*

    nūllā . . . nūllīs . . . nūllīs: note the *asyndeton*, lack of conjunctions, and *anaphora*, repetition
        of words, to emphasize what was missing from Clodius' party.

    impedīmenta, -ōrum, n. pl., *baggage.*

12   **Graecīs comitibus**: dancers, musicians, party-people.

    quod numquam ferē: *which he almost never (was)*; **erat** is understood.

    cum hic īnsidiātor: *while this (so-called) highwayman*, speaking ironically of Milo.

13   **quī . . . apparāsset**: = **quī . . . apparāvisset**, *who (was the type of person who) would have pre-*
        pared. Note Cicero's sarcasm.

    *****caedēs, caedis**, gen. pl., **caedium**, f., *murder, killing.*

    cum uxōre: the preposition **cum** extends to **magnō et impedītō . . . comitātū**.

14   **paenulātus, a-, -um**, *wearing the **paenula** (a traveling cloak).*

    impedītus, -a, -um, *loaded down.* This and the following adjectives modify **comitātū**.

    muliebris, -is, -e, *womanly.*

    dēlicātus, -a, -um, *dainty, effeminate.*

    ancillārum puerōrumque: perhaps youths for the choral hymns at the religious ceremony in
        Lanuvium the following day.

15   *****comitātus, -ūs**, m., *company, retinue.*

Raeda Rōmāna

B. ON THE APPIAN WAY

Milō autem, cum in senātū fuisset eō diē quoad senātus est dīmissus, domum vēnit, 8
calceōs et vestīmenta mūtāvit, paulisper, dum sē uxor, ut fit, comparat, commorātus est, 9
dein profectus id temporis, cum iam Clōdius, sī quidem eō diē Rōmam ventūrus erat, 10
redīre potuisset. Obviam fit eī Clōdius, expedītus, in equō, nūllā raedā, nūllīs im- 11
pedīmentīs, nūllīs Graecīs comitibus, ut solēbat, sine uxōre, quod numquam ferē: cum 12
hic īnsidiātor, quī iter illud ad caedem faciendam apparāsset, cum uxōre veherētur in 13
raedā, paenulātus, magnō et impedītō et muliebrī ac dēlicātō ancillārum puerōrumque 14
comitātū. 15

8. Describe Milo's activities prior to his departure for Lanuvium. (8–9)
9. What humorous aside does Cicero make in line 9?
10. Describe the traveling style of Clodius according to Cicero, and then compare it with that described by Asconius. (11–12; Chapter 58:4–6)
11. In the same way, describe Milo's traveling style, according to both Cicero and Asconius. Do they agree? (12–15; Chapter 58:6–9)
12. Demonstrate the extent of the balance and symmetry between lines 11–12 and 13–15. Why does Cicero employ these devices?
13. How or why does Cicero's description of Milo's manner of travel make his use of the word **īnsidiātor** ironical? (12–15)
14. How does the parade of ablatives in lines 14–15 contribute to this irony?
15. Why would Cicero's word **īnsidiātor** (13) apply more appropriately to Clodius, given his description of the latter?
16. Summarize the differences between the accounts of Cicero and Asconius with respect to the traveling styles of Clodius and Milo. What has Cicero added, omitted, or interpreted? What insight do these differences give us into Cicero's oratorical ability?

The Appian Way

16 **fit obviam**: see note on the previous passage, line 11. Note the use of the historic present throughout this passage. Although the action described took place in past time, the present tense is used to suggest to the listeners/readers that they are present as witnesses.

•**ūndecimus, -a, -um**, *eleventh*.

nōn multō secus: *not much later*, literally, *not otherwise by much*.

17 **complūrēs**: substantive use of the adjective, = **complūrēs hominēs**.

*****tēlum, -ī**, n., *weapon*.

hunc: = Milo, as **hic** and **hunc**, below. Imagine that Cicero is gesturing toward Milo at these points.

faciunt . . . impetum: *they make an attack*.

superior, superiōris: comparative of **superus, -a, -um**, *high*.

*****adversī**: the adjective **adversus, -a, -um**, used substantively here, means *those standing opposite, those in the way* (of the carriage).

18 **reiciō, reicere, reiēcī, reiectus**, *to throw back, throw off*.

reiectā: take with **paenulā** in an ablative absolute.

paenula, -ae, f., *traveling cloak*.

•**dēsiliō, dēsilīre, dēsiluī**, *to leap down*.

ācrī animō: *with stout heart*.

19 **dēfenderet**: a continuation of the circumstantial clause **cum . . . dēsiluisset** begun in the previous line.

partim, adv., *partly* or *some*, when used as a noun; with **illī** = *some of those*. The next **partim** will then mean *others*.

recurrere . . . caedere (21): dependent on **incipiunt** (21).

20 •**adorior, adorīrī, adortus sum**, *to rise up against, attack*.

quod . . . putārent: this causal clause gives the reasoning of the slaves. The verb is in the subjunctive to show that Cicero is giving the reason as theirs, not his.

*****interficiō, interficere, interfēcī, interfectus**, *to kill*.

interfectum: = **interfectum esse**.

21 *****caedō, caedere, cecīdī, caesus**, *to cut down, kill*.

•**incipiō, incipere, incēpī, inceptus**, *to begin*.

Salūs populī suprēma lēx est. *The safety of the people is the supreme law.* (Cicero, *De legibus* III.8)

C. THE ATTACK

    Milō fit obviam Clōdiō ante fundum eius hōrā ferē ūndecimā aut nōn multō secus: 16
statim complūrēs cum tēlīs in hunc faciunt dē locō superiōre impetum; adversī 17
raedārium occīdunt; cum autem hic dē raedā, reiectā paenulā, dēsiluisset sēque ācrī 18
animō dēfenderet, illī, quī erant cum Clōdiō, gladiīs ēductīs, partim recurrere ad rae- 19
dam, ut ā tergō Milōnem adorīrentur, partim, quod hunc iam interfectum putārent, 20
caedere incipiunt eius servōs, quī post erant. 21

17. How does the time of the attack, as presented here, differ from that given by Asconius? (16; Chapter 58:2)
18. How does Cicero claim the fight began? How does this compare with the version presented by Asconius? (17; Chapter 58:9–10)
19. After the attack had begun, what happened first? (17–18)
20. Describe how Milo reacted to the attack, according to Cicero. (18–19) What has been our impression of him up to this point?
21. After drawing their swords, what did Clodius' men do? (19–21)

Cicero
Chiaramonti Museum, the Vatican

22 **Ex quibus servīs**: *of those slaves*, referring to those of Milo under attack in lines 20–21.
animō fidēlī . . . et praesentī: *loyal at heart and steadfast*, ablative of description.
partim . . . partim: in contrast with the description of Clodius' men in lines 19–21.

23 **cum . . . pugnārī vidērent**: *when they saw that (it) was being fought*, an impersonal use of the passive infinitive, which serves here as the direct object of **vidērent**. **Cum** governs **vidērent** (23), **prohibērentur** (23), **audīrent** (24), and **putārent** (24). Note the cumulative effect of these **cum** clauses, which heighten the confusion and uncertainty of Milo's slaves.
succurrō, succurrere, succurrī, succursūrus + dat., *to assist, help*.
*****prohibeō, -ēre, uī, -itus**, *to prevent, prevent from* (+ infinitive).

24 **occīsum**: = **occīsum esse**.
rē vērā, *really, actually*.
rē vērā putārent: = supply **Milōnem occīsum esse**.
id: the antecedent of **quod** in line 26.
servī Milōnis: superfluous after the second **partim** in line 23, but included to emphasize Cicero's claim that it was not Milo himself who had killed Clodius, but Milo's slaves.

25 **apertē**, adv., *openly*.
dērīvō, -āre, -āvī, -ātus, *to divert, turn aside, shift*.
*****crīmen, crīminis**, n., *charge, accusation* (i.e., against Milo).
nec . . . nec . . . nec: note the effective anaphora here.
*****imperō, -āre, -āvī, -ātus**, *to order, command*.
imperante . . . dominō: *at the bidding of (their) master*, part of an extended ablative absolute.

26 *****praesēns, praesentis**, *present, at hand*.
*****quisque, quaeque, quidque**, indefinite pronoun, *each person, everyone*.
quod . . . quisque . . . voluisset: *what everyone would have wanted*. This clause describes the general type of behavior masters expected from their slaves. In this case, such behavior meant Milo's slaves taking a life to avenge the (reported) death of their master and to save their own lives. Cicero addresses here a point raised by the prosecution. After the events of 18 January, Milo had manumitted his slaves, according to Cicero, as a reward for saving his life, but according to the prosecution, to prevent them from being tortured into testifying against their master, which was within the jurisdiction of the prosecution.

Cēdant arma togae, concēdat laurea linguae. *Let arms yield to the toga, let the (general's) laurels yield to the (orator's) tongue.* (Cicero, *De consultatu suo*)

D. CLODIUS' DEATH

Ex quibus servīs quī animō fidēlī in dominum et praesentī fuērunt, partim occīsī 22
sunt, partim, cum ad raedam pugnārī vidērent, dominō succurrere prohibērentur, 23
Milōnem occīsum et ex ipsō Clōdiō audīrent et rē vērā putārent, fēcērunt id servī 24
Milōnis—dīcam enim apertē nōn dērīvandī crīminis causā, sed ut factum est—nec im- 25
perante nec sciente nec praesente dominō, quod suōs quisque servōs in tālī rē facere 26
voluisset. 27

—Cicero, *Pro Milone* X

22. What Latin phrases describe the behavior of Milo's men during the fight? (22)
23. What happened to some of Milo's slaves? (22–23)
24. What combination of circumstances led Milo's men to attack Clodius? List these
    circumstances in the sequence of their occurrence. (23–24)
25. According to Cicero, was Milo himself involved in the decision to kill Clodius?
    (25–26) How does this differ from Asconius' account? (Chapter 58:13–16)
26. What is the dramatic effect of the repeated use of **partim** in this and the previous
    passage? (19, 20, 22, 23)
27. If you were a member of Milo's jury, would you accept a plea of self-defense, based
    on the account of Cicero? On the account of Asconius?

A sarcophagus (stone coffin) with a relief showing a funeral procession

E. THE VERDICT

*During the first day of Milo's five-day trial, some 81 potential jurors had been selected by Pompey. After the summations and before the vote was taken on the final day, both prosecution and defense rejected five jurors from each of the three classes, 30 in all, leaving 51 to decide the verdict. Each juror was given a voting tablet which had **A (absolvō)** on one side and **C (condemnō)** on the other. To vote, he erased one of the letters. Here is the decision:*

Senātōrēs condemnāvērunt duodecim, absolvērunt sex; equitēs condemnāvērunt 1
trēdecim, absolvērunt quattuor, tribūnī aerāriī condemnāvērunt trēdecim, absolvērunt 2
trēs. Vidēbantur nōn ignōrāvisse iūdicēs īnsciō Milōne initiō vulnerātum esse Clō- 3
dium, sed compererant, postquam vulnerātus esset, iussū Milōnis occīsum. Milō in 4
exsilium Massiliam intrā paucissimōs diēs profectus est. Bona eius propter aeris aliēnī 5
magnitūdinem sēmunciā vēniērunt. 6

—Asconius, *Oratio in Milonianum Ciceronis* (extract)

1. What was the total vote for, and against, acquittal? (1–3)
2. On what grounds did the jury convict Milo? (3–4)
3. What happened to Milo himself? (4–5)
4. What happened to his property? (5–6)

2 **tribūnī aerāriī**: *officials of the treasury.*
3 **Vidēbantur**: the subject is **iūdicēs**.
   •**ignōrō, -āre, -āvī, -ātus**, *to be unaware.*
   iūdex, iūdicis, m., *judge, member of the jury.*
   īnsciō Milōne: ablative absolute.
   initiō: *in the beginning, early on.*
4 **comperiō, comperīre, comperī, compertus**, *to find out for certain.*
   iussū, *by order.*
   occīsum: = **occīsum esse**. Supply the pronoun **eum** (= **Clōdium**) as subject of the infinitive.
5 *exsilium, -ī*, n., *exile.*
   Massilia, -ae, f., *Massilia* (a city, modern Marseilles, in Gaul; see the map on page 17).
   •**bona, -ōrum**, n. pl., *"goods," property, possessions.*
   aes aliēnum: *debt*, literally, *another's money*, where **aes, aeris**, n., refers to bronze and copper coins.
6 **sēmuncia, -ae**, f., *a coin worth one twenty-fourth of an* ***as***.
   sēmunciā: *for a song.*
   vēneō, vēnīre, vēniī, vēnitūrus, irreg., *to be sold.*

BUILDING THE MEANING
The Gerundive or Verbal Adjective

Look at this example:

> Milō domum vēnit ad **vestēs mūtandās.**
> *Milo came home for **his clothes about to be changed.***
> (better English) *Milo came home **for (the purpose of) changing his clothes/to change his clothes.***

Note how the *gerundive* **mūtandās** serves as a *verbal adjective* by modifying the noun **vestēs.** The gerundive, because it is future and passive in meaning, is also referred to as the *future passive participle.* It is formed in the same manner as the gerund except that it has all the endings of 1st and 2nd declension adjectives, i.e., those of **magnus, -a, -um.** Here are the forms of the gerundive.

1st	conj.	para***ndus, -a, -um***
2nd	conj.	habe***ndus, -a, -um***
3rd	conj.	mitte***ndus, -a, -um***
3rd	conj. *-iō*	iacie***ndus, -a, -um***
4th	conj.	audie***ndus, -a, -um***

As with the gerund, the gerundive and the noun it modifies can function in any of the usual constructions of nouns in the various cases (see pages 48–49). Remember that, in form and function, *the gerundive is an adjective*, which means that it will modify a noun or pronoun.

The Romans preferred a gerundive to a gerund when the thought required a direct object. For example, the sentence "The citizens went to the Forum for the sake of hearing the speech" could be translated with a gerund in the genitive case ("of hearing"), dependent on **causā**, and a direct object of the verbal idea contained in the gerund ("the speech"):

> Cīvēs ad Forum vēnērunt **ōrātiōnem audiendī** causā.
> *The citizens went to the Forum for the sake **of hearing the speech*** (better English, ***to hear the speech***).

A juror drops his ballot into an urn on this coin from the Roman Republic.

The Romans, however, preferred to put the direct object of the gerund (i.e., **ōrātiōnem**) into the genitive case, dependent upon **causā**, and to modify it with a gerundive (a verbal adjective):

Cīvēs ad Forum vēnērunt **ōrātiōnis audiendae** causā.
*The citizens went to the Forum for the sake **of the speech about to be heard*** (better English, ***to hear the speech***).

Study the comparative chart below and be sure that you understand the differences between gerund (verbal noun) and gerundive (verbal adjective).

The Gerund	The Gerundive
is a verbal noun;	is a verbal adjective;
is equivalent to the English verbal noun in *-ing*;	agrees with a noun or pronoun;
is present and active in meaning;	is future and passive in meaning;
and has only the neuter singular gen., dat., acc., and abl. cases.	and has all the case forms of the adjective **magnus, -a, -um**

Exercise 59a
Read aloud and translate:

1. Competītōrēs cōnsilia capiēbant potestātis obtinendae causā.
2. Necesse erat competītōribus ad multa perīcula subeunda sē parāre.
3. Itaque Pompeiō rogantī cūr ipse cōnsul factus esset Cicerō respondit, "Reī pūblicae dēfendendae causā."
4. Num Clōdius vir idōneus gubernandae reī pūblicae fuit?
5. Cōnābāturne Milō Clōdiō necandō rem pūblicam cōnservāre?
6. Ad corpus Clōdiī cremandum scelestī Cūriam flagrāvērunt.
7. Num Cūria locus idōneus cremandō corporī Clōdiī fuit?
8. Ōrātiōnibus habendīs Cicerō spērābat sē senātōribus persuāsūrum esse.

Exercise 59b
Read each of the following sentences aloud and determine whether it contains a gerund or a gerundive. Then translate:

1. Necesse erat Clōdiō ad contiōnem adesse ad ōrātiōnēs habendās.
2. Milōne cōnsule, Clōdius scīvit sē cōnsilia capere nōn posse ad dēlendam rem pūblicam.
3. Crēdisne Clōdium competītōris necandī causā īnsidiās collocāvisse?

4. Servīs occīsīs, Clōdius cōnātus est sē ipsum servāre fugiendō.
5. Complūrēs hominēs in Milōnem dīcendō invidiam plēbis augēre cōnātī sunt.
6. Cicerō putābat sē Milōnem cōnservāre posse ōrātiōne habendā.
7. Milōnī quaerentī Cicerō respondit, "Vēra dīcendō līberāberis."

Exercise 59c

Complete each of the following sentences with the correct form of the gerundive and then translate the sentence. The infinitive is provided.

1. Comitia cōnsulis _____ grātiā habērī dēbent. (creāre)
2. Dictātōrēs ā cōnsulibus ad rem pūblicam _____ nōminātī sunt. (custōdīre)
3. Praetōrēs scelestī _____ multum temporis dant. (iūdicāre)
4. Ōrātōrēs convocātī sunt ad ōrātiōnēs _____. (habēre)
5. Dēlēbuntne factiōnēs rem pūblicam impetū in cīvēs _____? (facere)

    comitia, -ōrum, n. pl., *electoral assembly*
    in, prep. + acc., *against*

Gerundive of Obligation (Passive Periphrastic)

Look at these examples:

    Scelestī pūniendī sunt.
    Criminals have to be (must be) punished.

    Epistula erat scrībenda.
    The letter had to be written.

    Vēra dīcenda erunt.
    The truth will have to be spoken.

You will recognize the forms **pūniendī, scrībenda,** and **dīcenda** as gerundives. When used with a form of **esse**, provided or understood, the gerundive is known as a *gerundive of obligation* or *passive periphrastic*, and is translated *must be . . . , should be . . . ,* or *has to be . . .*

An *impersonal* gerundive of obligation is found with intransitive verbs (those that do not take a direct object). In Chapter 48 you met the following:

    Nunc domum nōbīs **redeundum est.** (48:20)
    *Now we **must return** home* (literally, *Now there **must be a returning** home by us.*)

There is no expressed subject; the gerundive is neuter and so ends in **-um**. The best procedure is to translate such impersonal gerundives of obligation actively in English. Here is another example:

    Milōnī Rōmā **discēdendum erit.**
    *Milo **will have** to leave Rome* (literally, *There **will have to be a leaving** from Rome by Milo).*

Dative of Agent

Consider the following example:

> Milō **Cicerōnī** dēfendendus est.
> *Milo must be defended **by Cicero.***
> ***Cicero** must defend Milo.*

This use of the dative case, called the *dative of agent*, expresses the person or agent by whom the action of the gerundive of obligation is to be carried out; it serves the same function as an ablative of agent (**ā/ab** + abl.) with other passive forms of the verb. Compare the following with the example above:

> Milō **ā Cicerōne** dēfenditur. (ablative of agent)
> *Milo is being defended **by Cicero.***

Exercise 59d
Read aloud and translate:

1. Lēgēs omnibus cīvibus observandae sunt.
2. Pompeius dē Cicerōne quaerēbat quae cōnsilia capienda essent dē Milōne.
3. Quis negābit Milōnem Rōmā dīmittendum esse?
4. Multa perīcula candidātīs semper cavenda erunt.
5. Cupiditās interficiendī omnibus vītanda est.
6. Pompeius cōnsul imperāvit ut omnēs quī caedem Clōdiī fēcissent pūniendī essent.
7. Num Rōma ab omnibus bonīs relicta est?
8. Clōdiō occīsō, Milō intellēxit sibi poenam dandam esse.
9. Cicerō iūdicibus persuādēre cōnātur nē Milō in exsilium mittendus sit.
10. Hoc mihi faciendum erat.

Exercise 59e
Supply the dative case of the pronoun in parentheses, then read aloud and translate:

1. Sī nōbīscum venīre nōn vīs, ____ domī manendum est. (tū)
2. Hic ōrātor ____ est laudandus quod mihi maximē placuit. (ego)
3. Cicerō in exsilium īre iussus erat. ____ igitur Rōmā erat ēgrediendum. (is)
4. Ubi Rōmam pervēneritis, Cūria incēnsa ____ vīsitanda erit. (vōs)
5. Fātum suum ____ est ferendum. (quisque)

Numquam . . . praestantibus in rē pūblicā gubernandā virīs laudāta est in ūnā sententiā perpetua permānsiō. *Persistence in a single view has never been regarded as a merit in political leaders.* (Cicero, *Epistulae ad familiares* I.9.21)

REVIEW XIV: Chapters 58–59

Exercise XIVa: Politics in the Late Republic
Answer the following questions:

1. Where was Julius Caesar and what was he doing during the political turmoil of the 50s B.C.? Who was his agent in Rome?
2. Who became the most influential leader in Rome during Caesar's absence? Who was one of his well-known agents?
3. For what office was Milo a candidate in 52? Clodius?
4. In what way could the events of 53–52 B.C. be seen as a foreshadowing of the years 49–45 B.C.?
5. Characterize the political life of Rome during the last century B.C. Cite a Latin **sententia** from this chapter in support of your observations.

Exercise XIVb: The Life of Cicero
Answer the following questions:

1. Give three facts about Cicero's political life.
2. Give the English equivalents of the following Latin titles of some of Cicero's most famous writings: *Epistulae ad familiares, De republica, Orationes in Catilinam, Epistulae ad Atticum, De officiis, Orationes in Verrem, Philippicae, Pro Archia,* and *De imperio Cn. Pompei.* Use a classical dictionary or other reference, as necessary.
3. How old was Cicero when he delivered his speech *Pro Milone*?

Exercise XIVc: Oratory
Answer the following questions:

1. Identify the following parts of a Roman speech: **exōrdium, partītiō, cōnfirmātiō, refutātiō,** and **perōrātiō.**
2. Name two Roman authors who wrote about oratory and give the titles of their works.
3. Do Cicero's speeches provide completely reliable accounts of people and events of the late Republic? Why or why not?
4. Identify the following terms: **Rostra, contiō, rēs pūblica, ambitiō, toga candida, iūdex.**

Exercise XIVd: Gerunds and Gerundives
Translate and identify all gerunds, gerundives, and gerundives of obligation:

1. Quot iūdicēs crēdidērunt Milōnem condemnandum esse?
2. Praetōrēs creātī sunt ad iūdicandum.
3. Cicerō reī pūblicae serviēbat bonīs ōrātiōnibus habendīs.

4. Milō Clōdium necāvit suī servandī causā.
5. Quis Clōdiō erat modus operandī? Eratne īnsidiae?
6. Inimīcō mortuō, Milō in raedam ā servīs sublātus est.
7. Catō semper dīcēbat Carthāginem dēlendam esse.
8. Īnsidiīs factīs, putāvitne Clōdius sē moritūrum esse?
9. Factiōnēs reī pūblicae servandae grātiā dēlendae sunt.
10. Ōrātiō prō Milōne Cicerōnī est cōnficienda.

The Senate House (**Cūria**), rebuilt by Caesar after the fire described in Chapter 58C. Its present form (as shown in this photograph)dates from the end of the third century A.D.

The abbreviation **Q.E.D.**, for **quod erat dēmōnstrandum**, *which was to be shown*, is often found following mathematical proofs and solutions to problems.

Carthāgō dēlenda est! *Carthage must be destroyed!*
(Exclaimed by Cato the Elder at Senate meetings prior to the Third Punic War.)

PART III
WARFARE IN THE LATE REPUBLIC

The supreme man of war during the late Republic was C. Julius Caesar. He fought a continuous war (58–51 B.C.) against the barbarians of Gaul, ostensibly to protect the northern frontier of Rome but also to win allies, increase his war chest, and build up an army personally loyal to him as commander. His achievements, which included the conquest of all Gaul, its addition to the Roman Empire, and Rome's first official contact with the far-flung shores of Britain, were chronicled in his famous *Commentarii de bello Gallico* (*Commentaries on the Gallic War*). Caesar's Gallic achievements and Pompey's rise to the sole consulship of Rome precipitated a confrontation between the two generals, which erupted on 10 January 49 B.C. when Caesar led his troops out of his province of Gaul and across the Rubicon River into Italy. There followed four years of bloody civil war between the Pompeians, who represented the Republic and the interests of the Senate, and the Caesarians, who favored radical political change and the transfer of power to the middle class. Pompey, along with many senators, fled to Greece. Caesar, postponing a march on Rome itself, first protected his flank by defeating Pompeian forces in Spain and then met Pompey in Greece at the battle of Pharsalus.

In his *Commentarii de bello civili* (*Commentaries on the Civil War*), Caesar provides memoirs or reports of the events of 49–48 B.C., in which he attempts to present himself and his cause in the best possible light. Cicero's letters to his friends and family during this period provide a personal counterpoint to the propaganda of Caesar's writing. Upon the outbreak of hostilities, Cicero found himself caught in a dilemma: should he support Pompey, who had helped in his recall from exile and now represented the cause of the Republic, or should he support Caesar to insure his own safety and that of his family?

Duae sunt artēs igitur quae possunt locāre hominēs in amplissimō gradū dignitātis: ūna imperātōris, altera ōrātōris bonī. *There are two professions that lead a man to the highest rank of office, that of general, and that of good orator.* (Cicero, *Pro Murena* 30)

Nec quemquam iam ferre potest Caesarve priōrem, Pompeiusve parem. *Caesar cannot tolerate a superior, nor Pompey an equal.* (Lucan, *De bello civili* I.125–126)

---

1 **Tullius**: the name by which Marcus Tullius Cicero was affectionately known to his wife Terentia.
   Tulliolae: Tullia was Cicero's daughter; Tulliola is a diminutive.
   duābus animīs suīs: in apposition to **Terentiae et . . . Tulliolae**.
   *****anima, -ae**, f., *soul, darling.*
2 **Suaviss.**: = **suāvissimae**; **suāvis, -is, -e**, *sweet.*
   S.P.D.: **salūtem plūrimam dīcit.**
3 •**valeō, -ēre, -uī, -itūrus**, *to be well.*
   cōnsilium: translate as *concern* rather than *plan.*
4 **ille**: = Caesar, as is **homō** in line 5.
   modestē, adv., *with restraint, under control.*
   rēctē . . . esse: *to be all right.*
   in praesentiā: *at present, for the time being.*
5 *****sīn**: = **sī + nē**, *but if, on the other hand.*
   *****āmēns, āmentis**, *mad, insane, mindless.*
   dīripiendam: *to be plundered* (by his soldiers).
   vereor ut . . . possit: *I am afraid that . . . will <u>not</u> be able.*
   Dolābella: P. Cornelius Dolabella, whom Tullia had married the previous year, was a supporter of Julius Caesar.
6 *****prōsum, prōdesse, prōfuī**, irreg. + dat., *to help, benefit.*
   illud metuō nē . . . interclūdāmur: *I fear this, that we may be cut off.*
   interclūdō, interclūdere, interclūsī, interclūsus, *to cut off, shut off.*
   ut . . . nōn liceat: a result clause; understand **vōbīs** with **liceat**.
7 **Reliquum est quod**: *There remains (a matter) which.*
   vestrī similēs: *like you*; **vestrī** is genitive of the pronoun **vōs**.
   sintne: *(whether) or not there are*; a double indirect question, with the first part omitted.
8 **videndum est**: *(you) must consider.*
   ut: *how* or *whether* in an indirect question.
   honestē, adv., *respectably, with honor.*
   Quōmodo quidem nunc sē rēs habet: *As things stand now*, literally, *How indeed the situation holds itself now.*
9 **modo ut**: *provided that*, followed by a subjunctive verb.
   haec . . . loca: i.e., the area of Campania, centering on Capua, where Cicero was in charge and where he owned several estates (see the map on page 12).
   bellissimē: *in great comfort.*
10 **praedium, -ī**, n., *estate, property.*
   illud verendum est, nē: *there should be concern that*, literally, *this must be feared, that.*
   •**famēs, famis**, f., *hunger.*
11 **velim . . . cōnsīderētis**: *I wish you would make plans.*
   Pompōniō . . . Camillō: T. Pomponius Atticus was Cicero's literary adviser and confidant. Camillus was a friend and fellow lawyer.
12 **ad summam**: *in short.*
   animō fortī: *courageous*, literally, *of brave spirit.*
13 **istīc**, adv., *over there* (i.e., in Rome).

EYEWITNESS TO CIVIL WAR

These four selections from Cicero's correspondence date from the early months of the civil war between Caesar and Pompey. They reveal his personal and political anxieties, as he witnessed what were to become the death throes of the Republic. In Reading A, Cicero is writing en route to Capua on 22 January 49 B.C., in reply to a letter from his wife Terentia. At Pompey's request, he had taken charge of levying troops in Campania, leaving his family in Rome.

A. FROM CICERO TO HIS FAMILY

Tullius Terentiae et pater Tulliolae, duābus animīs suīs, et Cicerō mātrī optimae, 1
suāviss. sorōrī S.P.D. 2
Sī vōs valētis, nōs valēmus. Vestrum iam cōnsilium est, nōn sōlum meum, quid sit 3
vōbīs faciendum. Sī ille Rōmam modestē ventūrus est, rēctē in praesentiā domī esse 4
potestis; sīn homō āmēns dīripiendam urbem datūrus est, vereor ut Dolābella ipse satis 5
nōbīs prōdesse possit. Etiam illud metuō nē iam interclūdāmur, ut, cum velītis, exīre 6
nōn liceat. Reliquum est quod ipsae optimē cōnsīderābitis, vestrī similēs fēminae sintne 7
Rōmae. Sī enim nōn sunt, videndum est ut honestē vōs esse possītis. Quōmodo qui- 8
dem nunc sē rēs habet, modo ut haec nōbīs loca tenēre liceat, bellissimē vel mēcum vel 9
in nostrīs praediīs esse poteritis. Etiam illud verendum est, nē brevī tempore famēs in 10
urbe sit. Hīs dē rēbus velim cum Pompōniō, cum Camillō, cum quibus vōbīs vidēbitur, 11
cōnsīderētis, ad summam, animō fortī sītis. Vōs, meae cārissimae animae, quam saepis- 12
simē ad mē scrībite et vōs quid agātis et quid istīc agātur. Valē. 13

—Cicero, *Epistulae ad familiares* XIV.14

1. Under what conditions does Cicero think his family can safely remain in Rome? (4–5)
2. What might happen when Caesar enters Rome? What does Cicero fear in this case? (5–6)
3. What additional fear does Cicero express? (6–7)
4. What fact should his family consider in deciding whether to stay in Rome? (7–8)
5. Where does Cicero suggest that his family seek refuge? Under what conditions will this be possible? (8–10)
6. What else does Cicero fear? (10–11)
7. What two pieces of advice does Cicero give everyone in lines 11–12?
8. What final request does Cicero make of his family? (12–13)

1 •**Sal.: Salūtem.** This letter was written on 8 or 9 February 49 B.C.
  Pedem: one **pēs**, or Roman foot, = .97 English feet or .29 meters.
  *istīus: genitive singular of **iste, ista, istud**, *that* (person or thing), a word frequently used to
     show contempt. The word refers to Caesar, here and in line 6 below.
  *potestās, potestātis, f., *power.*
2 **nisi in nāvem sē contulerit**: *unless he boards a ship*, literally, *unless he will have boarded a ship.*
  exceptum īrī: *will be captured*, the rare future passive infinitive.
  quid agam: *what should I do?*
3 •**persequor, persequī, persecūtus sum**, *to follow, pursue.*
  tūtō, adv., *safely.*
  Fac posse tūtō: = **Fac (mē) posse (trādere) tūtō**, *Suppose that I can surrender (to Caesar) safely.*
5 •**hortor, -ārī, -ātus sum**, *to encourage, urge on.*
  num . . . honestē?: = **num (mē trādere possum) honestē?**
  honestē, adv., *honorably.*
  *equidem, adv., *certainly.*
6 •**explicō, -āre, -āvī, -ātus**, *to unfold, explain, settle* (a difficulty).

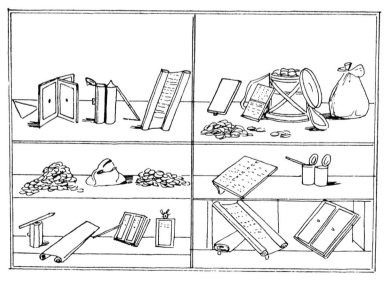

Writing materials (from a Pompeian wall-painting)

C. Iulius Caesar   M. Tullius Cicero   Cn. Pompeius Magnus

B. FROM CICERO TO ATTICUS

Cicerō Atticō Sal.   1
    Pedem in Italiā videō nūllum esse, quī nōn in istīus potestāte sit. Dē Pompeiō sciō   2
nihil, eumque, nisi in nāvem sē contulerit, exceptum īrī putō. Ego quid agam? Quā aut   3
terrā aut marī persequar eum, quī ubi sit, nesciō? Trādam igitur istī mē? Fac posse   4
tūtō (multī enim hortantur), num etiam honestē? Nūllō modō. Equidem ā tē petam   5
cōnsilium, ut soleō. Explicārī rēs nōn potest.   6

—Cicero, *Epistulae ad Atticum* VII.22 (extract)

1. According to Cicero, what progress has Caesar made during the war, thus far? (2)
2. In contrast, what does he write about Pompey? (2–3)
3. What emotion do lines 3–4 convey? Apathy? Fear? Frustration? Sorrow?
4. Discuss the options Cicero presents to Atticus. (3–5)
5. In what manner does Cicero discuss his options? Does he seem to be a decisive person?
6. What does Cicero's refusal to name Caesar imply about his sympathies? What is the force of the demonstratives **istīus** and **istī** (2 and 4)?
7. What reservation does Cicero have about delivering himself over to Caesar? (4–5)
8. What is Cicero's final request to Atticus? Why? (5–6)

1 **Cn. Magnus**: Pompey was called Magnus after 81 B.C. because of victories in Italy, Sicily, and Africa.

Prōcōs: Pompey was officially governor (**prōcōnsul**) of Spain.

Cicerōnī Imp.: Cicero is greeted as a victorious general (**imperātor**) by virtue of his conquest of native bandits while governing in Asia Minor the previous year. Pompey wrote this letter to Cicero on 20 February 49 B.C.

2 **S.V.B.**: = Sī valēs, bene (est).

Tuās litterās: this letter is in reply to one received from Cicero several days earlier, asking whether Cicero should stay in Capua or join Pompey.

****prīstinus, -a, -um**, *previous, former.*

****virtūs, virtūtis**, f., *courage, determination, strength.*

3 ****salūs, salūtis**, f., *safety.*

****commūnis, -is, -e**, *common, joint, public.*

Āpulia: still the name of a region of southeastern Italy.

4 •**magnopere**, adv., *greatly, seriously.*

•**prō**, prep. + abl., *for, on behalf of.*

singulāris, -is, -e, *outstanding, unique, extraordinary.*

•**studium, -ī**, n., *eagerness, enthusiasm, support.*

tē . . . cōnferās: *you should come,* literally, *you should bring yourself.*

5 ****afflīgō, afflīgere, afflīxī, afflictus**, *to strike down.*

****ops, opis**, f., *aid, help.*

6 ****cēnseō, cēnsēre, cēnsuī, cēnsus**, *to be of the opinion, think.*

cēnseō is followed by the indirect commands **ut . . . faciās** and **(ut) . . . veniās.**

1 **Caesar . . . Imp.**: Caesar wrote this letter in March 49 B.C.

2 **Cum**: *Although.*

•**properō, -āre, -āvī, -ātus**, *to hurry.*

essem in itinere: Caesar is on the march in pursuit of Pompey.

****praemittō, praemittere, praemīsī, praemissus**, *to send ahead.*

3 ****dubitō, -āre, -āvī, -ātus**, *to doubt, hesitate.*

nōn dubitāvī quīn + subjunctive: *I did not hesitate to.*

****grātiās agere** + dat., *to give thanks, to thank.*

****etsī**, conj., *even if, although.*

et saepius mihi factūrus (esse) videor: *and it seems to me that I will do this more often.*

4 ****mereor, merērī, meritus sum**, *to deserve, earn.*

Ita dē mē merēris: *You deserve this from me.*

In prīmīs: *First of all.*

petō: governs the indirect command **ut . . . videam.**

****cōnfīdō, cōnfīdere, cōnfīsus sum**, *to trust, believe.*

5 **ventūrum**: = ventūrum esse.

****grātia, -ae**, f., *favor, influence.*

****dignitās, dignitātis**, f., *prestige, good name, reputation.*

ope omnium rērum: *the help of all (your) resources.*

6 ****ūtor, ūtī, ūsus sum** + abl., *to use, make use of.*

festīnātiō, festīnātiōnis, f., *haste.*

brevitās, brevitātis, f., *brevity, shortness.*

****ignōscō, ignōscere, ignōvī, ignōtus** + dat., *to pardon.*

C. FROM POMPEY TO CICERO

Cn. Magnus Prōcōs. S. D. M. Cicerōnī Imp.   1
    S.V.B. Tuās litterās libenter lēgī. Recognōvī enim tuam prīstinam virtūtem etiam   2
in salūte commūnī. Cōnsulēs ad eum exercitum, quem in Āpuliā habuī, vēnērunt.   3
Magnopere tē hortor prō tuō singulārī perpetuōque studiō in rem pūblicam, ut tē ad   4
nōs cōnferās, ut commūnī cōnsiliō reī pūblicae afflictae opem atque auxilium ferāmus.   5
Cēnseō ut viā Appiā iter faciās et celeriter Brundisium veniās.   6

—Cicero, *Epistulae ad Atticum* VIII.11C

1. What comment does Pompey make about Cicero's letter? (2)
2. What news does Pompey provide about his own military status? (3)
3. What is Pompey urging Cicero to do? (3–4)
4. What is his justification for making this request? (4)
5. In what way does Pompey feel that Cicero can help? (5)
6. What final request does Pompey make? (6)

D. FROM CAESAR TO CICERO

Caesar Imp. S. D. Cicerōnī Imp.   1
    Cum properārem atque essem in itinere, praemissīs iam legiōnibus, tamen nōn   2
dubitāvī quīn et scrīberem ad tē et grātiās tibi agerem, etsī hoc et fēcī saepe et saepius   3
mihi factūrus videor. Ita dē mē merēris. In prīmīs ā tē petō, quoniam cōnfīdō mē ce-   4
leriter ad urbem ventūrum, ut tē ibi videam, ut tuō cōnsiliō, grātiā, dignitāte, ope om-   5
nium rērum ūtī possim. Festīnātiōnī meae brevitātīque litterārum ignōscēs.   6

—Cicero, *Epistulae ad Atticum* IX.6A (extract)

1. Under what circumstances is Caesar writing this letter? (2)
2. What news does Caesar provide about *his* military status? (2)
3. Why is Caesar writing to Cicero? (3)
4. What does he state about his previous relationship with Cicero? About his future relationship? (3–4)
5. What request does Caesar make of Cicero? (4–5)
6. How does Caesar feel that Cicero will help his cause? (5–6)
7. For what does he ask Cicero's pardon? (6)

After vacillating for several months in despair over what his position should be, Cicero finally wrote that he would "rather be conquered with Pompey than conquer with Caesar" and joined the Republican forces in Greece.

BUILDING THE MEANING
Clauses of Fearing

Thus far, you have learned that **ut** (or negative **nē**) introduces several different types of subjunctive clauses: indirect command, purpose, and result (negative **ut nōn**). A fourth type, clauses of *fearing*, is illustrated by the following sentences from the reading:

> . . . vereor **ut** Dolābella ipse satis nōbīs prōdesse **possit.** (A:5–6)
> . . . *I fear **that** Dolabella himself **cannot** be of sufficient help to us.*

> . . . metuō **nē** iam **interclūdāmur.** . . .(A:6)
> . . . *I am afraid **that we may be cut off** already.* . . .

You will note that a clause of fearing is introduced by a word expressing fear and uses **ut** or **nē** and a verb in the subjunctive (usually present or imperfect), following the regular rules for sequence of tenses. The word expressing fear is usually a verb such as **metuō, timeō,** or **vereor,** but it can be a noun such as **metus, timor,** or **perīculum.** Note in the examples above that in clauses of fearing, unlike other **ut** or **nē** clauses, **ut** is translated *that . . . not,* and **nē** is translated *that.*

The verbs above may also be accompanied by an infinitive, e.g.:

> Cicerō Terentiam **relinquere** timēbat.
> *Cicero was afraid **to leave** Terentia behind.*

Exercise 60a
Read aloud and translate:

1. Pompeius veritus est nē Caesar tōtam Italiam in eius potestāte iam habēret.
2. Terentia atque Tullia Rōmae diūtius manēre timēbant.
3. Equidem Caesar nōn verēbātur ut Pompeium vinceret.
4. Cicerō verērī vidētur nē Caesar cīvibus Rōmānīs noceat.
5. Timetne Cicerō ut Dolābella Tulliam servāre possit?
6. Atticus semper metuēbat nē Caesar dictātor fierī vellet.
7. Nē Cicerō ā Terentiā iam interclūsus esset summus metus fuit.
8. Cicerō timet ut Terentia epistulam accipiat.
9. Omnēs Rōmānī verēbantur nē bella cīvīlia fierent.
10. Caesar metuit nē Cicerō ad Pompeium trānseat.

Exercise 60b
Read aloud, translate, and identify the type of clause introduced by **ut** or **nē**.

1. Amīcī quīdam Cicerōnis hortābantur nē sē Caesarī trāderet.
2. Cicerō proficīscitur Capuam ut Pompeiī adiuvandī causā mīlitēs cōnscrībat.
3. Timēbatne Pompeius nē Cicerō auxilium Caesarī latūrus esset?
4. Tanta famēs Rōmae erat ut nēmō satis cibī habēret.
5. Pompeius, ut omnēs scītis, plūrēs mīlitēs quam Caesar habuit.
6. Pompeius Cicerōnī scrīpsit ut auxilium obtinēret.
7. Cicerō metuēbat ut familia sua tūta in urbe esset.
8. Cicerō uxōrem et fīliam monuit ut Rōmā esset proficīscendum.
9. Caesar adeō cupiēbat Cicerōnem sibi conciliāre ut epistulam adulantem ad eum mīsit.
10. Pompeius Cicerōnem ad Campaniam mittet ut mīlitēs cōnscrībat.

> **conciliō, -āre, -āvī, -ātus,** *to win over*
> **adulāns, adulantis,** *flattering*

Exercise 60c
Imagine that you are Cicero's daughter Tullia or son Marcus. Write in English a return letter to your father, responding to his concerns in reading A above. Describe what life is like in Rome, now that civil war has begun.

Exercise 60d
1. Compare the letter Pompey wrote to Cicero with the one Caesar wrote (Readings C and D). How are the content, language, and tone similar? How are they different?
2. What does each general hope to gain from Cicero? On what does each base his appeal?
3. What do these two letters reveal about the personalities of the opponents? How does each seem to feel about his cause?
4. What do all four letters tell us about Cicero as a private citizen? As a man of public affairs?

Exercise 60e
Cicero, indecisive for several months, finally determined to join Pompey in Greece. In a subsequent letter, Caesar replied the following. Translate:

Quod nē faciās, prō iūre nostrae amīcitiae ā tē petō. Postrēmō quid virō bonō et quiētō et bonō cīvī magis convenit quam abesse ā cīvīlibus contrōversiīs?

—quoted by Cicero in *Epistulae ad Atticum* X.8b

> **quod:** = to join Pompey
> **nē faciās:** indirect command dependent on **petō**
> **prō iūre:** *by right*
> **magis quid . . . convenit?:** *what is more appropriate?*

THE ROMAN ARMY

The Roman army was organized into units called legions (**legiōnēs**), each of which had a number and a name, such as the **LEGIŌ IX HISPĀNA**; Caesar's favorite was the 10th. A legion contained approximately 5,000 men organized into ten cohorts (**cohortēs**). Each cohort contained six centuries (**centuriae**), composed of about 80 men. A century was made up of 10 mess-tents (**contubernia**), each of which housed eight men. The century was commanded by a centurion (**centuriō**), an experienced veteran who carried a wooden swagger-stick with which to discipline his men.

The historian Tacitus, describing a mutiny that occurred in Germany during the first century A.D., tells this story about a centurion:

> A centurion named Lucilius was killed by his troops at the start of the mutiny. This man had earned their hatred because of the punishments he handed out among his men. They had nicknamed him **Cedo alteram** (*Gimme another*) because every time he broke his vine-stick on a soldier's back he called for another.
>
> —Tacitus, *Annales* I.23

The highest-ranking centurion (**prīmus pīlus**) of each legion headed the senior centurions (**prīmī ōrdinēs**), all of whom served in the First Cohort. By the beginning of the Empire, the Roman armed forces numbered some 390,000 men (10,000 Italian forces, 150,000 Roman legionaries, and 230,000 allied infantry, cavalry, and irregular troops).

The legion and its units were identified by particular standards or insignia (**signa mīlitāria**). The standard (**signum**) of each century was borne by a standard-bearer (**signifer**), and the silver eagle (**aquila**) of each legion by an "eagle-bearer" (**aquilifer**). A legion could be dissolved after losing its standard in battle, as happened when Crassus lost the eagles to the Parthians in 53 B.C. (see 57B:6 and the coin on page 37). Caesar describes the bravery of an **aquilifer** who led a charge during the Roman landing in Britain in 54 B.C.:

> The Romans were hesitant because of the depth of the water when the eagle-bearer of the 10th legion, after praying to the gods that his action might bring them luck, cried: "Jump down, comrades, unless you want to surrender the eagle to the enemy. I at least intend to do my duty to my country and my general." With these words he jumped from the ship and advanced on the enemy with the eagle in his hands. When the other soldiers saw this, they urged each other not to allow such a disgrace to happen and also jumped while the men in the ships followed them.
>
> —Caesar, *Commentarii de bello Gallico*, V.1

Signa from Trajan's Column

Subordinate to the legionary commander (**lēgātus**) were six staff officers or tribunes (**tribūnī mīlitum**), five of whom commanded the ten legionary cohorts and the sixth of whom, as senior tribune, served as second-in-command. The term **imperātor**, source of the English word "emperor," served as a title of honor reserved for those generals (**ducēs**) who had won a major victory.

Battle cavalry (**equitēs** or **equitātus**) was provided by auxiliaries (**auxilia**) recruited from Rome's provincial allies or from peoples or tribes loyal to a particular general. These horse-soldiers, who were commanded by a Roman officer (**praefectus**), served on the legion's flanks as support. Under Augustus, the cavalry was regularly organized into units of 1,000 men called wings (**alae**), subdivided into squadrons (**turmae**). The auxiliary forces also provided other support troops such as archers (**sagittāriī**), slingers (**funditōrēs**), and light-armed soldiers (**numerī**). Soldiers in these units could receive Roman citizenship upon discharge.

Legionary footsoldiers (**peditēs**) of the Republic were equipped for both offensive and defensive fighting. Offensive weapons (**tēla**) included a javelin (**pīlum**), which was thrown from a distance before the charge into the enemy, and a short sword (**gladius**) used for hand-to-hand combat. The point of the spear was made of soft metal to enable it to bend when it penetrated an enemy shield, making the shield heavy and unwieldly. The defensive equipment consisted of a bronze and iron helmet (**galea**) and body armor (**lōrīca**) worn over a woolen tunic. Each footsoldier also carried a four-foot, slightly curved shield (**scūtum**) of wood covered with leather and bound with metal.

In battle the ranks of infantry (**ōrdinēs**) were organized into battle lines (**aciēs**). The most popular formation was the triple battle line (**aciēs triplex**), with the cavalry and support troops on the right and left wings (**cornua**). The signals for maneuvering battle formations were given (**signum dare**) by war trumpets (**tubae**) and by movement of the unit insignia.

Legionary soldier of the Republic

Roman soldiers carried with them all equipment necessary for battle and for life on the march. Their 45-pound packs led to the nickname "Marius' mules." The organization of the Roman army enabled it to make camp (**castra pōnere**) quickly and efficiently while on the march. Each soldier had a specialized task for which he carried the appropriate tools. Each campsite was laid out in a square with the two main camp roads intersecting within the fort and the general's tent (**praetōrium**) at the center. The camp's perimeter was secured by a ditch (**fossa**) dug by soldiers and by an earthen rampart constructed from the excavated earth and topped by a palisade (**vallum**) of upright pointed logs. (See the illustration on page 89.) The men's leather tents (**tabernācula**) were then set up in fixed positions within the fortress. These temporary camps, when placed in particularly strategic locations along the frontier, often were turned into permanent stone forts, which became centers of Romanization in the provinces. These centers eventually became towns and cities that modeled themselves on Rome and that could apply for citizenship and other rights. Many modern British place names, such as Manchester, Leicester, and Newcastle, take their names from the Roman word **castra**. Other cities of the Roman Empire, such as Colonia Agrippinensis (modern Cologne, in Germany) derived from permanent settlements of retired legionaries (**colōniae**).

1 **cum**: conjunction *when*, not preposition *with*.
mīlitārī mōre: *according to the custom of war*, i.e., as generals usually did.
***cohortor, -ārī, -ātus sum**, *to exhort, encourage*.
suaque in eum perpetuī temporis officia: *his (i.e., Caesar's) constant services toward them (the army)*.
2 **officia, -ōrum**, n. pl., *services*.
***praedicō, -āre, -āvī, -ātus**, *to set forth, relate*.
imprīmīs, adv., *especially, particularly*.
commemorō, -āre, -āvī, -ātus, *to recall, remind*.
testis, testis, gen. pl., **testium**, m., *witness*.
testibus: take in apposition to **mīlitibus**, *soldiers as witnesses*.
3 **petīsset**: = **petīvisset**, subjunctive in an indirect question.
abūtor, abūtī, abūsus sum + abl., *to abuse, misuse*.
4 **alteruter, alterutra, alterutrum**, *one of two, either*.
***prīvō, -āre, -āvī, -ātus** + abl., *to deprive of*.
•**ōrātiōnem habēre**, *to deliver a speech*.
exposcō, exposcere, expoposcī, *to insist, implore*.
5 **tuba, -ae**, f., *war horn, trumpet*.
6 **ēvocātus, -ī**, m., *reenlisted or veteran soldier*.
•**superior, superiōris**, *higher, previous; earlier* (of time).
apud eum: *under him (Caesar)*.
7 **prīmum pīlum . . . dūxerat**: *had led the **prīmus pīlus***. The **prīmus pīlus** was a unit of the Roman army, the first century of the first cohort of a legion. This unit derived its name from **pīlum**, *spear, javelin*, because the javelin throwers of the **prīmus pīlus** usually led the attack. The name **prīmus pīlus** came to be associated with the centurion who led that unit.
singulārī virtūte: *of remarkable courage*.
8 **manipulāris, manipulāris**, m., *member of the same maniple (a unit of 200 men), comrade-in-arms*.
•**imperātor, imperātōris**, m., *commander, general*.
quam cōnstituistis operam date: *give the service that you pledged*.
9 ***supersum, superesse, superfuī**, irreg., *to be left, remain*.
10 ***recuperō, -āre, -āvī, -ātus**, *to recover, regain*.
lībertātem recuperābimus: Caesar and his men were technically outlaws, having entered Rome under arms.
Faciam: *I will see to it*. **Faciam** introduces a substantive clause of result.
12 •**dexter, dextra, dextrum**, *right* (the direction).
•**cornū, -ūs**, n., *horn; wing of an army*.
prōcurrō, prōcurrere, prōcucurrī, prōcursūrus, *to run ahead*.
ēlēctus, -a, -um, *picked, select, chosen*.
***circiter**, adv., *around, about*.
•**eiusdem**: genitive of **īdem, eadem, idem**, *the same*.
13 **centuria, -ae**, f., *century (unit of [nominally] 100 men)*.
prōsequor, prōsequī, prōsecūtus sum, *to follow*.

CHAPTER
61

THE BATTLE OF PHARSALUS (PART I)

Caesar defeated Pompey's armies in Spain and then crossed over into Greece. After losing a preliminary engagement at the coastal town of Dyrrachium, Caesar met Pompey on the plain of Pharsalus in 48 B.C. Caesar himself tells the story of the ensuing battle in this and the next chapter.

A. CAESAR EXHORTS HIS MEN TO BATTLE

Exercitum cum mīlitārī mōre ad pugnam cohortārētur suaque in eum perpetuī tem- 1
poris officia praedicāret, imprīmīs commemorāvit testibus sē mīlitibus ūtī posse, quantō 2
studiō pācem petīsset, neque sē umquam abūtī mīlitum sanguine neque rem pūblicam 3
alterutrō exercitū prīvāre voluisse. Hāc habitā ōrātiōne, exposcentibus mīlitibus et stu- 4
diō pugnae ardentibus tubā signum dedit. 5
Erat C. Crāstinus ēvocātus in exercitū Caesaris, quī superiōre annō apud eum 6
prīmum pīlum in legiōne X dūxerat, vir singulārī virtūte. Hic, signō datō, "Sequiminī 7
mē," inquit, "manipulārēs meī quī fuistis, et vestrō imperātōrī quam cōnstituistis ope- 8
ram date. Ūnum hoc proelium superest; quō cōnfectō et ille suam dignitātem et nōs 9
nostram lībertātem recuperābimus." Simul respiciēns Caesarem, "Faciam," inquit, "ho- 10
diē, imperātor, ut aut vīvō mihi aut mortuō grātiās agās." Haec cum dīxisset, prīmus ex 11
dextrō cornū prōcucurrit, atque eum ēlēctī mīlitēs circiter CXX voluntāriī eiusdem 12
centuriae sunt prōsecūtī. 13

—Caesar, *Commentarii de bello civili* III.90–91

1. What did a Roman general usually do before a battle? (1)
2. What was Caesar's initial point in his speech? (1–2)
3. What three additional points could he call upon his soldiers to witness? (2–4)
4. How did Caesar's men react to his speech? (4–5)
5. What does Caesar tell about Crastinus' background? (6–7)
6. What is the substance of Crastinus' speech? (7–10)
7. What does Crastinus say to Caesar himself? (10–11)
8. What does Crastinus do to demonstrate his valor? (11–13)

1   **cum**: conjunction, not preposition.

    *īnfestus, -a, -um, *hostile* (i.e., prepared to attack). For details of the battle, see the plan on page 83.

    pīlum, -ī, n., *spear, lance.*

2   •**concurrō, concurrere, concurrī, concursūrus**, *to run together, attack.*

    nōn concurrī ā Pompeiānīs: *an attack was not being made by Pompey's men, Pompey's men were not attacking.*

    ūsū perītī: *skilled through practice.*

    exercitō, -āre, -āvī, -ātus, *to train.*

    *suā sponte: *of one's own accord, voluntarily.*

3   ***cursus, -ūs**, m., *a charge* (literally, *a running*).

    reprimō, reprimere, repressī, repressus, *to check, stop, cease.*

    *spatium, -ī, n., *space* (between the two armies).

    •**cōnsistō, cōnsistere, cōnstitī**, *to halt, take a stand.*

    cōnsūmptīs vīribus: *with their strength drained, worn out.*

4   •**renovō, -āre, -āvī, -ātus**, *to renew.*

5   **mīsērunt**: = iēcērunt.

    •**praecipiō, praecipere, praecēpī, praeceptus**, *to order, instruct.*

    erat praeceptum: *(it) had been instructed.*

    •**stringō, stringere, strīnxī, strictus**, *to draw* (pull a sword from its sheath).

6   ***dēsum, dēesse, dēfuī**, irreg. + dat., *to be lacking, be unable to deal with.*

    •**excipiō, excipere, excēpī, exceptus**, *to receive, withstand.*

    •**impetus, -ūs**, m., *attack.*

7   **tulērunt**: *they endured, they withstood.*

    *ōrdō, ōrdinis, m., *line, rank* (of soldiers).

    servārunt: = servāvērunt.

    ad gladiōs rediērunt: *resorted to* (literally, *returned to*) *their swords.*

8   •**eques, equitis**, m., *horse-soldier*, pl., *cavalry.*

    •**sinister, sinistra, sinistrum**, *left.*

    •**imperō, -āre, -āvī, -ātus**, *to order, command.*

    ūniversī: *all together.*

9   **sagittārius, -ī**, m., *archer.*

    prōfundō, prōfundere, prōfūdī, prōfūsus, *to pour forth.*

10 ***equitātus, -ūs**, m., *cavalry.*

    •**paulātim**, adv., *little by little, gradually.*

    locō: = ē locō.

    mōtus: perfect passive participle of **moveō**.

    •**cēdō, cēdere, cessī, cessūrus**, *to give way, retreat.*

    hōc ācrius: *all the more fiercely.*

11 •**īnstō, īnstāre, īnstitī**, *to press on, attack.*

    turmātim, adv., *by squadrons.* A **turma** was a squadron of 30 cavalrymen.

    •**explicō, -āre, -āvī, -ātus**, *to unfold, arrange, deploy.*

    •**aciēs, aciēī**, f., *battle line, arrangement of cohorts side by side.*

    *latus, lateris, n., *side, flank.*

    apertus, -a, -um, *open, exposed, unprotected.*

Contrary to the standard tactics of the time, Pompey had ordered his men to stand their ground, instead of hurling their javelins and then charging. Pompey hoped that Caesar's charge would exhaust his men and increase the advantage of Pompey's already-superior numbers.

B. CAESAR'S MEN REACT TO POMPEY'S TACTIC

Sed nostrī mīlitēs datō signō cum īnfestīs pīlīs prōcucurrissent atque animadvertis- 1
sent nōn concurrī ā Pompeiānīs, ūsū perītī ac superiōribus pugnīs exercitātī suā sponte 2
cursum repressērunt et ad medium ferē spatium cōnstitērunt, nē cōnsūmptīs vīribus ap- 3
propinquārent, parvōque intermissō temporis spatiō ac rūrsus renovātō cursū pīla 4
mīsērunt celeriterque, ut erat praeceptum ā Caesare, gladiōs strīnxērunt. Neque vērō 5
Pompeiānī huic reī dēfuērunt. Nam et tēla missa excēpērunt et impetum legiōnum 6
tulērunt et ōrdinēs suōs servārunt pīlīsque missīs ad gladiōs rediērunt. 7

Eōdem tempore equitēs ab sinistrō Pompeiī cornū, ut erat imperātum, ūniversī 8
prōcucurrērunt, omnisque multitūdō sagittāriōrum sē prōfūdit. Quōrum impetum 9
noster equitātus nōn tulit, sed paulātim locō mōtus cessit, equitēsque Pompeiī hōc 10
ācrius īnstāre et sē turmātim explicāre aciemque nostram ā latere apertō circumīre 11
coepērunt. 12

1. How did Caesar's men first react to Pompey's stalling tactic? (2–3)
2. What factors does Caesar say were responsible for this reaction? (2)
3. What did Caesar's men then do, after a brief interval? (4–5)
4. How did Pompey's men respond? (5–7)
5. What happened on Pompey's left wing, as his legionaries defended themselves against Caesar's onrush? (8–9)
6. How did Caesar's cavalry reply to this new attack? (9–10)
7. What danger did the threat of Pompey's cavalry pose to Caesar's position? (10–12)
8. Describe, in general terms, the tactics and weapons used when a Roman army attacked an enemy.
9. Find the Latin words in Reading B for the following military terms: *cavalry* (2 different words), *battle line*, *wing*, *legion*, *javelin*, *sword*, *archer*, and *rank*.

Funditor

1   **Quod**: this refers to Pompey's attack with cavalry on Caesar's right flank, as described in the previous passage.

    quārtae aciēī: Caesar's battle formation normally consisted of three battle lines (**aciēs triplex**).

    *¹**īnstituō, īnstituere, īnstituī, īnstitūtus**, *to set up, arrange*.

    sex cohortium: *from six cohorts*, more than half of a legion.

2   **īnfestīsque signīs**: *in attack formation*, literally, *with hostile standards*. **Signa** were the insignia or "colors" of a unit and were used to direct formations in battle. (See the illustration on page 76.)

    in: *against*.

3   **ut . . . cōnsisteret . . . excēderent**: result clauses, following **tantā vī**.

    convertō, convertere, convertī, conversus, *to turn*.

    nōn sōlum . . . sed (etiam): *not only . . . but (also)*.

    excēdō, excēdere, excessī, excessūrus, *to withdraw, depart*.

    conversī . . . locō excēderent: *turned tail and ran from the field*.

4   ***prōtinus**, adv., *immediately*.

    incitātī fugā: *driven in flight, routed*.

    Quibus: i.e., Pompey's cavalry.

    •**summoveō, summovēre, summōvī, summōtus**, *to move away, drive off*.

5   **funditor, funditōris**, m., *slinger*.

    sagittāriī funditōrēsque: archers and slingers were auxiliary troops who supported the legionary soldiers and who generally served on the wings or behind the last line.

    dēstituō, dēstituere, dēstituī, dēstitūtus, *to abandon, desert*.

    ***inermis, -is, -e**, *unarmed* (**in + arma**).

    ***praesidium, -ī**, n., *guard, protection*.

    sine praesidiō: i.e., by the cavalry.

6   **sinistrum cornū**: direct object of **circumiērunt**.

    pugnantibus . . . ac resistentibus . . . Pompeiānīs: ablative absolute.

    etiam tum: *even then* (when the cavalry had been routed.)

7   •**adorior, adorīrī, adortus sum**, *to rise up against, attack*.

10. What tactic did Caesar use to meet the attack of Pompey's cavalry on his right wing? (1–2)
11. What was the result of the battle between Pompey's cavalry and Caesar's fourth line? (2–4)
12. What happened to Pompey's archers and slingers and why? (4–5)
13. Where did Caesar's fourth battle line attack next? (5–7)

C. CAESAR'S MEN GAIN THE ADVANTAGE

Quod ubi Caesar animadvertit, quārtae aciēī, quam īnstituerat sex cohortium, dedit 1
signum. Illī celeriter prōcucurrērunt īnfestīsque signīs tantā vī in Pompeiī equitēs im- 2
petum fēcērunt, ut eōrum nēmō cōnsisteret, omnēsque conversī nōn sōlum locō excē- 3
derent, sed prōtinus incitātī fugā montēs altissimōs peterent. Quibus summōtīs omnēs 4
sagittāriī funditōrēsque dēstitūtī inermēs sine praesidiō interfectī sunt. Eōdem impetū 5
cohortēs sinistrum cornū pugnantibus etiam tum ac resistentibus in aciē Pompeiānīs 6
circumiērunt eōsque ā tergō sunt adortī. 7

—Caesar, *Commentarii de bello civili* III.93

(to be concluded in Chapter 62)

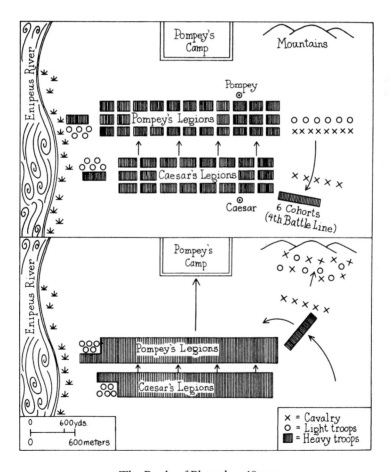

The Battle of Pharsalus, 48 B.C.

ROMAN BULLETS

Lead shots were the projectiles used by slingers (**funditōrēs**), auxiliary soldiers who provided protection for troops during battle or construction of siege-works. The bullets, which the Romans called "acorns" (**glandēs**) were pointed ovals inscribed with the name of the commanding general, the corps of slingers, or the maker of the bullet. Often the inscription contained curses or insults directed at the enemy. A bullet with this inscription was used against Caesar in the civil war:

Cn. Mag(nus) Imp(erātor)

In 91 B.C. Pompeius Strabo, father of Pompey the Great, laid a two-year siege against Asculum, an allied Italian city that had revolted against Roman domination. Here are inscriptions from several bullets found there:

Ferī (side 1) **Pomp(eiu)m** (side 2)
Asc(u)lānīs (d)ōn(um).   **feriō, ferīre**, *to strike*
Fugitīvī perīstis.   **pereō, perīre**, irreg., *to die*
Em tibi malum malō.   **Em**: *Here's. . . .*

BUILDING THE MEANING
Ablative with Special Verbs

Several deponent verbs and their compounds are used with the ablative case: **fruor, fungor, potior, ūtor**, and **vēscor**, of which **ūtor** is the most commonly found. You met **vēscor** in Chapter 49 of Book II:

> Trēs annōs ego et leō in eādem spēluncā habitābāmus, **eōdem cibō** vēscentēs. (49:18)
> *For three years the lion and I lived in the same cave, eating **the same food**.*

In the current passage we have:

> (Caesar) commemorāvit **testibus** sē **mīlitibus** ūtī posse. . . . (A:2)
> *Caesar reminded (his men) that he could make use of **his soldiers as witnesses**. . . .*

Be sure you know the principal parts and meanings of these special verbs that are used with the ablative case:

    fruor, fruī, frūctus sum, *to enjoy, have benefit of*
    fungor, fungī, fūnctus sum, *to perform, discharge*
    potior, potīrī, potītus sum, *to get possession of, obtain*
    ūtor, ūtī, ūsus sum, *to use, make use of*
    vēscor, vēscī, *to eat, feed on*

Exercise 61a

Read aloud and translate:

1. Signō datō, Crāstinus exclāmāvit, "Iacite pīla atque gladiīs ūtiminī!"
2. Cum maximīs labōribus perfūnctī essent, centuriōnēs ā Caesare laudātī sunt.
3. Equitibus repulsīs, Caesaris cohortēs castrīs potītae sunt.
4. In proeliō Pharsālicō, Caesar quattuor aciēbus ūtēbātur.
5. Licēbatne umquam mīlitibus Rōmānīs fēstīs diēbus fruī?
6. Quarta aciēs, quā Caesar contrā equitēs Pompeiī sē ūtī posse spērābat, sex cohortēs habuit.
7. Nōnne Crāstinus officiō suō fungētur?
8. Exercitus Caesaris cōnābātur agrō Pharsālicō potīrī.

Exercise 61b

Complete each sentence with the correct form of the word in parentheses, then read aloud and translate the entire sentence:

1. Necesse est senātōrēs semper _____ ūtī. (prūdentia)
2. Fungēturne pessimus mīles _____ _____? (pessimī labōrēs)
3. Caesare imperātōre, Rōmānī _____ _____ potītī sunt. (flūmen Rhēnum)
4. Peditēs in sinistrō cornū _____ funditōrum fruēbantur. (praesidium)
5. Arma _____ mīlitēs Pompeiānī ūtēbantur gravissima vidēbantur. (quī)

A CASUALTY OF WAR

In A.D. 9, three Roman legions under the command of Quinctilius Varus were annihilated by the Germans. This epitaph commemorates a centurion who fell in this battle. It was inscribed on a cenotaph (a tomb with no remains) probably erected shortly after the disaster. Translate it:

M CAELIO T F LEM BON
O LEG XIIX ANN LIII
CECIDIT BELLO VARIANO OSSA
INFERRE LICEBIT P CAELIVS T F
LEM FRATER FECIT

Marcō Caeliō Titī fīliō, Lemōniā tribū, domō Bonōniā, centuriōnī Legiōnis XIIX, annōrum LIII sēmissis; cecidit bellō Variānō. Ossa īnferre licēbit. Pūblius Caelius Titī fīlius, Lemōniā tribū, frāter fēcit.

Lemōnia, one of 16 tribes into which Roman citizens were divided
tribus, -ūs, f., *tribe*
Bonōnia, -ae, f., *Bonōnia* (modern Bologna)
O: = **centum,** for **centuriō**

sēmis, sēmissis, m., *one-half*
Variānus, -a, -um, *of Quinctilius Varus*
os, ossis, n., *bone*
īnferō, īnferre, intulī, illātus, irreg., *to put, place in or on*

1　**Eōdem tempore**: i.e., as the fourth line made its encircling maneuver.
　　ad id tempus: *up to this time, until then.*
　　locō: = in locō.
2　***recēns, recentis**, *fresh, new.*
　　•**integer, integra, integrum**, *unhurt, intact, vigorous.*
　　　recentēs atque integrī: only Caesar's front lines had engaged in the charge. The third line
　　　　was held in reserve as reinforcement.
　　•**succēdō, succēdere, successī, successūrus** + dat., *to come up, follow, aid.*
　　　aliī: = aliī mīlitēs Caesaris.
3　***sustineō, sustinēre, sustinuī, sustentus**, *to hold out, withstand.*
　　terga vertērunt: *turned tail, retreated.*
4　***fallō, fallere, fefellī, falsus**, *to deceive, mislead.*
　　　Neque . . . Caesarem fefellit: impersonal; *Nor did it mislead Caesar = Nor was Caesar wrong.*
　　***quīn**: *that*; quīn introduces a subordinate clause with the subjunctive.
5　•**collocō, -āre, -āvī, -ātus**, *to station, post, locate.*
　　•**initium, -ī**, n., *beginning, origin.*
　　•**orior, orīrī, ortus sum**, *to arise, begin, originate from.*
　　•**ut**: *as.*
　　in cohortandīs mīlitibus: for part of this speech, see Chapter 61, Reading A, lines 1–4.
6　***prōnūntiō, -āre, -āvī, -ātus**, *to declare, state.*
　　Ab hīs: = Ab hīs cohortibus, i.e., the cohorts mentioned in line 4.
　　***pellō, pellere, pepulī, pulsus**, *to drive away, dislodge.*
　　factae: = factae sunt.
　　•**caedēs, caedis**, gen. pl., **caedium**, f., *massacre, slaughter.*
7　**ā sinistrā parte**: i.e., on the left wing.
　　•**circumeō, circumīre, circumiī, circumitūrus**, irreg., *to surround.*
　　　circumita . . . factum: = circumita est . . . factum est.
9　**ut**: *when.*
　　•**cōnfīdō, cōnfīdere, cōnfīsus sum** + dat., *to trust in, rely on.*
10　**perterritam**: = perterritam esse, indirect statement.
　　diffīdō, diffīdere, diffīsus sum + dat., *to have no confidence in.*
　　sē . . . equō contulit: *he rode*, literally, *he took himself by horse.*
11　***statiō, statiōnis**, f., *post, station, duty.*
　　praetōriam portam: the praetorian gate of a camp was across from the camp headquarters or
　　　general's tent.
12　**clārē**: *in a loud voice, loudly.*
　　***tueor, -ērī, -itus sum**, *to watch over, guard.*
　　sī quid dūrius acciderit: *if anything worse happens*, literally, *if anything worse will have
　　　happened.*
13　•**reliquus, -a, -um**, *remaining, other.*
　　•**cōnfirmō, -āre, -āvī, -ātus**, *to establish firmly, strengthen, encourage.*
14　**praetōrium, -ī**, n., *headquarters, general's tent.*
　　summae reī: *outcome*, literally, *high point of the affair.*
　　ēventus, -ūs, m., *outcome, result.*

THE BATTLE OF PHARSALUS (PART II)

A. CAESAR'S THIRD LINE ENTERS THE ACTION

Eōdem tempore tertiam aciem Caesar, quae quiēta fuerat et sē ad id tempus locō 1
tenuerat, prōcurrere iussit. Ita cum recentēs atque integrī dēfessīs successissent, aliī 2
autem ā tergō adorīrentur, sustinēre Pompeiānī nōn potuērunt atque ūniversī terga 3
vertērunt. Neque vērō Caesarem fefellit quīn ab eīs cohortibus, quae contrā equitātum 4
in quartā aciē collocātae essent, initium victōriae orīrētur, ut ipse in cohortandīs mīliti- 5
bus prōnūntiāverat. Ab hīs enim prīmum equitātus est pulsus, ab eīsdem factae caedēs 6
sagittāriōrum ac funditōrum, ab eīsdem aciēs Pompeiāna ā sinistrā parte circumita atque 7
initium fugae factum. 8

Sed Pompeius, ut equitātum suum pulsum vīdit atque eam partem cui maximē cōn- 9
fīdēbat perterritam animadvertit, aliīs quoque diffīsus aciē excessit prōtinusque sē in 10
castra equō contulit et eīs centuriōnibus quōs in statiōne ad praetōriam portam po- 11
suerat, clārē, ut mīlitēs exaudīrent, "Tuēminī," inquit, "castra et dēfendite dīligenter, sī 12
quid dūrius acciderit. Ego reliquās portās circumeō et castrōrum praesidia cōnfirmō." 13
Haec cum dīxisset, sē in praetōrium contulit summae reī diffīdēns et tamen ēventum 14
exspectāns. 15

—Caesar, *Commentarii de bello civili* III.94

1. What order did Caesar give to the third line? (1–2)
2. Describe Pompey's position, given the movements of Caesar's third and fourth lines. (Consult the battle plan on page 83.)
3. Why did the men of Caesar's third line have an advantage over Pompey's troops? (2)
4. Describe the effect of this attack on Pompey's army. (3–4)
5. Explain Caesar's reasoning about his victory. (4–8)
6. How did Pompey himself react to the realization that Caesar had gained the upper hand in the battle? (9–11)
7. To whom did Pompey speak? Where were they? (11–12)
8. What order did Pompey give them? (12–13)
9. How did Pompey break his word, as narrated in lines 13–15?

1   **ex fugā**: *in retreat.*
     *vāllum, -ī, n., *stockade around a camp* (consisting of a rampart built of pointed logs supported by an earthen embankment on the outside).
     compellō, compellere, compulī, compulsus, *to drive back.*
     perterritīs: take with **Pompeiānīs . . . compulsīs.**
2   ***exīstimō, -āre, -āvī, -ātus**, *to think.*
     beneficium, -ī, n., *favor, generosity, kindness.* Why ablative?
3   ***oppugnō, -āre, -āvī, -ātus**, to attack, storm.
     Quī: the antecedent is **mīlitēs** (2).
     •etsī, conj., *although, even though.*
     •aestus, -ūs, m., *heat.*
     magnō aestū: ablative absolute.
     •merīdiēs, merīdiēī, m., *midday, noon.*
     rēs: *action, engagement.*
     perdūcō, perdūcere, perdūxī, perductus, *to prolong.*
4   **animō parātī**: *with a ready spirit*, literally, *prepared in spirit.*
     •imperium, -ī, n., *command, order.*
     •pareō, parēre, paruī + dat., *to obey, carry out.*
5   **praesidiō**: dative of purpose, *for the purpose of guarding, on guard.*
     •relinquō, relinquere, relīquī, relictus, *to leave behind.*
     industriē, adv., *zealously, eagerly, with energy.*
     multō . . . ācrius: *much more fiercely.*
6   **Thrācibus barbarīsque auxiliīs**: the Thracians were from northeastern Greece. The auxiliaries (**auxilia**) of a Roman army were support troops and were generally noncitizens.
     quī: the antecedent is **mīlitēs**, which comes later in the sentence.
     aciē: = **ex aciē.**
7   **lassitūdō, lassitūdinis**, f., *exhaustion.*
     cōnfectī: *worn out, finished off, done in.*
     missīs . . . signīsque mīlitāribus: for a legion to lose its insignia in battle was a disgrace.
     *plērīque, plēraeque, plēraque, *very many, a large part.*
     •magis, adv., *more.*
8   **dēfēnsiō, dēfēnsiōnis**, f., *defense, protection.*
     quī: the antecedent is **mīlitēs**, understood from line 6 above, which serves as the subject of **potuērunt** (9), **relīquērunt** (10), and **cōnfūgērunt** (11).
10   **dūcibus ūsī**: *under the leadership of*, literally, *using as leaders.*
     ūsī: perfect participle of **ūtor.**
     tribūnīs mīlitum: military tribunes, of which there were six per legion. Each commanded the unit for two months of the year.
11   ***pertineō, pertinēre, pertinuī, pertentus**, *to extend to, reach.* See the battle plan on page 83.

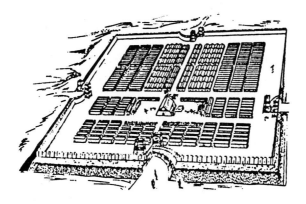

Layout of a camp

B.   CAESAR ATTACKS POMPEY'S CAMP

Caesar Pompeiānīs ex fugā intrā vāllum compulsīs nūllum spatium perterritīs dare   1
oportēre exīstimāns, mīlitēs cohortātus est ut beneficiō fortūnae ūterentur castraque   2
oppugnārent.   Quī, etsī magnō aestū (nam ad merīdiem rēs erat perducta), tamen ad   3
omnem labōrem animō parātī imperiō pāruērunt.   4

Castra ā cohortibus quae ibi praesidiō erant relictae industriē dēfendēbantur, multō   5
etiam ācrius ā Thrācibus barbarīsque auxiliīs.   Nam quī aciē refūgerant mīlitēs, et ani-   6
mō perterritī et lassitūdine cōnfectī, missīs plērīque armīs signīsque mīlitāribus, magis   7
dē reliquā fugā quam dē castrōrum dēfēnsiōne cōgitābant.   Neque vērō diūtius quī in   8
vāllō cōnstiterant multitūdinem tēlōrum sustinēre potuērunt, sed cōnfectī vulneribus   9
locum relīquērunt, prōtinusque omnēs ducibus ūsī centuriōnibus tribūnīsque mīlitum   10
in altissimōs montēs, quī ad castra pertinēbant, cōnfūgērunt.   11

—Caesar, *Commentarii de bello civili* III.95

1. Why did Caesar order an attack on Pompey's camp? (1–3)
2. Under what conditions were the soldiers fighting? (3)
3. Did Caesar's men obey his order? What frame of mind were they in? (3–4)
4. How did Pompey's men respond to the attack? (5)
5. What additional support did Pompey's men have in the crisis? (5–6)
6. Describe the state of mind and actions of Pompey's men who had been on the battlefield. (6–8)
7. What two factors drove Pompey's men from their defensive positions along the ramparts? (8–10)
8. Where did Pompey's men take refuge? Who led them in their retreat? (10–11)

1 **trichila, -ae**, f., *arbor* (of trees and vines, for shade).
   struō, struere, strūxī, strūctus, *to erect, build, set up.*
   ***argentum, -ī**, n., *silver* (i.e., eating utensils).
   pondus, ponderis, n., *weight.*
   expōnō, expōnere, exposuī, expositus, *to set out, lay out.*
2 **caespes, caespitis**, m., *turf, sod.*
   tabernāculum, -ī, n., *tent.*
   cōnsternō, cōnsternere, cōnstrāvī, cōnstrātus, *to pave.*
   Lūcī . . . Lentulī: L. Cornelius Lentulus, consul of 49 B.C., was a vigorous anti-Caesarian.
   •**nōnnūllī, -ae, -a**, *several, some others.*
3 **prōtegō, prōtegere, prōtēxī, prōtēctus**, *to cover.*
   hedera, -ae, f., *ivy.*
   nimius, -a, -um, *too much, excessive.*
4 ***fidūcia, -ae**, f., *confidence in* (+ gen.).
   eōs: = **Pompeiānōs**, the subject of **timuisse** in indirect statement.
5 ***conquīrō, conquīrere, conquīsīvī, conquīsītus**, *to obtain, procure.*
   ***voluptās, voluptātis**, f., *pleasure, comfort.*
   patiēns, patientis, *long-suffering* (from **patior**).
   exercituī Caesaris lūxuriam obiciēbant: *continually taunted Caesar's army with (their) self-indulgence.* **Exercituī** is dative with the compound verb **obiciō**, *to throw out against.*
6 **cui**: the antecedent is **exercitus**.
   cui . . . dēfuissent: *to which . . . had been lacking* = *which had lacked.*
   omnia ad necessārium ūsum: *every necessity.*
7 **nostrī**: a substantive (adjective used as a noun) = **nostrī mīlitēs**.
   ***versor, -ārī, -ātus sum**, *to move about, operate.*
   ***nancīscor, nancīscī, nactus sum**, *to obtain, procure, get.*
   dētrahō, dētrahere, dētraxī, dētractus, *to remove, tear away.*
   ***īnsigne, īnsignis**, gen. pl., **īnsignium**, n., *insignia, badge.*
8 **decumānā portā**: the gate of the Roman camp farthest from the enemy, so called because the 10th cohort of each legion was stationed there.
   citō, -āre, -āvī, -ātus, *to spur on, rouse up.*
   Lārīsam: *Larisa* (a town in Thessaly, near Pharsalus).
9 ***contendō, contendere, contendī, contentus**, *to strain, exert, hurry.*
   suōs: = **suōs mīlitēs**.
10 •**comitātus, -ūs**, m., *company, retinue.*
   nāvis frūmentāria, *a grain ship.*
11 **cōnscendō, cōnscendere, cōnscendī, cōnscēnsus**, *to board, embark on.*
   ***queror, querī, questus sum**, *to complain, lament.*
   tantum sē opīniōnem fefellisse: *that he had been so terribly mistaken,* literally, *that his expectation had deceived him so much.*
12 **ā quō genere**: correlates with **ab eō (genere)** in the next line.
   spērāsset: = **spērāvisset**.
   •**prōdō, prōdere, prōdidī, prōditus**, *to hand over, betray.*
      prōditus: = **prōditus esse**.

C. DESCRIPTION OF POMPEY'S CAMP; POMPEY FLEES

In castrīs Pompeiī vidēre licuit trichilās strūctās, magnum argentī pondus exposi- 1
tum, recentibus caespitibus tabernācula cōnstrāta, Lūcī etiam Lentulī et nōnnūllōrum 2
tabernācula prōtēcta hederā, multaque praetereā quae nimiam lūxuriam et victōriae 3
fīdūciam dēsignārent, ut facile exīstimārī posset nihil eōs dē ēventū eius diēī timuisse, 4
quī nōn necessāriās conquīrerent voluptātēs. At hī miserrimō ac patientissimō exercituī 5
Caesaris lūxuriam obiciēbant, cui semper omnia ad necessārium ūsum dēfuissent. 6

Pompeius, iam cum intrā vāllum nostrī versārentur, equum nactus dētractīs īnsigni- 7
bus imperātōris decumānā portā sē ex castrīs ēiēcit prōtinusque equō citātō Lārīsam 8
contendit. Neque ibi cōnstitit, sed eādem celeritāte paucōs suōs ex fugā nactus, noc- 9
turnō itinere nōn intermissō, comitātū equitum trīgintā ad mare pervēnit nāvemque 10
frūmentāriam cōnscendit, saepe, ut dīcēbātur, querēns tantum sē opīniōnem fefellisse, 11
ut, ā quō genere hominum victōriam spērāsset, ab eō, initiō fugae factō, paene prōditus 12
vidērētur. 13

—Caesar, *Commentarii de bello civili* III.96

1. Describe the luxuries in Pompey's camp. (1–3)
2. What conclusion about Pompey and his men did Caesar draw from what he observed? (3–5)
3. How does Caesar characterize the condition of his own army? What made this condition especially unendurable? (5–6)
4. Describe, in sequence, Pompey's actions after Caesar's men had stormed the rampart. (7–9)
5. Describe Pompey's flight to the sea. By what means did he make his final escape from Greece? (9–11)
6. Why did Pompey claim to have been "betrayed"? (11–13)
7. What picture of Pompey do we get from Caesar's narrative? What picture do we get of Caesar himself?

Caesar pursued the remnant of Pompey's forces and accepted their surrender the next morning with leniency. Caesar reports that Crastinus (see 61A:6–13) perished in the fighting but that what he said as he set forth to battle did not prove false, in that Caesar was grateful to his bravery and service. Pompey fled to Egypt, where he was treacherously slain by the king's prefect and a Roman military tribune, Lucius Septimius, who had served under Pompey in his campaign against the pirates. After defeating Pompey, Caesar spent the next three years secur- ing his final victory, which came with the defeat of Pompey's sons in Spain in 45 B.C. Lavish entertainments of games and public banquets were held to celebrate the end of the civil war. Within a year, Caesar was assassinated.

BUILDING THE MEANING
Passive Verbs Used Impersonally

Look at the following examples from the readings:

Complūrēs hōrās ācriter **pugnābātur.** (48:18)
The fighting went on fiercely *for several hours.*

Coniūrātum est in eum ā sexāgintā . . . senātōribus. (55D:4–5)
A conspiracy was made *against him by sixty senators.*

. . . ut **erat praeceptum** ā Caesare . . . . (60B:5)
. . . *as* **instructions had been given** *by Caesar* . . . .
. . . *as Caesar* **had instructed**. . .

In these examples we find verbs in the passive voice, 3rd person singular, with no noun or pronoun as the subject. The subject is the action expressed by the verb; thus **pugnā-bātur** = *a fight was being fought, fighting went on.* We say that such verbs (usually intransitive) are used *impersonally* because no personal subject is expressed. Verbs are used impersonally when the writer wishes to emphasize the *action*, rather than the person or persons performing the action. These verbs can often be translated by an English abstract noun (*the fighting, a conspiracy*); sometimes it is best to use an English active verb (*were attacking*). Here are two more examples:

Nōn **concurritur** ā Pompeiānīs.
An attack ***is*** *not* ***being made*** *by Pompey's men. Pompey's men* ***are*** *not* ***attacking***.

Cum . . . animadvertissent nōn **concurrī** ā Pompeiānīs. . . . (61B:12)
When they had noticed that ***an attack was*** *not* ***being made*** *by Pompey's men* . . . .
. . . *that Pompey's men* ***were*** *not* ***attacking***. . .

When an impersonal passive is used as part of an indirect statement, as in the last example, the impersonal passive verb changes to the corresponding passive infinitive (i.e., **concurritur** changes to **concurrī**).

Exercise 62a
Read aloud and translate into good English:

1. Ad Forum Caesaris videndī causā ā nōbīs concurritur.
2. Mox ad summum montem perventum est.
3. Omnibus quī Cūriam incenderint Rōmā discēdendum erit.
4. Quīdam crēdēbant in Milōnem ā Clōdiō coniūrātum esse.
5. Cum Pompeiānīs usque ad noctem fortiter pugnātum est.
6. Caesar scrīpsit ab omnibus mīlitibus suīs nōn prōcurrī.
7. Ā Pompeiō ipsō ad mare contendēbātur.
8. Centuriōnibus ducibus, ad montēs altissimōs cōnfugitum est.
9. Pompeiō occīsō, dolēbāturne vehementer?

Genitive and Dative with Special Verbs

In addition to the verbs that take the ablative case (pages 84–85), there are also special verbs that take the genitive and dative cases.

1. Genitive with Special Verbs

There are some special verbs that are used with the *genitive case:*

    meminī, meminisse, irreg., *to remember* (this verb is found only in the perfect, pluperfect, and future perfect tenses; the perfect is translated as a present, the pluperfect as a perfect, and the future perfect as a simple future)
    misereor, -ērī, -itus sum, *to pity, feel sorry for*
    oblīvīscor, oblīvīscī, oblītus sum, *to forget*
    potior, potīrī, potītus sum, *to get control of, get possession of*

Thus,

    Meminit **mīlitum.** *He is mindful* **of the soldiers.** *He remembers* **the soldiers.**

When the object is a person, as in the example above, the genitive is always used. When the object is not a person, **oblīvīscor** and **meminī** can take either genitive or accusative:

    Oblīvīscor **nōmina** *or* Oblīvīscor **nōminum.** *I forget* **names.** *I am forgetful* **of names.**

The verb **potior** can be found with either the genitive or the ablative case (see page 84):

    Caesar **castrīs** potītus est *or* Caesar **castrōrum** potītus est. *Caesar got control* **of the camp.**

2. Dative with Special Verbs

These verbs fall into four groups:
a. Certain special intransitive verbs may be found with the *dative of indirect object.* These verbs cannot take a direct object in Latin:

Caesar **nēminī** cēdit.	**Bonīs** nocet quī **malīs** parcit.
Caesar yields **to no one.**	*He does harm* **to the good** *who is sparing* **to the bad.**

Among the most important of these verbs are:

cēdere, *to yield*	**ignōscere,** *to pardon*	**parcere,** *to spare*
cōnfīdere, *to rely on, trust*	**imperāre,** *to order*	**parēre,** *to obey*
crēdere, *to believe*	**licēre,** *to be allowed*	**persuādēre,** *to persuade*
diffīdere, *not to trust*	**nocēre,** *to harm*	**placēre,** *to please*
favēre, *to favor*	**nūbere,** *to marry*	**praecipere,** *to instruct, order*

When verbs in this category are used in the passive voice, they must be made *impersonal* (see definition on page 92) and the dative object is retained:

Mīlitibus persuāsum est ut contrā hostēs pugnārent.
The soldiers were persuaded to fight against the enemy (literally, *Persuasion was effected to **the soldiers** to fight . . .)*

b. The second group consists of intransitive verbs that are compounded with prepositions:

Urbī appropinquābant.   *They were approaching **the city**.*

Verbs in this category include:

appropinquāre, *to approach**	**succēdere**, *to relieve*
occurrere, *to meet*	**succurrere**, *to come to the aid*
resistere, *to resist*	

* This verb may also take **ad** + acc.

c. The third group consists of compound transitive verbs that can take a dative in addition to a direct object in the accusative (in the passive, these verbs have only a dative):

Octāviānus C. Cornēlium Gallum **Aegyptō** praeposuit.
*Octavian put C. Cornelius Gallus in charge of **Egypt***

. . . praepositusque (est) **eī** C. Cornēlius Gallus. (56B:4)
. . . *and C. Cornelius Gallus was put in charge of **it** (Egypt).*

This group includes **impōnere**, *to place X upon Y*, and **praeficere**, *to place X in charge of Y.*

d. The fourth group consists of compounds of the verb **esse**, including **dēesse**, *to be lacking*, **praeesse**, *to be in charge of*, and **prōdesse**, *to benefit*:

Haec rēs **Caesarī** prōfuit. *This situation was beneficial **to Caesar**.*

Notice that the verb **dēesse** requires the person who lacks to be in the dative, and the thing lacked to be the subject:

. . . (exercitus) **cui** semper **omnia** . . . dēfuissent. (61C:9–10)
. . . *(the army) **which** always lacked **everything*** (literally, **to which** everything was always lacking).

Aliquandō **virtūs ducibus** dēest.
*Sometimes **leaders** lack **courage*** (literally, *Sometimes **courage** is lacking **to leaders**).*

The verb **esse** can be used in a similar way with the dative case. This is called the *dative of possession*:

Sunt **Caesarī** paucī equitēs.
***Caesar** has few cavalry* (literally, *There are few cavalry **to Caesar**).

Erant **Antōniō** nāvēs magnae.
***Antony** had large ships* (literally, *Large ships were **to Antony**).

Exercise 62b

Read aloud and translate each of the following sentences, paying careful attention to the use of special verbs:

1. Necesse est bonōs cīvēs scelestīs cōnsulibus quam saepissimē resistere.
2. Nihil plūrimī mīlitēs pessimō imperātōrī prōsunt.
3. Gravī vulnere acceptō, mīles amīcōrum suōrum meminisse nōn poterat.
4. Tarquiniō expulsō, nōn iam erant Rōmānīs rēgēs.
5. Pompeius quidem spērābat Caesarem suīs castrīs nōn potītūrum esse.
6. Caesarī victōrī placēbat Pompeiī miserērī.
7. Lēgātus Caesarem rogāvit quem quārtae cohortī praefēcisset.
8. Aliquandō pecūnia etiam praeclārissimīs senātōribus dēerat.
9. Caesarem pudet nōmen huius centuriōnis oblīviscī.
10. Pompeius prīmum pīlum quendam fortissimum reliquīs manipulāribus praefēcit.

Exercise 62c

Complete each sentence with the proper form of the word in parentheses, and then read aloud and translate. The nominative singular or plural is given:

1. Meminit _____, sed oblīvīscitur _____. (ego) (tū)
2. Centuriōnēs semper pārent _____. (imperātor)
3. Caesar praefēcit Marcum Antōnium _____ _____. (multī mīlitēs)
4. Miserēminī _____ quī in proeliō mortuī sunt. (hominēs)
5. Pompeius imperāvit _____ ut _____ pārērent. (omnēs suī) (tribūnī)
6. Potestne Caesar meminisse _____ ūnīus cuiusque centuriōnis? (nōmen)
7. Cum Pompeiānī acerrimē pugnāvissent, Caesariānī _____ parcere voluērunt. (eī)
8. _____ nōn licet oblīviscī _____. (nōs) (Caesar)
9. Pompeiānī _____ fortiter resistēbant; _____ nōn iam persuāsum est ut arma dēpōnerent. (hostēs) (eī)
10. Caesar _____ Pompeiī appropinquāvit et dīxit "Hoc _____ placet." (castra) (ego)

Exercise 62d

Town and city names such as Cheshire, Lancaster, Winchester, and Worcester, all of which derive from the Latin word **castra**, *army camp*, reflect the Roman military presence in Britain. Use an atlas to assist you in finding as many additional place-names in Britain as you can that derive from this word.

THE DEATHS OF CAESAR AND CICERO

THE IDES OF MARCH

On 15 March 44 B.C., Julius Caesar was murdered by a faction of the senatorial nobility because, as dictator, he threatened senatorial control of the government of the Republic. Of the events that took place on the Ides of March, no eyewitness account survives. However, Nicolaus of Damascus came to Rome sometime during Augustus' reign and had the opportunity to interview those who may have witnessed the murder. He wrote as follows:

> The Senate rose in respect for his position when they saw him entering. Those who were to have a part in the plot stood near him. Right next to him went Tullius Cimber, whose brother had been exiled by Caesar. Under pretext of a humble request on behalf of his brother, Cimber approached and grasped the mantle of his toga, seeming to want to make a more positive move with his hands upon Caesar. Caesar wanted to get up and use his hands, but was prevented by Cimber and became exceedingly annoyed. That was the moment for the men to set to work. All quickly unsheathed their daggers and rushed at him. Caesar rose to defend himself. They were just like men doing battle against him. Under the mass of wounds, he fell at the foot of Pompey's statue. Everyone wanted to seem to have had some part in the murder, and there was not one of them who failed to strike his body as it lay there, until, wounded thirty-five times, he breathed his last.

> —Nicolaus of Damascus, *Historici Graeci minores* XXIV

L. Minucius Basilus was an officer in Gaul under Caesar and was one of his assassins. The following hasty note of congratulations to Basilus is thought to have been written by Cicero on the day of the assassination, in reply to a report received from Basilus. Translate Cicero's message:

CICERO BASILO SAL.

Tibi grātulor, mihi gaudeō; tē amō, tua tueor, ā tē amārī et quid agās quidque agātur certior fierī volō.

> —Cicero, *Epistulae ad familiares* VI.15

tē amō, *I am your friend.*
tueor, -ērī, -itus sum, *to look out for, protect.*
certior fierī, *to be informed.*

Nam sī violandum est iūs, rēgnandī grātiā violandum est. *If you must break the law, do it only to seize power.* (Cicero, quoting Caesar in *De officiis* III.12)

The Folger Shakespeare Library, Washington, D. C.

THE DEATH OF CICERO

On 7 December 43 B.C., Cicero bravely faced death at the hands of assassins sent by Mark Antony, who was angry at Cicero for having delivered a series of speeches, called the *Philippics*, attacking him. Livy describes his death as follows:

Cicero, realizing that he could not be rescued from the hands of Antony, first made for his estate at Tusculum and, from there, by traveling crossways across the peninsula, he set out for Formiae to board a ship leaving Gaeta. There, weariness of both flight and life itself seized him, for, having set out to sea several times, contrary winds had brought him back and then the tossing of the ship had become unendurable. On returning to his villa, he exclaimed, "I will now die in the land I have so often served." It is a fact that he ordered his slaves, willing to fight bravely and loyally to the finish, to put down his litter and to endure without resistance what an unjust fate had laid upon them all. As he stretched himself out from his litter and offered his neck without hesitation, his head was cut off. Charging that his hands had written things against Antony, the assassins cut off those as well. And so the head was carried back to Antony and by his order was placed between Cicero's two hands on the Rostra where, as former consul, he had spoken with remarkable eloquence against Antony that very year.

—Livy, *Periochae* CXX

REVIEW XV: CHAPTERS 60–62

Exercise XVa: Review of the Late Republic
Answer the following questions:

1. What were the general causes of the civil war of 49–45? (Recall the political background of the late Republic presented in Part II.) What was the immediate cause of the war?
2. What political position did the Caesarians represent in the war? The Pompeians? How did Cicero react to the outbreak of war (see the readings in Chapter 60)?
3. Does Crastinus (61A:7–11) seem to be fighting as a patriot of Rome or to please his general, Caesar? What does this reveal about a soldier's loyalties during the late Republic? What light does this shed on reasons for the downfall of the Roman Republic in the 1st century B.C.?
4. How is Pompey portrayed in the readings in Chapters 61 and 62? What does a passage such as 62C imply about Caesar's purpose in writing his commentaries?
5. Characterize Caesar as a man and as a general, giving evidence from the readings.
6. How were the deaths of Caesar and Cicero similar? How do their deaths reflect the temper of the times in the late Republic?

Exercise XVb: Clauses of Fearing, Impersonal Passives, and Special Verbs
Read aloud and translate:

1. Cicerō verēbātur nē Caesar rem pūblicam dēlētūrus esset.
2. Timetne Caesar ut ipse Cicerōnem Rōmae vīsūrus sit?
3. Nē brevī tempore famēs in urbe sit cīvibus est verendum.
4. Cicerō metuit nē iam Terentia Tulliaque interclūdantur.
5. Proeliō commissō, omnibus Caesariānīs imperātum est ut pīlīs ūterentur.
6. Multās hōrās prope castra Pompeiāna ācriter pugnābātur.
7. Misereor eius quī aliīs nocet.
8. Caesar, cum commentāriōs dē bellō cīvīlī scrīberet, vēra dīcere semper nōn meminerat.
9. Aciēbus īnstrūctīs, Caesar Labiēnum decimae legiōnī praefēcit.
10. Rēs male gestae vōbīs oblīvīscendae sunt.

Exercise XVc: Identification of Forms
In Cicero's letter to his family (Reading 60A), find at least one example of each of the following forms or constructions. Do not use any example more than once:

superlative adjective and adverb, imperative verb, fear clause, result clause, present active subjunctive verb, gerundive of obligation (passive periphrastic), deponent verb, dative of agent, circumstantial clause, future active participle, indirect question, dative object of a compound verb, ablative of description, and gerundive used as a future passive participle.

PART IV

EMPEROR AND EMPIRE: THE RISE OF THE ROMAN PRINCIPATE

As you learned in Part I, it was near Actium, in Greece, that Octavian defeated the combined naval forces of Antony and Cleopatra to become master of the Mediterranean world. After his victory, Octavian gradually assumed supreme power under the guise of restoring the Republic and ushered in a period of **Pāx Rōmāna**. Command of the entire Roman Empire thus came into the hands of this one man, Gaius Julius Caesar Octavianus, called **Augustus** (*worthy of respect, venerable*). His rule, which ended the Republic (509–27 B.C.), has come to be known as the Principate, from the unofficial title **prīnceps**, *first citizen*, which Augustus used to describe himself. The next 500 years of Roman history were dominated by over ninety-five rulers, or emperors, who reigned over the more than fifty million people of the Empire. The emperor, whose official title was **Imperātor**, was formally granted his powers by senatorial decree and by ratification by the people, but the real basis of his power was the allegiance of the military. The role of the Senate gradually became ceremonial, and its functions were assumed by a vast bureaucracy, mainly dependent upon the **auctōritās**, or personal prestige, of the emperor himself.

Beginning with Augustus, both the military and civilian populations of the Empire swore an oath of allegiance to the new emperor and renewed it on each anniversary of his accession. The following oath was sworn to the Emperor Gaius (better known as Caligula) by a community in Spain in A.D. 37:

> I solemnly swear that I will be an enemy to those who I learn are enemies to Gaius Caesar Germanicus. If anyone brings or shall bring danger to him and his welfare, I will not cease to pursue him with arms and deadly war on land and on sea until he has paid the penalty to him; I will hold neither myself nor my children dearer than his welfare; and I will regard as enemies of mine those who have hostile intentions against him. If I knowingly swear or shall swear falsely, then may Jupiter Optimus Maximus and the deified Augustus and all the other immortal gods cause me and my children to be deprived of fatherland, safety, and all good fortune.
>
> —*Corpus inscriptionum Latinarum* II.172

In addition to oaths of allegiance, the relationship between ruler and ruled was fostered by emperor worship, through the imperial cult established by Augustus, and by emperor deification. Julius Caesar was the first Roman ruler to be declared a god posthumously by the Senate, and emperors as early as Caligula began to seek divinity during their reigns.

Putō deus fīō. *I think I'm becoming a god!* Spoken by the emperor Vespasian on his deathbed. (Suetonius, *Vespasian* XXIII)

Above: the goddess Pax from the Ara Pacis, built in thanksgiving for Augustus' return from his military campaigns. Right: a marble statue of the Emperor Augustus found in the villa of his wife Livia at Prima Porta, just outside Rome. Note the cupid riding a dolphin at the emperor's feet, suggesting Augustus' descent from the goddess Venus. What other messages are sent by the gesture and pose, facial expression, and dress?

IMPERIAL PROPAGANDA

The breastplate of the Prima Porta statue (shown in detail on the opposite page) offers symbolic messages that suggest the same imperial plan seen elsewhere in the art and architecture, coinage, and literature of the Augustan Age. The central figures of the scene depict a Parthian returning the legionary standard lost in the East at Carrhae by Crassus in 53 B.C., an achievement of which Augustus was justly proud (see the coin on page 37). In a more general way, this scene represents the new imperial ideology of prosperity through peace. Below the central figures Mother Earth (or possibly the goddess Pax) reclines holding an overflowing cornucopia. Barely visible at each side are figures of the deities Apollo and Diana. At the top left of the breastplate's pectoral zone hover Sol, riding in his chariot, and at right, the goddess Luna carrying a torch and the winged figure of Dawn. Above all, Caelus supports the vault of heaven. These earth and sky deities represent the eternal in nature. Their presence symbolically sug-

gests that the gods approve of and protect Augustus; that the new **saeculum aureum** or Golden Age of Augustus is an event of cosmic significance.

The symbolic linking of military victory, internal order, and happiness through divine providence that is present in this sculpture is seen everywhere in the art and literature of the Augustan era. Another good example of Augustan propaganda is the Ara Pacis, about which you will read in Chapter 64. The detail on the opposite page shows Pax; from another part of the altar comes a relief showing the family and friends of Augustus in a sacrificial procession (reproduced on pages iv and v at the front of this book).

These same virtues of the Augustan regime, which reach their highest form of expression in Vergil's epic poem the *Aeneid*, are celebrated in a hymn written by the imperial poet Horace in honor of the Secular Games of 17 B.C.

> And whatever the illustrious descendant of Anchises and Venus, accompanied by the sacrifice of milk-white oxen, asks of you (Apollo and Diana), may he, triumphant over the war-maker but merciful to the fallen, obtain his request.
>
> Now the Parthian fears the power, mighty on land and sea, and the Alban axes and now the Indians and Scythians, but recently disdainful, are asking our answer.
>
> Now Faith and Peace and Honor and Modesty of old and neglected Virtue venture to return, and blessed Plenty appears with a full horn.
>
> —Horace, *Carmen saeculare* 49–60

RES GESTAE DIVI AUGUSTI

The passages in the initial chapter of this section come from an inscription which records the achievements of the forty-one-year reign of Augustus. Called "the queen of Latin inscriptions," it was found carved on the interior walls of the Temple of Rome and Augustus in what is now Ankara, Turkey. It is known as the *Res gestae divi Augusti* (*The Deeds of the Deified Augustus*). The text of this inscription is a copy of the one that was ordered cut in bronze and erected in front of Augustus' mausoleum in Rome as a testament to his principate. The text was composed by the emperor himself, just months before his death on 19 August A.D. 14. Here is a portion of it:

Et colōnīs mīlitum meōrum cōnsul qu]īntum ex manibiīs virīt[im mīllia nummum singula dedī; accēpēru]nt id triumphāle congiā[rium in colōnīs hominum circiter centum et] vīgint mīllia. Cōnsul [tertium decimum sexāgēnōs dēnāriōs plēbēī] quae tum frūmentum pūb[licum accipiēbat dedī; ea mīllia hominum paul]lō plūra quam dūcenta fu[ērunt.

And to every one of the colonists drawn from my soldiers I gave 1,000 sesterces out of booty during my fifth consulship (29 B.C.). At the time of my triumph about 120,000 men in the colonies received this donation. In my thirteenth consulship (2 B.C.) I gave 60 denarii each to the plebs who were then receiving public grain; this made up a few more than 200,000 people.

—*Res gestae* 15

A ROMAN SENATOR OF THE EMPIRE

C. Plinius Secundus, or Pliny the Younger, was born to a prosperous landowning family at Comum, in the Cisalpine province of northern Italy. Although a lawyer by vocation, Pliny published hundreds of letters, including his official correspondence with the Emperor Trajan, who ruled A.D. 98–117. These letters—perhaps the most famous of which is Pliny's eyewitness account of the eruption of Mt. Vesuvius in A.D. 79—provide an intimate look at the personal and professional life of a member of the Roman ruling class during the reigns of the emperors Domitian and Nerva, as well as Trajan. Pliny was privileged to witness the reconciliation between Senate and Emperor after the tyrannical rule of Domitian and the transition of the Empire in what Gibbon called "the period in the history of the world during which the condition of the human race was most happy and prosperous." As an advocate for the Senate, Pliny prosecuted or defended a number of Roman officials accused of maladministration and embezzlement in their provinces. This, coupled with the fact that he was knowledgeable about financial affairs, having served as head of the state treasury, led to his commission in A.D. 110 as special envoy of the Emperor Trajan, with the title **lēgātus Augustī cōnsulārī potestāte**, to deal with problems of inefficiency and corruption in the province of Bithynia-Pontus. The last of Pliny's ten books of epistles contains over 100 letters to and from Trajan, in which Pliny asks for advice on such matters as procedure, law, finance, building projects, and security. It is believed that Pliny died in office in Bithynia just before A.D. 114.

Here is a translation of part of an inscription that was placed in the baths at Comum, Pliny's home town, in recognition of his civic generosity:

> Gaius Plinius Caecilius Secundus, son of Lucius of the tribe Oufentina, consul, augur, praetorian commissioner with full consular power for the province of Pontus and Bithynia, sent to that province in accordance with the Senate's decree by the Emperor Nerva Trajan Augustus, curator of the bed and banks of the Tiber and the sewers of Rome, official of the Treasury of Saturn, official of the military Treasury, praetor, tribune of the people, quaestor of the Emperor, commissioner for the Roman knights, military tribune of the Third Gallic Legion, magistrate of the Board of Ten, left by his will public baths at a cost of . . . and an additional 300,000 sesterces for furnishing them, with 1,866,666 sesterces to support a hundred of his freedmen, and subsequently to provide an annual dinner for the people of the city. . . . Likewise in his lifetime he gave 500,000 sesterces for the maintenance of boys and girls of the city and also 100,000 for the upkeep of the library.

> —*Corpus inscriptionum Latinarum* V.5262

1 **Annōs ūndēvīgintī nātus**: *at the age of 19*, literally, *born for 19 years*; this was in 44 B.C.
   prīvātō cōnsiliō: *on my own responsibility.*
   impēnsa, -ae, f., *expense.*
   •**comparō, -āre, -āvī, -ātus**, *to get ready.*

2 ***factiō, factiōnis**, f., *political gang, faction.* Augustus is referring here to Mark Antony, who had challenged his rights as Caesar's heir in 44 B.C.
   in lībertātem vindicāvī: *I emancipated, I set free.* This refers to the battle of Mutina in 43 B.C., when Octavian defeated Antony.
   Eō nōmine: *On that account.*

3 **dēcrētum, -ī**, n., *decree, edict.*
   honōrificus, -a, -um, *honorary.*
   •**ōrdō, ōrdinis**, m., *rank, order.*
   adlegō, adlegere, adlēgī, adlēctus, *to elect, enroll.*
   C. Pansā et A. Hirtiō cōnsulibus: Hirtius and Pansa were consuls in 43 B.C.

4 **cōnsulārem locum sententiae dīcendae tribuēns**: the consuls had the privilege of being the first to speak in any debate; this privilege was also extended to Augustus.
   ***sententia, -ae**, f., *opinion.*
   •**imperium, -ī**, n., *the right to command armies.*

5 **Rēs pūblica nē quid dētrīmentī caperet . . . prōvidēre**: *to see to it that the state should come to no harm.*
   prō praetōre: *as propraetor*, i.e., as a magistrate with the powers of a praetor.
   •**praetor, praetōris**, m., *praetor (a magistrate with judicial functions).*

6 **iussit**: the subject is **Senātus** in line 3.
   cōs.: inscriptional abbreviation for **cōnsul**.
   •**uterque, utraque, utrumque**, *each of two.*

7 **cecidisset**: from **cadō**.
   triumvir, triumvirī, m., *triumvir (one of a special commission of three men).* The First Triumvirate had been composed of Julius Caesar, Pompey, and Crassus (see Introduction to Part I, pages 3–4); the Second Triumvirate consisted of Octavian, Mark Antony, and Lepidus (review Reading 55A, pages 27–29).
   reī pūblicae cōnstituendae: *for the reestablishment of the state, i.e.,* after the civil wars.
   •**creō, -āre, -āvī, -ātus**, *to choose, elect, appoint.*

8 **Quī**: *Those who* (= Brutus and Cassius).
   parentem meum: = Julius Caesar.
   trucidō, -āre, -āvī, -ātus, *to murder.*
   •**expellō, expellere, expulī, expulsus**, *to drive out, banish.*
   iūdiciīs lēgitimīs: *by due process of law.*
   ***ulcīscor, ulcīscī, ultus sum**, *to avenge, punish.*

9 •**facinus, facinoris**, n., *crime, wicked deed.*
   •**bellum īnferre**, idiom + dat., *to make war on.*
   vīcī bis aciē: this refers to the two battles at Philippi, in Greece, where Brutus and Cassius were defeated in 42 B.C.

10 **Iūrāvit in mea verba**: *Swore allegiance to me.* This oath taken in 31 B.C. became the precedent for the imperial oath of allegiance (page 99).
   •**sponte suā**: *of its own accord, voluntarily.*
   ducem: take in apposition to **mē**.

11 **dēposcō, dēposcere, dēpoposcī**, *to demand.*

AUGUSTUS

A. AUGUSTUS BEFORE THE PRINCIPATE (44–31 B.C.)

Annōs ūndēvīgintī nātus exercitum prīvātō cōnsiliō et prīvātā impēnsā comparāvī, 1
per quem rem pūblicam ā dominātiōne factiōnis oppressam in lībertātem vindicāvī. Eō 2
nōmine Senātus dēcrētīs honōrificīs in ōrdinem suum mē adlēgit, C. Pansā et A. Hirtiō 3
cōnsulibus, cōnsulārem locum sententiae dīcendae tribuēns, et imperium mihi dedit. 4
Rēs pūblica nē quid dētrīmentī caperet, mē prō praetōre simul cum cōnsulibus 5
prōvidēre iussit. Populus autem eōdem annō mē cōnsulem, cum cōs. uterque in bellō 6
cecidisset, et triumvirum reī pūblicae cōnstituendae creāvit. 7

Quī parentem meum trucidāvērunt, eōs in exsilium expulī iūdiciīs lēgitimīs ultus 8
eōrum facinus, et posteā bellum īnferentēs reī pūblicae vīcī bis aciē. 9

Iūrāvit in mea verba tōta Italia sponte suā, et mē bellī quō vīcī ad Actium ducem 10
dēpoposcit; iūrāvērunt in eadem verba prōvinciae Galliae, Hispāniae, Āfrica, Sicilia, 11
Sardinia. 12

—Augustus, *Res gestae* 1, 2, 25 (excerpts)

1. At what age did Augustus enter public affairs? (1)
2. Against whom was his first conquest? In what manner does he represent this victory? (1–2)
3. In what three ways did the Senate reward Augustus for his services? (2–4)
4. What special responsibility was Augustus given as propraetor? (5–6)
5. Identify the circumstances under which Augustus was first elected consul. (6–7)
6. What does he claim was his mission as triumvir? (7)
7. In what two ways did Augustus exact justice from Caesar's assassins? (8–9)
8. From which areas of the Empire did Augustus receive votes of confidence before Actium? (10–12)

1   **In cōnsulātū sextō et septimō**: 28 and 27 B.C.
    •**exstinguō, exstinguere, exstīnxī, exstīnctus**, *to exstinguish.*
    per cōnsēnsum ūniversōrum: *by universal consent.*

2   **rem pūblicam . . . trānstulī**: by laying aside all the extraordinary powers that the Senate had granted him during the civil wars, Augustus restored the Republic in form; however, he retained the powers of a tribune, which included the right to veto legislation, and the power to command soldiers (**imperium**).
    •**potestās, potestātis**, f., *power.*

3   **arbitrium, -ī**, n., *mastery, control.*
    trānstulī: deduce from **trāns + ferre.**
    Quō prō meritō meō: *For this service of mine.*
    •**cōnsultum, -ī**, n., *decree.*
    Augustus: as an ordinary adjective, **augustus, -a, -um** means *worthy of respect* or *venerable* and is a word that has religious overtones. Augustus is said to have considered the name Romulus also. Some ancient writers date the beginning of the imperial monarchy to 16 January 27 B.C., when Octavian received the title Augustus.

4   •**appellō, -āre, -āvī, -ātus**, *to call by name.*
    laurea, -ae, f., *(leaves of) the bay tree;* "*laurels,*" *symbols of victory.*
    •**aedēs, aedis**, gen. pl., **aedium**, f., *building, temple*; pl., *house.*
    vestiō, -īre, -īvī, -ītus, *to dress, adorn.*
    corōna . . . cīvica: a crown of oak leaves was awarded to a citizen soldier for saving the life of a comrade in battle. Augustus had saved lives by bringing the civil wars to an end.

5   •**fīgō, fīgere, fīxī, fīxus**, *to fasten, attach.*
    clipeus, -ī, m., *a round shield.*
    Cūria Iūlia: the Senate House was rebuilt by Julius Caesar after the Clodian fire (see Part II, page 47).
    positus: = positus est.
    quem . . . testātum est per eius clupeī īnscrīptiōnem: *(and) that the Senate and Roman people gave it to me . . . is proclaimed* (literally, *has been witnessed*) *by the inscription on that shield.*
      Testātum est: this verb governs an indirect statement with **Senātum populumque Rōmānum** as subject and **dare** as verb.

6   **clēmentia, -ae**, f., *mercy, forgiveness.* This and other Augustan virtues were represented on coins and inscriptions.
    •**testor, -ārī, -ātus sum**, *to bear witness, give evidence.*

7   •**auctōritās, auctōritātis**, f., *influence, prestige.*
    auctōritāte omnibus praestitī: during the Republic, the leading citizens had influence. Augustus, as leading citizen (**prīnceps**), claims to have ruled more through influence (**auctōritās**), as a result of his pre-eminent services to Rome, than through power (**potestās**).
    •**praestō, praestāre, praestitī, praestitūrus** + dat., *to stand ahead of, excel, surpass.*
    potestātis . . . nihilō amplius: *no more power.*

8   •**magistrātus, -ūs**, m., *magistracy, office.*
    •**collēga, -ae**, m., *colleague, fellow official.*

B. AUGUSTUS AT THE TIME OF TRANSITION TO THE PRINCIPATE (28–27 B.C.)

In cōnsulātū sextō et septimō, postquam bella cīvīlia exstīnxeram, per cōnsēnsum 1
ūniversōrum potītus rērum omnium, rem pūblicam ex meā potestāte in Senātūs po- 2
pulīque Rōmānī arbitrium trānstulī. Quō prō meritō meō Senātūs cōnsultō Augustus 3
appellātus sum et laureīs postēs aedium meārum vestītī pūblicē corōnaque cīvica super 4
iānuam meam fīxa est et clipeus aureus in Cūriā Iūliā positus, quem mihi Senātum 5
populumque Rōmānum dare virtūtis clēmentiaeque et iūstitiae et pietātis causā testātum 6
est per eius clipeī īnscrīptiōnem. Post id tempus auctōritāte omnibus praestitī, po- 7
testātis autem nihilō amplius habuī quam cēterī quī mihi quoque in magistrātū collēgae 8
fuērunt. 9

—Augustus, *Res gestae* 34

1. What does Augustus claim to have done in lines 2–3? Is what you know of his subsequent career consistent with this statement?
2. At what point did he do this? (1)
3. How did Octavian obtain the title Augustus? (3–4) How did this title reflect his position in Rome?
4. What other honors did the Senate and people bestow on him? (4–5)
5. According to Augustus, for what qualities was he honored? (5–7)
6. What claim did Augustus make in lines 7–9? What seems to be the distinction between **auctōritās** and **potestās** (7)?
7. According to Augustus, from whom did he derive his power? (1–3, 7) What other source of power does he avoid mentioning?

The obverse of this coin of Augustus shows the **corōna cīvica** (above: 4) with the legend **OB CĪVĪS SERVĀTŌS** (**cīvīs** is an alternate spelling for **cīvēs**). The reverse shows the laurel branches that were also granted to Augustus (above: 4).

1 •**bellum gerere**, idiom, *to wage war.*
  externus, -a, -um, *outside, foreign.*
  •**orbe terrārum**: *the world.*
2 **venia, -ae,** f., *pardon.*
  •**parcō, parcere, pepercī, parsūrus** + dat., *to spare.*
  •**gēns, gentis,** f., *nation, people.*
  •**tūtō,** adv., *safely.*
  quibus tūtō ignōscī potuit: *who could be safely pardoned,* literally, *to whom it could be safely pardoned.* **Ignōscī** is the passive infinitive and is used impersonally.
3 **excīdō, excīdere, excīdī, excīsus,** *to exterminate.*
4 *finitimus, -a, -um,* *neighboring.*
  fīnis, fīnis, gen. pl., **fīnium,** m., *end, boundary;* pl., *territory.*
  •**augeō, augēre, auxī, auctus,** *to increase, enlarge.*
5 **gestīs**: perfect participle of **gerere,** *to do, manage.*
  •**prōsperē,** adv., *prosperously, successfully.*
  Ti. Nerōne P. Quīntiliō cōnsulibus: Nero and Quintilius were consuls in 13 B.C.
6 •**āra, -ae,** f., *altar.*
  āram . . . senātus . . . cōnsecrandum (esse) cēnsuit: *the Senate resolved that an altar should be dedicated.*
  •**reditus, -ūs,** m., *return, homecoming.*
  cōnsecrō, -āre, -āvī, -ātus, *to consecrate, dedicate.*
7 •**cēnseō, cēnsēre, cēnsuī, cēnsus,** *to resolve, decide.*
  sacerdōs, sacerdōtis, m., *priest.*
  virginēs . . . Vestālēs: the Vestal Virgins were the six chief priestesses of the state cult of Vesta, chosen from the most aristocratic Roman families. Vesta was the goddess of the home and hearth; a fire burned continuously in her temple, symbolizing the state as one "family." The most important job of the Vestal Virgins was to keep this fire burning.
8 **anniversārius, -a, -um,** *annual.*
9 **Iānum Quirīnum**: this serves as the subject of the infinitive **claudendum esse** (12) in indirect statement after **senātus . . . cēnsuit** (12).
  Iānum Quirīnum, quem clausum esse . . . voluērunt: the shrine of Janus Quirinus was apparently an arched gate in the Roman Forum. There are no remains of this structure, and its exact location and purpose are uncertain.
  maiōrēs, maiōrum, m. pl., *ancestors.*
10 *pariō, parere, peperī, partus,* *to produce, secure.*
  cum: *although.*
  prius quam nāscerer: Octavian was born in 63 B.C.
11 *omnīnō,* adv., *altogether.*
  prōdātur memoriae: *tradition records,* literally, *is handed down to memory.*
  ter, adv., *three times.* The three closings took place in 29 B.C., 25 B.C., and at another unknown date.
  mē prīncipe: ablative absolute.

C. PĀX RŌMĀNA: THE AUGUSTAN PEACE (27 B.C.–A.D. 14)

Bella terrā et marī cīvīlia externaque tōtō in orbe terrārum saepe gessī, victorque 1
omnibus veniam petentibus cīvibus pepercī. Externās gentēs, quibus tūtō ignōscī po- 2
tuit, cōnservāre quam excīdere māluī. Omnium prōvinciārum populī Rōmānī quibus 3
fīnitimae fuērunt gentēs quae nōn pārērent imperiō nostrō fīnēs auxī. 4

Cum ex Hispaniā Galliāque, rēbus eīs prōvinciīs prōsperē gestīs, Rōmam rediī, Ti. 5
Nerōne P. Quīntiliō cōnsulibus, āram Pācis Augustae senātus prō reditū meō cōnse- 6
crandam cēnsuit ad campum Martium, in quā magistrātūs et sacerdōtēs virginēsque 7
Vestālēs anniversārium sacrificium facere iussit. 8

Iānum Quirīnum, quem clausum esse maiōrēs nostrī voluērunt cum per tōtum im- 9
perium populī Rōmānī terrā marīque esset parta victoriīs pāx, cum prius quam nāsce- 10
rer ā conditā urbe bis omnīnō clausum fuisse prōdātur memoriae, ter mē prīncipe senā- 11
tus claudendum esse cēnsuit. 12

—Augustus, *Res gestae* 3, 12, 13, 26 (excerpts)

1. What types of wars did Augustus fight? (1)
2. Give examples of Augustus' clemency. (2–3) Where else previously have you seen
   mention of this quality?
3. What claim does Augustus make in lines 3–4?
4. In what special way was Augustus honored upon his return to Rome from Spain
   and Gaul? (5–7)
5. What provisions did the Senate make regarding the **āra**? (7–8)
6. To what custom does Augustus refer in lines 9–10?
7. How many times previously had the gateway been closed since Rome's origin?
   (10–11)
8. How many times was the gateway shut during the principate of Augustus? (11–12)
   What does this imply about his reign?
9. Is Augustus' claim to have expanded the Empire consistent with his claim to have
   brought peace to the world?

The shrine of Janus. The legend on this coin of
Nero reads **Pāce p(opulī) R(ōmānī) terrā
marīq(ue) partā Iānum clūsit**; compare this
with Augustus' language in lines 9–10 above.

Ara Pacis

1   **Capitōlium, -ī**, n., *the Capitolium* (the temple of Jupiter, Juno, and Minerva on the Capitoline Hill).

    Pompeium theātrum: built by the great general Pompey, this was the first and most important stone theater in Rome; Julius Caesar was assassinated here.

    *****opus, operis**, n., *(public) work.*

    •**grandis, -is, -e**, *great.*

    *****reficiō, reficere, refēcī, refectus**, *to rebuild, restore.*

    sine ūllā īnscrīptiōne nōminis meī: it was customary for the emperor (or other individual) responsible for the erection of a structure to claim recognition by having his name and titles inscribed in the stone.

2   •**rīvus, -ī**, m., *stream, water channel of an aqueduct* (**aqua**).

    vetustās, vetustātis, f., *old age.*

    lābentēs: *falling (into disrepair).*

3   **duplicō, -āre, -āvī, -ātus**, *to double.* Augustus means that he doubled the capacity of the Aqua Marcia, one of Rome's chief aqueducts.

    fōns, fontis, m., *spring, source.*

    •**immittō, immittere, immīsī, immissus**, *to join, connect.*

    Forum Iūlium: the Julian Forum (also called the Forum of Caesar), named after Julius Caesar, was dedicated in 47 B.C., along with the Basilica Julia (see the plan of the imperial fora on page 120).

4   **basilicam**: the Basilica Julia, in the Forum Romanum.

    aedem Castoris: the temple of Castor and Pollux, the Gemini. (See the plan on page 47.)

    aedem Saturnī: the temple of Saturn, the mythical god-king of early Rome.

    coeptus, -a, -um, *begun.*

    prōflīgātus, -a, -um, *nearly completed.*

5   **perficiō, perficere, perfēcī, perfectus**, *to finish, complete.*

    •**cōnsūmō, cōnsūmere, cōnsūmpsī, cōnsūmptus**, *to destroy.*

    cōnsūmptam incendiō: in A.D. 12.

6   *****ampliō, -āre, -āvī, -ātus**, *to enlarge, increase.*

    solum, -ī, n., *floor, foundation.*

    titulus, -ī, m., *title.*

    sub titulō nōminis fīliōrum meōrum: Augustus means that he gave his (adopted) sons, Gaius and Lucius, all the credit in the inscription.

    incohō, -āre, -āvī, -ātus, *to begin, undertake.*

    vīvus: *while still living, during my lifetime.*

7   **perficī**: do not confuse with **perfēcī**; likewise, distinguish **reficī** from **refēcī** (8).

    •**hērēs, hērēdis**, m., *heir.*

    octōgintā, *eighty.*

    deum: = **deōrum**.

    cōnsul sextum: *in my sixth consulship*, literally, *consul for the sixth time* (28 B.C.).

8   **nūllō praetermissō**: *omitting none.*

9   **Cōnsul septimum**: 27 B.C.

    viam Flāminiam: the Via Flaminia was the main northern route from Rome, leading to Ariminum (modern Rimini) on the Adriatic coast. (See the map on page 12.)

    pontēs . . . Mulvium et Minūcium: these were bridges over the Tiber River.

    •**praeter**, prep. + acc., *except.*

D. AUGUSTUS DURING THE PRINCIPATE: THE BUILDING PROGRAM

Capitōlium et Pompeium theātrum, utrumque opus impēnsā grandī, refēcī sine ūllā 1
īnscrīptiōne nōminis meī. Rīvōs aquārum complūribus locīs vetustāte lābentēs refēcī, et 2
aquam quae Marcia appellātur duplicāvī fonte novō in rīvum eius immissō. Forum 3
Iūlium et basilicam quae fuit inter aedem Castoris et aedem Saturnī, coepta prō- 4
flīgātaque opera ā patre meō, perfēcī et eandem basilicam cōnsūmptam incendiō, 5
ampliātō eius solō, sub titulō nōminis filiōrum meōrum incohāvī, et, sī vīvus nōn perfē- 6
cissem, perficī ab hērēdibus meīs iussī. Duo et octōgintā templa deum in urbe cōnsul 7
sextum et auctōritāte Senātūs refēcī, nūllō praetermissō quod eō tempore reficī dēbēbat. 8
Cōnsul septimum viam Flāminiam ab urbe Arīminum refēcī et pontēs omnēs praeter 9
Mulvium et Minūcium. 10

—Augustus, *Res gestae* 20

1. Of what two public works is Augustus especially proud, and why? (1–2)
2. In what specific ways did he improve the public water supply? (2–3)
3. Which works begun by Caesar did Augustus complete? (3–5)
4. What special provisions did he make for the Basilica Julia? What had happened to this building? (5–7)
5. How many temples did Augustus restore? (7–8) How does this fact reflect the values of his regime?
6. What improvements in public works did Augustus make during his seventh consulship? (9–10)
7. In what ways might a building program have helped Augustus to maintain power?
8. Study the picture of Augustus on page 100 and then evaluate its message. Does it support or conflict with the impressions left by his own words, as presented in the previous passages?
9. Review Eutropius' assessment of Augustus, presented in Chapter 57. Is this consistent with Augustus' picture of himself?

Urbem excoluit adeō ut iūre sit glōriātus marmoream sē relinquere quam latericiam accēpisset. *He improved Rome to such an extent that he could rightly boast of having found it brick and left it marble.* (Said of Augustus, Suetonius, *Augustus* XXVIII.3)

Tū regere imperiō populōs, Rōmāne, mementō
(hae tibi erunt artēs), pācīque impōnere mōrem,
parcere subiectīs et dēbellāre superbōs.

You must remember, Roman, to rule the nations with your power (this will be your special skill),
and to impose the habit of peace, to spare the conquered and to make war on the proud.
(Vergil, *Aeneid* VI.851–853)

BUILDING THE MEANING
Indefinite Pronouns and Adjectives

In Chapter 28 you learned the forms of the relative pronoun **quī, quae, quod**. In Chapter 29 you learned that the indefinite adjective **quīdam, quaedam, quoddam**, *a certain*, pl., *some*, is a compound of **quī** plus the suffix **-dam**. You have also met another indefinite, **aliquis, aliquis, aliquid**, *someone, something*, a compound of the prefix **ali-** and the pronoun **quis**:

Catilīna . . . coniūrāvit cum **quibusdam** clārīs virīs. (55A:2–3)
*Catiline . . . formed a conspiracy with **certain** eminent men.*

Titus noster **aliquid** malī accēpit. (54:8)
*Our Titus experienced **something** bad.*

In the first example, **quibusdam** is an indefinite adjective; in the second, **aliquid** is an indefinite pronoun. Note that the meaning of **quīdam** is less vague, or "less indefinite," than that of **aliquis**; writers use **quīdam** when they know who is involved but may not wish to identify him. Observe the following sets of indefinite pronouns and adjectives:

Servus **aliquid** portat.	*The slave is carrying **something**.*
Servus **aliquās** epistulās portat.	*The slave is carrying **some** letters.*
Exīstimō **quōsdam** bonōs nātūrā esse.	*I think that **certain** people are naturally good.*
Quīdam mīles frātrem suum necāvit.	***A certain** soldier slew his brother.*
Quisque sē optimum esse exīstimat.	***Each one** thinks that he is the best.*
Mercātor **cuique** nautae pecūniam dedit.	*The merchant gave **each** sailor money.*
Iūstitia numquam nocet **cuiquam**.	*Justice never harms **anyone**.*

(The adjectival form of **quisquam** is rarely found.)

On the following page is a summary of indefinite pronouns and adjectives; for a complete list of the forms, refer to the charts at the end of this book (page 176). Note that it is only the **quis** or **quī** part of the word that changes.

| Pronoun | Adjective |
| m.   f.   n. | m.   f.   n. |

Pronoun

m.   f.   n.

ali**quis**, ali**quis**, ali**quid**
    (*someone, something, anyone, anything*)
quīdam, **quae**dam, **quod**dam
    (*a certain one*)
quisque, **quis**que, **quid**que
    (*each one, every one*)
quisquam, **quis**quam, **quid**quam
    (*someone, something, anyone, anything*)

Adjective

m.   f.   n.

ali**quī**, ali**qua**, ali**quod**
    (*some, any*)
quīdam, **quae**dam, **quod**dam
    (*a certain*)
quisque, **quae**que, **quod**que
    (*each, every*)
same as pronoun but rarely found
    (*any*)

Notes

1. Forms of **quīdam** are commonly found with the preposition **ex** and meaning *some of* when a partitive idea is expressed, e.g., **quīdam ex mīlitibus**, *some of the soldiers.*
2. The Romans used forms of **quis**, instead of **aliquis** or **quisquam**, after **sī, nisi, num,** and **nē**. The forms of **quis** are declined like **aliquis** without the prefix **ali-**. For example, **Sī quis in Forum ierit, multōs hominēs vidēbit.** *If anyone goes into the Forum, he/she will see many people.*
3. **Quisquam** is usually found in a negative context; that is, the sentence contains a word such as **nōn, nec, numquam,** or **negāre**. See the last example on page 112 and the **sententia** at the bottom of this page.

Exercise 63a

Read aloud and translate:

1. Potestne iūstitia alicui umquam nocēre?
2. "Estne aliquis domī?" clāmāvit praedō.
3. Augustus praecipiēbat nē quis sē deum esse dīceret.
4. Quīdam ē senātōribus voluērunt Octāviānum appellāre Rōmulum.
5. Neque quisquam est quī sine metū in proeliō pugnet.
6. Alicui quidem rogantī quam iubentī libentius pārēmus.
7. "Quot hominēs, tot sententiae; suus cuique mōs," scrīpsit Terentius.
8. Nūlla causa iūsta cuiquam esse potest contrā patriam arma capiendī.
9. Vidēmus quōsdam adesse quī ad Actium pugnāvērunt.
10. Augustus, quamquam reī pūblicae potītus erat, tyrannus nōn erat.
11. Sī quis imperātōrī "Minimē" dīxerit, pūniētur.
12. Datane est corōna triumphālis quoque Augustō?

Cum dēbēre carnufex cuiquam quidquam quemquam, quemque quisque conveniat, neget. *Since the rascal denies that anyone owes anything to anyone, let each one sue the other.*

(Ennius, fragment of a comedy)

---

2   •**pietās, pietātis,** f., *devotion, sense of duty.*
    ***sānctus, -a, -um,** *sacred, venerable, revered.*
    •**optō, -āre, -āvī, -ātus,** *to wish; to require, demand.*
        optāverat: followed by an indirect command.
        quam tardissimē: *at the latest possible moment.*
    •**succēdō, succēdere, successī, successūrus** + dat., *to come after, take the place of, succeed.*
3   **virtūtēs tuās:** here this means *virtue* rather than *courage.* The thought is that the gods have
        given Trajan the opportunity to rule sooner than anticipated because of Nerva's untimely
        death.
    gubernāculum, -ī, n., *rudder, helm.*
        ad gubernācula reī pūblicae: this metaphor depicts the State as a ship, with the
        Emperor at the helm. The "ship of state" is a common image in ancient literature.
    quam: the antecedent is **reī pūblicae.**
4   •**suscipiō, suscipere, suscēpī, susceptus,** *to undertake, take on.*
        quam suscēperās: as Nerva's officially adopted heir, Trajan had already begun to assume
        some of the duties of state.
    precor, -ārī, -ātus sum, *to beg, beseech, pray.*
    Precor . . . ut . . . omnia . . . contingant: *I pray that all things may turn out;* **ut . . . contin-
    gant** is an indirect command after **precor.**
5   **digna saeculō tuō: dignus** requires an ablative of respect, where we say "worthy of"; **digna**
        elaborates on the meaning of **prospera.**
    saeculum, -ī, n., *age, reign.*
    •**hilaris, -is, -e,** *cheerful, happy, successful.*
    optime: in addressing the Emperor as **optimus,** Pliny foreshadows what will later become the
        extraordinary title Optimus, granted to Trajan alone among all Caesars. Trajan enjoyed the
        association with Jupiter Optimus Maximus that this title brought, even celebrating it on his
        coins, such as the one reproduced below.
    prīvātim et pūblicē: i.e., both as a private individual and as a public official.

On coin A, Jupiter Optimus Maximus, addressed as **Cōnservātor Patris Patriae,** is shown dressed in a toga
and standing protectively over Trajan. On coin B, look for the small globe just below the bust of Trajan.
This coin is about the size of an American nickel.

CHAPTER

64

EMPEROR AND EMPIRE

Marcus Ulpius Traianus (Trajan), Roman Emperor A.D. 98–117, was born in Spain, a fact that shows the extent to which the Empire had become "Romanized." His personal qualities led to accomplishments similar to those of Augustus. As you read, compare the two emperors in an attempt to draw some conclusions about Roman imperial rule.

The letter in Reading A was written by Pliny to Trajan in A.D. 98, in celebration of the Emperor's accession after the sudden death of his adoptive father Nerva.

A. C. PLINIUS TRAIANO IMPERATORI   1

Tua quidem pietās, imperātor sānctissime, optāverat ut quam tardissimē succēderēs 2
patrī; sed dī immortālēs festīnāvērunt virtūtēs tuās ad gubernācula reī pūblicae quam 3
suscēperās admovēre. Precor ergō ut tibi et per tē generī hūmānō prospera omnia, id 4
est digna saeculō tuō, contingant. Fortem tē et hilarem, imperātor optime, et prīvātim 5
et pūblicē optō. 6

—Pliny, *Epistulae* X.1

1. With what title does Pliny
   address the Emperor? (2) What had
   this title meant during the Republic?
   What does the use of this title during
   imperial times imply?
2. According to Pliny, which of Trajan's
   qualities makes him a worthy successor
   to his father? (2)
3. What image does Pliny use to describe
   the Emperor's guidance of Rome? (3–4)
4. What hopes did Pliny have for Trajan's
   reign? (4–5)
5. What does Pliny's closing salutation
   imply about his purpose in writing this
   letter? (5–6)

The Emperor Trajan

2   **•meritō**, adv., *deservedly.*

   praeferātur: deduce from **prae + ferō.**

   inūsitātus, -a, -um, *unusual.*

   cīvīlitās, cīvīlitātis, f., *behavior as an ordinary person, civility.*

     inūsitātae cīvīlitātis et fortitūdinis: *(a man) of unusual courtesy and bravery.*

   •imperium, -ī, n., *empire* (in this context).

     Rōmānī imperiī . . . fīnēs: the territory of the Roman Empire reached its greatest extent under Trajan.

3   **dēfēnsum . . . fuerat**: = **dēfēnsum erat.**

   nōbiliter, adv., *grandly, impressively.*

   longē lātēque: *far and wide.*

   *diffundō, diffundere, diffūdī, diffūsus, *to spread out, extend.*

4   **moderātiō, moderātiōnis,** f., *temperance, self-control.*

5   **aequālis, -is, -e,** *equal in status.*

   exhibeō, -ēre, -uī, -itus, *to show, demonstrate.*

   frequentō, -āre, -āvī, -ātus, *to visit often.* By the fourth century, when Eutropius wrote, Roman emperors had established elaborate court rituals to distance themselves from their subjects and emphasize their absolute power. It is perhaps for this reason that Eutropius is so impressed that Trajan interacted socially with upper class citizens.

   vel . . . vel, conj., *either . . . or*

6   **īsdem**: *the same (friends).*

   indiscrētus, -a, -um, *without prejudice or social distinction.*

   vicissim, adv., *in turn, in exchange.*

7   **•laedō, laedere, laesī, laesus,** *to injure, harm.*

   iniūstus, -a, -um, *improper, unjust.*

   fiscus, -ī, m., *purse; treasury, the Emperor's private funds* (as opposed to **aerārium**, the state treasury).

8   **immūnitās, immūnitātis,** f., *exemption from* **mūnera** (public duties and taxation).

   cīvitās, cīvitātis, f., *citizenship; state; city* (in late Latin).

   immūnitātēs cīvitātibus tribuēns: by Eutropius' time, both taxes and other obligations imposed by the government were more burdensome than they had been earlier in the Empire. Thus, it is not surprising that Eutropius admires Trajan for granting **immūnitātēs** to various cities.

9   **placidus, -a, -um,** *peaceful, peaceable.*

10 **venerātiō, venerātiōnis,** f., *respect.*

   •obeō, obīre, obiī or **obīvī, obitūrus,** irreg., *to depart, die.*

   •aetās, aetātis, f., *age.*

11 **dīvōs**: = **deōs.**

12 **conlāta**: perfect passive participle of **conferō.**

   Ossa . . . sub columnā posita sunt: Trajan's ashes were enshrined in the base of his column in his Forum, built just to the northeast of the Roman Forum. See the picture on page 119 and the plan on page 120. (The column is located between the Basilica Ulpia and Trajan's temple.)

13 **•dēferō, dēferre, dētulī, dēlātus,** irreg., *to bring down, hand down.*

14 **•usque ad** + acc., *up to, as far as.*

   *nōn aliter: *not otherwise, in no other way.*

   acclāmō, -āre, -āvī, -ātus, *to cry out in approval, acclaim publicly.*

B. A SUMMARY OF TRAJAN'S REIGN

Although Eutropius, the author of the next passage, lived several hundred years after Trajan, he nonetheless preserved at least the spirit of the popular attitude toward Trajan during that emperor's lifetime.

Marcus Ulpius Traiānus rem pūblicam ita administrāvit ut omnibus prīncipibus 1
meritō praeferātur, inūsitātae cīvīlitātis et fortitūdinis. Rōmānī imperiī, quod post Au- 2
gustum dēfēnsum magis fuerat quam nōbiliter ampliātum, fīnēs longē lātēque diffūdit. 3
Glōriam tamen mīlitārem cīvīlitāte et moderātiōne superāvit, Rōmae et per prōvinciās 4
aequālem sē omnibus exhibēns, amīcōs salūtandī causā frequentāns vel aegrōtantēs vel 5
cum fēstōs diēs habuissent, convīvia cum īsdem indiscrēta vicissim habēns, saepe in ve- 6
hiculīs eōrum sedēns, nūllum senātōrem laedēns, nihil iniūstum ad augendum fiscum 7
agēns, per orbem terrārum aedificāns multa, immūnitātēs cīvitātibus tribuēns, nihil nōn 8
tranquillum et placidum agēns. Ob haec per orbem terrārum deō proximus nihil nōn 9
venerātiōnis meruit et vīvus et mortuus. Obiit aetātis annō LXIII, mēnse IX, diē IV; 10
imperiī XIX, mēnse VI, diē XV. Inter dīvōs relātus est sōlusque omnium intrā urbem 11
sepultus est. Ossa conlāta in urnam auream in Forō, quod aedificāvit, sub columnā 12
posita sunt, cuius altitūdō CXLIV pedēs habet. Huius tantum memoriae dēlātum est ut 13
usque ad nostram aetātem nōn aliter in senātū prīncipibus acclāmētur nisi "Fēlīcior Au- 14
gustō, melior Traiānō." 15

—Eutropius, *Breviarium ab urbe condita* VIII.2–5 (extracts)

1. What characteristics of Trajan as a ruler does Eutropius mention? (1–2 and 4–5)
2. How did Trajan's foreign policy compare with that of Augustus? (2–3; Chapter 63, Reading C).
3. Describe Trajan's attitude toward: citizens, friends, senators, economic and financial affairs, and public works. (5–9)
4. What reputation did the Emperor enjoy as a result? (9–10)
5. What was Trajan's age at his death? For how long had he ruled? (10–11)
6. What honors were granted to Trajan? (11–12)
7. Describe the special location of Trajan's burial. (12–13)
8. What custom revealed Trajan's popularity, even two hundred years after his death? (13–15)

This coin of Trajan shows a bridge over the Danube River. The bridge was one of Trajan's many building projects (cf. **per orbem terrārum aedificāns multa**, line 8, above). Note the legend **Optimō Prīncipī**.

BUILDING THE MEANING
Impersonal Verbs II

1. Nōbīs **necesse est** statim <u>discēdere</u>. (9:13–14)
   It is necessary *for us <u>to leave</u> immediately.*

   Licetne nōbīs hīc <u>cēnāre</u>? ***Is it allowed*** *for us <u>to dine</u> here?* (20:7)

You learned in Chapter 20 that the boldface expressions are called *impersonal* because they are used only in the 3rd person singular and in the infinitive and are often translated with *it* as the subject. In the course of Book II you met several other impersonal verbs, which were summarized in Chapter 52. Here are some of the ones you have met:

decet, decēre, decuit, *it is becoming, fitting; should*
libet, libēre, libuit (+ dat.), *it is pleasing, it is agreeable*
licet, licēre, licuit (+ dat.), *it is allowed*
oportet, oportēre, oportuit, *it is fiting; ought*

All the verbs in the above list can be used either with an accusative and infinitive or with a subjunctive clause as subject:

<u>Festīnāre tē</u> **oportet.** (50:9)   **Oportet** <u>festīnēs</u>.   <u>That you hurry</u> **is fitting**.
                                                          It is fitting <u>*that you hurry*</u>.
                                                          You ought to hurry.

Libet, licet, and **necesse est** can also be used with a dative, as in the examples at the top of the page.

2. You met this verb in Chapter 50:

   Mē **taedet** solitūdinis. ***I am tired*** *of being alone* (literally, ***It tires*** *me of loneliness*).

This verb is one of several impersonals that deal with feelings:

miseret, miserēre, miseruit, *it makes one pity, feel sorry for something*
paenitet, paenitēre, paenituit, *it makes one regret something*
pudet, pudēre, puduit, *it makes one be ashamed of something*
taedet, taedēre, taesum est, *it bores, makes one tired of something*

These impersonal verbs are accompanied by the accusative of the person affected by the feeling and the genitive of the cause of the feeling, as the example above shows. It is usually better to translate such verbs personally in English:

<u>Tē</u> **pudet** <u>errōris</u>.
It makes <u>*you*</u> ***ashamed*** <u>*of your mistake*</u>. *You are ashamed of your mistake.*

Such verbs are also found with an infinitive phrase describing the cause of the feeling:
   Nōs **pudet** male <u>fēcisse</u>.   ***We are ashamed*** <u>*of having done*</u> *poorly.*

3. You have also met the verb **placēre** used impersonally:

Placetne hoc tibi? ***Does** this **please** you? Is this all right with you?*
Hic liber mihi **placet**. *This book **is pleasing** to me. I like this book.*
Placuit nē quis eam rem ēnūntiāret. (52:2–3)
***It was decided** that no one should reveal the matter.*

Note that in the perfect tense **placuit** means *it was decided*.

4. The verbs **iuvāre** and **vidērī** have special meanings when used impersonally:

Nōs ambulāre **iuvat**. *We **enjoy** walking* (literally, ***It delights** us to walk*).
Nōbīs abīre **vidētur**. ***It seems best** to us to go away.*

5. Many intransitive verbs can be used impersonally in the *passive voice* (see page 92):

. . . nōn aliter in Senātū prīncipibus **acclāmētur** nisi . . . (64B:14)
. . . *in no other way **is acclamation given** to emperors in the Senate except . . .*

Exercise 64a
Read aloud and translate into idiomatic English:

1. Senātum oportet lēgātōs mittere ad Dacōs.
2. Nervā mortuō, Traiānum necesse erat imperātōrem fierī.
3. Decet senātōrī imperātōris salūtandī causā Forum petere.
4. Oportet epistulam scrībās ut imperātōrī grātūlēris.
5. Mē stultitiae meae pudet.
6. Multīs epistulīs scrīptīs, Plīniō fēstīs diēbus fruī licēbit.
7. Taedet imperātōrem eadem semper audīre.
8. Traiānus amīcīs aegrōtantibus auxilium dabat quod sē miserēbat eōrum.
9. Licuit Rōmānīs ossa Traiānī intrā urbem sepelīre.
10. Plīnium laudāvisse Traiānum nōn paenitet.
11. Mīlitēs puduit in proeliō fūgisse.
12. Ad Forum imperātōris audiendī causā concurritur.
13. Optimī imperātōrēs nōn agunt quod libet sed quod decet.
14. Nec mē pudet concēdere mē nescīre quod nesciam.
15. Dē Traiānō optimē nārrātur.

Dācī, -ōrum, m. pl., *Dacians, people of Dacia (modern Rumania)*

Trajan's Column

TRAJAN'S BUILDING PROGRAM

Trajan extended the boundaries of the Roman Empire to the limits of the civilized world, with the exception of India and China. The wealth that poured into Rome from these imperial territories enabled Trajan to undertake a massive building program, to the extent that the Emperor Constantine later called him **Parietāria**, *Wallflower*, because his name was inscribed on so many walls. He built baths, aqueducts, roads, and bridges at home and abroad, and, in keeping with his imperial vision of Rome as a cosmopolis, he constructed a huge market, which was supplied by his new harbor at Ostia. His crowning achievement was the last and greatest of the imperial **fora**, Trajan's Forum, where the Emperor's remains were laid to rest at the foot of his column celebrating the defeat of the Dacians. It was the Emperor's hope that Rome would become the architectural showpiece of the world, much as the Athens of Pericles had been, and his coins often boast of this intention. In general, Roman rulers used their buildings as architectural propaganda, to symbolize the material rewards of prosperity under imperial rule and to portray such imperial virtues as **concordia, abundantia, fēlīcitās**, and **aeternitās**.

Provincial municipalities often competed for imperial favor by constructing baths, **fora**, theaters, and aqueducts in the image of Rome herself. Pliny, in writing to Trajan of the public works in Bithynia, several times refers to those "whose utility and beauty will be most worthy of your age."

The Arch of Trajan at Beneventum, along the extension built by Trajan of the Via Appia.

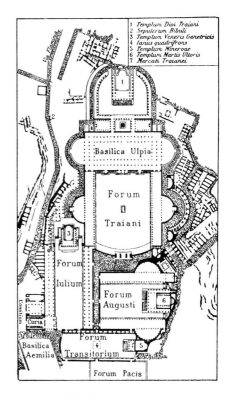

1 *Templum Diui Traiani*
2 *Sepulcrum Bibuli*
3 *Templum Veneris Genetricis*
4 *Ianus quadrifrons*
5 *Templum Mineroae*
6 *Templum Martis Ultoris*
7 *Mercati Traianei*

Basilica Ulpia

Forum Traiani

Forum Iulium

Forum Augusti

Curia

Basilica Aemilia

Forum Transitorium

Forum Pacis

The Imperial Fora

TWO INSCRIPTIONS FROM BRITAIN

As time went by, the various provinces of the Empire gradually became "Romanized"—that is, what were originally pieces of conquered territory (cf. **vincere**, the root of **prōvincia**) took on the language and customs of their conquerors. The Romans systematically encouraged this process by rewarding provincial leaders who adopted the Roman way of life. The following dedicatory inscription is from a Roman temple at Noviomagus (Chichester) in Britain (see the map below). It illustrates the influence of Rome on Cogidubnus, an important British client king of the first century A.D., who had been made a Roman official by the Emperor Claudius in A.D. 47.

> NEPTŪNŌ ET MINERVAE
>   TEMPLUM
> PRŌ SALŪTE DOMŪS DĪVĪNAE
> EX AUCTŌRITĀTE TI. CLAUD(Ī)
> CŌGIDUBNĪ R(ĒGIS) LĒGĀT(Ī) AUG(USTĪ) IN BRIT(ANNIĀ)
> COLLĒGIUM FABRŌRUM ET QUĪ IN EŌ
> SUNT DĒ SUŌ DEDĒRUNT DŌNANTE ĀREAM
> CLĒMENTE PUDENTĪNĪ FĪLIŌ

domūs dīvīnae: the family of the Emperor Claudius	**faber, fabrī**, m., *metalworker*
Cōgidubnus: king of the Regnenses tribe	**dē suō**, *at their own expense*
collēgium, -ī, n., *guild, union*	**ārea, -ae**, f., *open space, site*

Exercise 64b

Translate the inscription above, and then write answers to the questions below:

1. To what deities was this temple dedicated?
2. What Latin words reveal the feelings of the donors toward the emperor?
3. Under whose authority was this dedication made?
4. Who provided the funds for the temple?
5. Where did the land for the temple precinct come from?

Roman Britain

Roman gods were sometimes adopted wholesale in the provinces and fused with local deities. This can be seen clearly in Britain, where the Roman army was the main vehicle of Romanization. Here is an inscription from a small altar dedicated by a soldier in payment of a vow to **Mars Brāciāca**, *Mars in Pants*. The word **brācae** refers to the trousers worn by Gauls. Although the altar was found in Britain, the soldier was serving in a unit of provincial auxiliaries from Aquitania, in southwestern Gaul (see the map on page 17).

Deō Martī Brāciācae
Q. Sittius Caeciliān(us) praef(ectus) coh(ortī) I.
  Aquītānō
v(ōtum) s(olvit)

> **praefectus, -ī,** m., *prefect* (official in charge)
> **I.: = prīmae**
> **vōtum solvere,** *to pay a vow*

Gaul wearing **brācae**

GEOGRAPHY ANCIENT AND MODERN

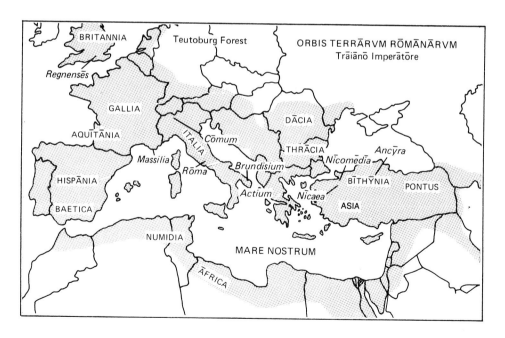

During the principate of Trajan, the Roman Empire reached its greatest size. The map above shows all the territory that was ruled by Rome at Trajan's death.

Exercise 64c

Compare the map on the opposite page with the map on page 17, which shows the boundaries of the Empire at Augustus' death. List those territories that had been added by Trajan's time.

Exercise 64d

Make a list of all the modern countries wholly or partly contained within the boundaries of the Roman Empire during the time of Trajan, as illustrated by the map on the opposite page. Consult a modern atlas for assistance, as necessary.

Exercise 64e

Many cities trace their origins to the Roman imperial period. For each city in the first column, find the modern city that corresponds to the Roman one. Then tell the country in which it is found (use an atlas as necessary).

	ROMAN CITY		MODERN CITY		MODERN COUNTRY*
1.	Ancyra	a.	London	A.	Austria
2.	Burdigala	b.	Cadiz	B.	England
3.	Carthago Nova	c.	Milan	C.	France
4.	Colonia Agrippinensis	d.	Vienna	D.	Germany
5.	Gades	e.	Cologne	E.	Israel
6.	Hierosolyma	f.	Ankara	F.	Italy
7.	Londinium	g.	Cartagena	G.	Rumania
8.	Mediolanum	h.	Naples	H.	Russia
9.	Neapolis	i.	Bordeaux	I.	Spain
10.	Vindobona	j.	Jerusalem	J.	Turkey

   * Some countries are used more than once.

This **Traiānēum** (temple of Trajan) was built at Pergamum in Asia Minor (modern Turkey) and was finished by Trajan's successor Hadrian.

1 **in eīs**: *in (the case of) those.*
  ***tamquam**, conj., *just as if, as.*
  •**dēferēbantur**: here, **dēferō** is a technical term meaning *to inform against, accuse.* Christians were identified by informers, presumably fellow provincials. Informers were common and notorious during the Empire.
2 **an essent**: *whether or not they were*; understand **utrum** in a double indirect question.
  cōnfiteor, cōnfitērī, cōnfessus sum, *to confess.*
3 ***supplicium, -ī**, n., *punishment.*
  ***minor, -ārī, -ātus sum**, *to threaten.*
  persevērāns, persevērantis, *being persistent, stubborn.*
  dūcī: *to be led (to execution).* Organized persecutions of Christians did not begin until the third century A.D., but provincial governors, under orders from the emperor to keep the peace, often used summary police powers to suppress Christians charged with disobedience, immorality, or treason.
  quāliscumque, quāliscumque, quālecumque, *of whatever kind.*
4 ***fateor, fatērī, fassus sum**, *to admit, confess.*
  pertinācia, -ae, f., *stubbornness.*
  obstinātiō, obstinātiōnis, f., *determination, obstinacy.*
  īnflexibilem obstinātiōnem: there had been no formal edict by Trajan to suppress Christians; Pliny was acting on his own in punishing them for their obstinate rejection of his authority.
5 **āmentia, -ae**, f., *madness, insanity.*
  adnotō, -āre, -āvī, -ātus, *to make a ruling.*
  adnotāvī in urbem remittendōs (esse): Roman citizens could appeal to Caesar for trial in Rome, as did Saint Paul to Nero.
7 **trāctātus, -ūs**, m., *investigation.*
  •**crīmen, crīminis**, n., *charge, accusation.*
  diffundente sē crīmine plūrēs speciēs incidērunt: *as the accusations spread, more cases came to light.*
8 **prōpōnō, prōpōnere, prōposuī, prōpositus**, *to put forth, publish.*
  libellus, -ī, m., *notice, poster, indictment.*
  sine auctōre: *anonymously.*
9 **cum**: introduces **appellārent** (9), **supplicārent** (10), and **maledīcerent** (11).
  praeeunte mē: *repeating the words after me*, literally, *with me going before*; Pliny dictated the formula of the oath or prayer.
  imāginī tuae: dative with **supplicārent** (10) and antecedent of **quam**. Emperor worship was not compulsory, but there was a cult of the emperor established in each province as a focus of political loyalty to Rome. Adoration of the emperor's statue, as a pledge of allegiance, was rejected by Christians as a form of idolatry.
10 **simulācrum, -ī**, n., *image, statue.*
  ***nūmen, nūminis**, n., *divine power, god.*
  tūs, tūris, n., *incense.*
  supplicō, -āre, -āvī, -ātūrus + dat., *to offer worship to, pray to.*
11 **maledīcō, maledīcere, maledīxī, maledictūrus** + dat., *to curse, revile.*
12 **dīmittendōs**: = **eōs** (i.e., those who had sacrificed to the Roman gods) **dīmittendōs esse.**

RELIGION AND THE STATE

In the following letter, Pliny asks Trajan for guidance in dealing with the Christians in his province of Bithynia and relates what initiatives he has taken thus far. The date is A.D. 110–112. At the beginning of his letter Pliny confesses, "I am not at all sure whether a pardon ought to be granted to anyone retracting his faith, or whether someone who has previously professed Christianity should gain nothing by renouncing it; whether it is the actual name 'Christian' which is punishable, even if no crime has been committed, or only the crimes associated with the name." He continues:

A. PLINY TO TRAJAN

Interim, in eīs quī ad mē tamquam Chrīstiānī dēferēbantur, hunc sum secūtus 1
modum. Interrogāvī ipsōs an essent Chrīstiānī. Cōnfitentēs iterum ac tertiō inter- 2
rogāvī supplicium minātus; persevērantēs dūcī iussī. Neque enim dubitābam, quāle- 3
cumque esset quod fatērentur, pertināciam certē et īnflexibilem obstinātiōnem dēbēre 4
pūnīrī. Fuērunt aliī similis āmentiae, quōs, quia cīvēs Rōmānī erant, adnotāvī in urbem 5
remittendōs. 6

Mox ipsō tractātū, ut fierī solet, diffundente sē crīmine plūrēs speciēs incidērunt. 7
Prōpositus est libellus sine auctōre multōrum nōmina continēns. Quī negābant esse sē 8
Chrīstiānōs aut fuisse, cum praeeunte mē deōs appellārent et imāginī tuae, quam prop- 9
ter hoc iusseram cum simulācrīs nūminum adferrī, tūre ac vīnō supplicārent, praetereā 10
maledīcerent Chrīstō, quōrum nihil cōgī posse dīcuntur quī sunt rē vērā Chrīstiānī, 11
dīmittendōs putāvī. 12

(continued)

1. How were Christians identified in Bithynia? (1)
2. What were Pliny's methods of investigation? (2–3)
3. What was the penalty for those who admitted being Christian? (3)
4. Why did Pliny think that Christians deserved to be punished? (3–5)
5. What happened to Christians who were Roman citizens? (5–6)
6. What was the reason for the sharp increase in accusations? (7–8)
7. What tests were suspects required to pass in order to prove their "innocence"? (8–12)

13 *index, indicis, m., *sign, proof; informer, spy.*

14 *dēsinō, dēsinere, dēsiī, *to stop, cease.*
   triennium, -ī, n., *three years.*

15 veneror, -ārī, -ātus sum, *to worship.*

16 affirmō, -āre, -āvī, -ātus, *to declare, assert.*
   Affirmābant: governs **fuisse** in indirect statement. The subject is those Christians who
   had been accused but were no longer participating. Pliny now describes the main
   elements of Christian liturgy.

17 **quod essent solitī**: *the fact that they had been accustomed*; explaining **hanc summam** in line 16.
   The verb **essent solitī** governs the infinitives in the next three lines.
   status, -a, -um, *fixed, appointed.*
   statō diē: Sunday, the day after the Jewish Sabbath.
   *carmen, carminis, n., *poem, song, hymn.*

18 **sēcum invicem**: i.e., chanting back and forth, in alternate verses.
   sacrāmentum, -ī, n., *oath, vow.*
   in: *for the purpose of.*
   obstringō, obstringere, obstrīnxī, obstrictus, *to bind.*

19 *fūrtum, -ī, n., *theft, fraud.*
   *latrōcinium, -ī, n., *robbery.*
   nē fūrta (18–19) . . . committerent, etc.: These are indirect commands after **sēque** . . .
   sacrāmentō . . . obstringere which parallel **nōn in scelus aliquod**.
   •fallō, fallere, fefellī, falsus *to betray, deceive.*
   nē dēpositum appellātī abnegārent: a **dēpositum** is something entrusted. In the absence of
   banks, property could be left with friends for safekeeping and then returned on demand, a
   trust apparently often abused.

20 peragō, peragere, perēgī, perāctus, *to carry through, complete.*
   mōrem . . . fuisse and **quod . . . dēsiisse** (20–21): continuations of the indirect statement
   after **affirmābant** in line 16.
   coeō, coīre, coiī or coīvī, irreg., *to come together, gather.*

21 prōmiscuus, -a, -um, *common, ordinary.*
   innoxius, -a, -um, *harmless.*
   cibum, prōmiscuum tamen et innoxium: Christians were suspected of ritual murder,
   cannibalism, and the drinking of blood, all associated with the Eucharist.

22 ēdictum, -ī, n., *edict, public order.*
   secundum, prep. + acc., *according to.*
   secundum mandāta tua hetaeriās esse vetueram: these **hetaeriae** (Greek word) or
   collēgia (Latin) were social clubs, which often became focal points for social unrest.
   Trajan had sent Pliny to Bithynia to deal in part with political disturbances, and Pliny
   had issued an edict suppressing **hetaeriae** in the province.

23 **ancillīs, quae ministrae dīcēbantur**: **ancilla** and **ministra** are Latin translations of the feminine form of *diakonos*, the Greek word for servant, which gives the English *deacon(ness)*. The
   witnesses whom Pliny was questioning spoke Greek, the primary language of Bithynia.
   per tormenta quaerere: slaves could be tortured to give evidence.

24 prāvus, -a, -um, *depraved, perverse.*
   immodicus, -a, um, *excessive.*

Aliī ab indice nōminātī esse sē Chrīstiānōs dīxērunt et mox negāvērunt; fuisse 13
quidem sed dēsiisse, quīdam ante triennium, quīdam ante plūrēs annōs, nōn nēmō 14
etiam ante vīgintī. Hī quoque omnēs et imāginem tuam deōrumque simulācra venerātī 15
sunt et Chrīstō maledīxērunt. Affirmābant autem hanc fuisse summam vel culpae suae 16
vel errōris, quod essent solitī statō diē ante lūcem convenīre, carmenque Chrīstō quasi 17
deō dīcere sēcum invicem sēque sacrāmentō nōn in scelus aliquod obstringere, sed nē 18
fūrta, nē latrōcinia, nē adulteria committerent, nē fidem fallerent, nē dēpositum appel- 19
lātī abnegārent. Quibus perāctīs mōrem sibi discēdendī fuisse rūrsusque coeundī ad 20
capiendum cibum, prōmiscuum tamen et innoxium; quod ipsum facere dēsiisse post 21
ēdictum meum, quō secundum mandāta tua hetaeriās esse vetueram. Quō magis neces- 22
sārium crēdidī ex duābus ancillīs, quae ministrae dīcēbantur, quid esset vērī, et per tor- 23
menta quaerere. Nihil aliud invēnī quam superstitiōnem prāvam et immodicam. 24

—Pliny, *Epistulae* X.96 (excerpts)

8. From what particular group of those named by informers did Pliny obtain information about Christians? (13–14)
9. How long ago had these people been active in the religion? (14–15)
10. According to Pliny's informants, what were the main elements of Christian worship? (16–20)
11. What did the Christians do after their worship service was over? (20–21)
12. What Roman misconception about Christian beliefs do the words **prōmiscuum**
and **innoxium** reveal? (21)
13. What concession did the Christians make to Roman law? (21–22)
14. How did Pliny attempt to confirm what he had learned from former Christians?
(22–24)
15. What might have led the Emperor to become suspicious of Christians?
16. What do the words **ēdictum** and **mandāta** tell us about the source of law during
the Empire? (22)
17. What seems to have been Pliny's attitude toward the Christians? Apathy? Fear?
Hatred? Curiosity? Do you think his treatment of them was just?

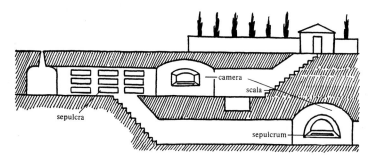

Christians and Jews were buried in catacombs (**catacumbae**, *down in the hollows*), a series of narrow under-
ground galleries and tomb-chambers. The catacombs in Rome, which stretch for some 350 miles, housed
the bodies of tens of thousands, including those of popes and saints.

2   **āctus, -ūs**, m., *procedure.*

      mī Secunde: note the familiar use of Pliny's cognomen **Secundus**.

      excutiō, excutere, excussī, excussus, *to examine, inspect.*

      •**causa, -ae**, f., *reason, cause; case* (legal term).

3   **dēlātī fuerant**: = **dēlātī erant.** See note for line 1, page 124.

      Neque . . . aliquid: = **Nihil.**

      in ūniversum: *in all respects, in every detail.*

      quod quasi certam fōrmam habeat: *which might provide, as it were, a fixed rule.*

4   *****conquīrō, conquīrere, conquīsīvī, conquīsītus**, *to hunt down, seek out.*

      arguō, arguere, arguī, argūtus, *to prove guilty, convict.*

5   **ut . . . impetret**: result clause.

      *****manifestus, -a, -um**, *clear.*

6   *****quamvīs**, conj., *however much.*

      suspectus: = **suspectus est.**

      in praeteritum; *formerly, previously.*

      •**venia, -ae**, f., *pardon.*

7   **paenitentia, -ae**, f., *repentance.*

      *****impetrō, -āre, -āvī, -ātus**, *to obtain, secure, gain.*

8   **et pessimī exemplī nec nostrī saeculī est**: *(characteristic) of the worst sort of precedent, and not (characteristic) of our age.*

      saeculum, -ī, n., *generation, age.*

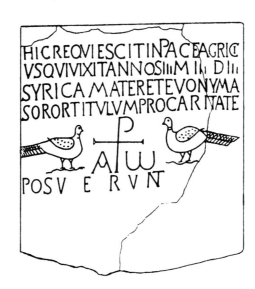

Hīc requiēscit in pāce Agricius quī vīxit annōs III, mēnsēs III, diēs III, Syrica māter et Euōnyma soror titulum prō cāritāte posuērunt.

    titulus, -ī, m., *title, notice, inscription, epitaph*

    cāritās, cāritātis, f., *love*

B. TRAJAN'S REPLY

Traiānus Plīniō.

Āctum quem dēbuistī, mī Secunde, in excutiendīs causīs eōrum, quī Chrīstiānī ad tē dēlātī fuerant, secūtus es. Neque enim in ūniversum aliquid, quod quasi certam formam habeat, cōnstituī potest. Conquīrendī nōn sunt; sī dēferantur et arguantur, pūniendī sunt, ita tamen ut, quī negāverit sē Chrīstiānum esse idque rē ipsā manifestum fēcerit, id est supplicandō dīs nostrīs, quamvīs suspectus in praeteritum, veniam ex paenitentiā impetret. Sine auctōre vērō prōpositī libellī in nūllō crīmine locum habēre dēbent. Nam et pessimī exemplī nec nostrī saeculī est.

—Pliny, *Epistulae* X.97

1. How does Trajan feel about the way in which Pliny has been handling the situation thus far? (2–3)
2. What does Trajan's statement in lines 3–4 imply about his methods as a ruler?
3. Is Pliny to seek out Christians? (4)
4. What is to happen to the Christians who are found guilty? (4–5)
5. How does Trajan address Pliny's uncertainty about Christians who deny their beliefs? (5–7)
6. What practice described by Pliny will Trajan not tolerate? (7–8) What is his reasoning for feeling this way? (8)
7. Given Trajan's advice on the matter of the Christians, how would you assess his qualities as a ruler? Do his own words support his reputation for fairness, as described by Eutropius in the previous chapter?

This coin shows the temple dedicated to the deified Trajan by his successor Hadrian (number 1 in the plan on page 120). **S C** stands for **Senātūs cōnsultō**, *by a decree of the Senate*, and **SPQR** stand for **Senātūs populusque Rōmānus**. What does the rest of the legend say?

BUILDING THE MEANING
Relative Clauses of Characteristic

Observe the following examples:

> Iste est **quem** omnēs **timent.**
> *He is a man **whom** everyone **fears.***

> Iste est **quem** omnēs **timeant.**
> *He is the type of man **whom** everyone **fears (would fear).***

In the second example, the verb in the relative clause is in the subjunctive. This type of clause is called a *relative clause of characteristic*, because it characterizes or describes an antecedent as a general or indefinite type, rather than as a specific and definite person or thing.

The relative clause of characteristic is especially common after such expressions as **est quī, sunt quī, nēmō est quī,** and **quis est quī,** and it is usually translated with phrases such as *of the sort that. . . . , the kind that. . . . ,* or *of such a kind that. . . .* Here are some further examples:

> Quis est **quī** hoc **faciat?**
> *Who is there of the sort who would do this?*

> Sunt **quī dīcant. . . .**
> *There are those who say (would say). . . .*

> Is nōn est **quī** hoc **dīcat.**
> *He is not the kind of person who says (would say) this.*

> Nēmō est **quī sciat. . . .**
> *There is no one **who knows.** . . .*

Exercise 65a
Read aloud and translate:

1. Sunt quī putent Bīthȳniam molestissimam omnium prōvinciārum esse.
2. Traiānus erat quī iniūriae ignōsceret.
3. Quid est quod in hāc prōvinciā Plīnium nōn vexet?
4. Num tū es quī Chrīstiānōs condemnēs?
5. Nēmō est imperātor quī omnēs senātōrēs cognōverit.
6. Quis est cui possessiō lībertātis nōn sit cāra?
7. Sunt quī dīcant Chrīstiānōs multīs deīs nōn supplicāre.
8. Quī imperātōrī pāreant fēlīciter et quiētē vīvent.
9. Traiānus erat quī rem pūblicam bene gerere esse vellet.

Exercise 65b

Read aloud and translate the following pairs of sentences to demonstrate your understanding of the distinction between regular relative clauses and relative clauses of characteristic:

1. (a) Vīdī nihil quod timēbam.
   (b) Vīdī nihil quod timērem.
2. (a) Nēmō est quī vīderit quī tē adiuvat.
   (b) Nēmō est quī vīdit quī tē adiuvet.
3. (a) Est is quem Traiānus saepe laudet.
   (b) Est is quem Traiānus saepe laudat.

Exercise 65c

Read aloud, translate, and identify the uses of the subjunctive in the following sentences (not every sentence contains a subjunctive verb):

1. Plīnius ā Traiānō quaerēbat quae cōnsilia capienda essent dē Chrīstiānīs.
2. Estne aliquī imperātor quī sē pessimum omnium esse putet?
3. Cum eī plūrēs mīlitēs essent, Pompeius spērābat proelium breve futūrum esse.
4. Licēbat cīvibus Rōmānīs quī Chrīstiānī erant petere ut Rōmam remitterentur.
5. Traiānus rem pūblicam ita administrat ut deō proximus esse videātur.
6. Senātus Octāviānum iussit prōvidēre nē rēs pūblica quid dētrīmentī caperet.
7. Metuitne Plīnius ut Chrīstiānī imperātōrī fidēlēs futūrī essent?
8. Comparābatne Octāviānus exercitum ut rem pūblicam ā dominātiōne Antōnī līberāret?
9. Pompeius, cum nostrōs intrā vāllum esse vīdisset, equum nactus sē ē castrīs ēiēcit.
10. Plīnius, ut imperāverat Traiānus, ad Bīthȳniam statim nāvigāvit.

Exercise 65d

Coins were used by Roman emperors as instruments of propaganda. Through their coins, which have been found as far away from Rome as India and China, Roman emperors were able to communicate to their subjects the virtues of Roman imperial rule. Study the coin pictured and be ready to discuss its "message." What messages did they send to those who possessed, used, or saw them? What do the other coins pictured in this book tell us? What kinds of messages do modern coins send?

A coin of Augustus of 27 B.C., minted at Ephesus, in what is now Turkey. Note the eagle of Jupiter clutching the **corōna cīvica** and the laurel trees in the background.

REVIEW XVI: CHAPTERS 63–65

Exercise XVIa: History of the Early Empire

Answer the following questions in English:

1. Name the emperors who ruled between Augustus and Trajan, and give the length of each emperor's reign. (Consult the timeline on page viii.)
2. Discuss the sources that historians use for reconstructing Roman history during the period of the Empire.
3. What political and military conditions during the late Republic led to the transition from Republic to Empire? (Consider what you learned in Part III.) What specific military event eventually led to the concentration of power in the hands of Octavian?
4. What are the traditional dates for the beginning and end of the Roman Republic? Why is 27 B.C. considered by historians to be the beginning of imperial rule in Rome?
5. What term characterizes the condition of the Roman world during Augustus' reign? Identify a Roman monument that celebrates this Augustan achievement.
6. What messages do Augustus' own words in the *Res gestae* send us? What messages do we receive from the Prima Porta statue on page 100? Are these messages consistent?
7. How does the correspondence between Pliny and Trajan reflect the relationship between Rome and her provinces under imperial rule? How does the tone of Pliny's letters in Chapters 64 and 65 suggest Pliny's personal dependence upon the emperor's **auctōritās**?
8. Compare and contrast the careers of Augustus and Trajan. In what ways were they similar? In what ways different? Comment both on personal characteristics and on qualities of leadership and support your observations from the readings.
9. Identify some of the means by which the provinces of the Empire were Romanized.

Bust of the emperor Trajan

Exercise XVIb: The Price of Empire

Imagine that Rome is on trial in an international court of law and is being asked to defend her place in world history. Read the following quotations and then, from the point of view of either the prosecuting or defense attorney, discuss which of these best presents an accurate assessment of Roman imperial rule. Be sure to support your observations by referring to the materials in Part IV:

1. O Rome, the world is yours and you its queen. Far distant tribes become one fatherland beneath your power, which brought to conquered men the rule of law; and through this common right, you made a city out of all the world.

   —Rutilius Namatianus, *On His Return* I.62–66

2. Plunderers of the world, now that there are no more lands for their all-devastating hands, they search even the sea. If the enemy is rich, they are rapacious, if poor they lust for dominion. Not East, not West has satisfied them; alone of all mankind they covet riches and poverty with equal passion. They rob, butcher, plunder, and call it *empire*; and where they make a desolation, they call it *peace*.

   —Attributed to Calgathus, leader of the Caledonians in Scotland, by Tacitus, *Life of Agricola* 30

Exercise XVIc: Indefinite Pronouns and Adjectives, Impersonal Verbs, and Relative Clauses of Characteristic

Read aloud and translate:

1. Plīnius negāvit quemquam quī deōs Rōmānōs appellāret Chrīstiānum esse posse.
2. Cum eī nūllus fīlius esset, oportēbat Augustum hērēdem adoptāre.
3. Caesar, ā quō Octāviānus per testāmentum erat adoptātus, mox mortuus est.
4. Catilīna ad dēlendam patriam coniūrāverat cum quibusdam audācibus virīs.
5. Erantne quī dīcerent Augustum pessimum prīncipem esse?
6. Cuique Chrīstiānō quī dīs Rōmānīs supplicāret Plīnius veniam dedit.
7. Certē nēmō est quī sciat quot aedificia ā Traiānō aedificāta sint.
8. Traiānō amīcōs quōsdam salūtandī causā frequentāre maximē placuit.
9. Cicerō erat quī spērāret rem pūblicam quam diūtissimē dūratūram esse.
10. Līvia erat quam quīdam ē senātōribus timērent.
11. Plīnius quidem nōn est quem pudeat imperātōrem laudāre.
12. Sī quis columnam Traiānī vīsitāverit, cognōscet quō modō exercitus Rōmānus contrā Dācōs bellum gesserit.
13. Quis est quī crēdat imperātōrem esse deum vīvum?

PART V
THREE INDIVIDUALS OF THE EARLY EMPIRE

The readings in Parts I–IV traced the development of Roman politics and history from the late Republic to the early Empire. In this Part, we will focus on the lives of individuals who lived during the early Empire. Chapters 67 and 68 will contain two letters of Pliny, whose work is already familiar to you. Chapter 66 presents extracts from the *Satyricon*, a satiric novel of the first century A.D.

The author of this work is usually identified with the C. Petronius described by the historian Tacitus as a man who held a privileged but dangerous position as unofficial "Arbiter of Elegance" at the court of Nero. Yet, as governor of Bithynia and later consul, he showed himself a capable and energetic administrator. Eventually, he aroused Nero's suspicions and died by suicide (a form of imperial execution), surrounded by friends who comforted him "not with philosophical doctrines but with frivolous songs and light verse."

The longest and most famous of the surviving fragments of the *Satyricon* is the *Cena Trimalchionis (Banquet of Trimalchio)*. It describes an elaborate dinner party given by the ex-slave and self-made millionaire Trimalchio. An army of slaves serves a vast array of dishes, most of them disguised as something other than what they are: for example, glowing "coals" made of sliced damsons and pomegranates, a roast boar with sausages for entrails, and a sow with pastry "piglets." From time to time the guests are entertained by musicians, actors, or singing waiters of various degrees of awfulness.

Some of the most interesting and amusing passages of the *Cena* are those in which Petronius lets us eavesdrop on the conversations of Trimalchio and his guests. These conversations are unique in Latin literature for the vividness with which they portray the habits of speech and thought of ordinary people in the ancient Roman world. But the real heart of the *Cena* is the brilliant comic portrait of Trimalchio himself. Every aspect of the banquet reveals some facet of Trimalchio's life and personality: the culinary extravaganzas, the service and entertainment, and the guests' comments on their host and his fabulous wealth.

Of all the ways Petronius brings to life this great comic figure, Trimalchio's own speeches are the most revealing. The passage contained in readings A and B of this chapter, in which Trimalchio describes the preparations he has made for his own death, is an example of this kind of self-characterization. As you read it, try to share Petronius' double vision: on the one hand, the way Trimalchio sees himself (i.e., the image he thinks he is presenting to others) and on the other hand the way we the readers see him. In this double vision lies much of the humor and humanity of the *Cena*.

Relief from the tomb of Q. Haterius Tychicus, a rich building contractor of the late first century A.D. A tomb-temple is shown, every inch of its surface crammed with sculpture. A crane (operated by slaves on a treadwheel) symbolizes the owner's trade. The upper right-hand corner gives an interior view of the temple. Haterius himself reclines on a couch while his three children play on the floor and his old nurse lays a sacrifice on an altar. To their right is a shrine of Venus with ancestor-masks above.

Ascyltos, one of the main characters in the *Satyricon*, has come to Trimalchio's house for dinner. He is met by an outlandishly dressed doorkeeper and a magpie in a golden cage:

> While I was staring at all these things, I almost fell and broke my leg. For at the left as you entered, not far from the doorkeeper's room, there was a huge dog, tied up with a chain, painted on the wall and above it in square letters was written BEWARE OF THE DOG. For sure my friends laughed, but I, after catching my breath, continued to persue the whole wall. There was a slave market painted with captions, and Trimalchio himself, with the long hair of a young slave, was holding a caduceus and entering Rome while Minerva lead the way. Next it showed how he had learned to keep accounts and then had become steward; the careful painter had rendered everything diligently with labels. Indeed, in the painting at the end of the portico Mercury had picked up Trimalchio by his chin and was raising him onto the high magistrates' platform. The goddess Fortune was on hand with her horn of plenty and the three Fates spinning golden threads.

> —Petronius, *Satyricon* XXIX.1–6

What facts about Trimalchio's life can you determine or infer from this passage? What kind of person do you think Trimalchio is? Watch to see whether your impressions are confirmed by the Latin readings in this chapter.

1   **et servī**: *slaves, too.*

   aequē: *equally*, i.e., with us free men.

   lāc, lactis, n., *milk.*

      lactem = lāc; Trimalchio confuses the gender of nouns; he treats both **lāc** and **fātum** in the following clause as if they were masculine, not neuter.

2   **fātum, -ī**, n., *fate, destiny.*

   mē salvō: *as long as I'm alive, while I'm around.*

   *****cito**, adv., *quickly, soon.*

   gustō, -āre, -āvī, -ātus, *to taste.*

      aquam līberam gustābunt: *they will taste the water of freedom*, a cliché. Trimalchio in his confusion has jumbled together two incompatible ideas, since the slaves will not be free until Trimalchio is dead.

3   **manū**: one meaning of the word **manus** is the *power* that a Roman father exercised over all members of his household; hence **manū mittere** (sometimes written as one word), *to send from one's power*, meant to free from slavery.

   ideō, adv., *for this reason, therefore.*

   pūblicō, -āre, -āvī, -ātus, *to make public.*

5   *****oblīvīscor, oblīvīscī, oblītus sum** + gen., *to forget.*

   nūgae, nūgārum, f. pl., *jokes, trifles.*

      oblītus nūgārum: *getting down to business* (literally, *forgetting trifles*).

   exemplar, exemplāris, n., *copy.*

6   **ingemēscō, ingemēscere, ingemuī**, *to groan, lament, sigh.*

7   **Habinnam**: Habinnas, one of Trimalchio's friends, a stonemason.

8   **quemadmodum**, conj., *in what way, as.*

   secundum, prep. + acc., *by, beside.*

9   *****catella, -ae**, f., *puppy.*

   pingō, pingere, pīnxī, pictus, *to paint, portray, represent.*

   Petraitis: genitive of **Petraitēs**, a real gladiator of the 1st century A.D.

10 **contingō, contingere, contigī, contāctus**, *to befall, happen to.*

   beneficium, -ī, n., *kindness.*

   ut sint: continuing the indirect command construction from **rogō** (8).

   in fronte: *wide.*

   in agrum: *deep.*

11 **dūcentī, -ae, -a**, *two hundred.*

   pōmum, -ī, n., *fruit tree.*

      Omne genus . . . pōma: *Every kind of fruit tree.*

   sint: supply **ut**.

   circā, prep. + acc., *around.*

   *****cinis, cineris**, m., *ashes.*

12 **vīneārum largiter**: *plenty of grapevines.*

   *****vīvus, -a, -um**, living.

      vīvō . . . esse: *for a living man to have*; **vīvō** is dative of possession, and the infinitives (**esse** and **cūrārī**) are the subjects of **falsum est**, *it is wrong.*

   cultus, -a, -um, *cultivated, elegant.*

13 **Hoc . . . sequātur**: *Let this monument not pass to* (literally, *follow*). This formula was intended to prevent sale or unauthorized use of the tomb by the heirs of the deceased; it did not "pass to" them (**sequātur**) with the rest of his possessions.

THE MILLIONAIRE

A. TRIMALCHIO'S TOMB

At this point in the dinner, Trimalchio has just invited his slaves to share the dining couches with his guests; as they scramble to accept this offer, the dining room is thrown into confusion. Trimalchio then addresses his friends and defends his liberal gesture with bits of ill-digested "philosophy."

Trimalchiō, "Amīcī," inquit, "et servī hominēs sunt et aequē ūnum lactem bibērunt, 1
etiam sī illōs malus fātus oppresserit. Tamen mē salvō, cito aquam līberam gustābunt. 2
Ad summam, omnēs illōs in testāmentō meō manū mittō. Et haec ideō omnia pūblicō, 3
ut familia mea iam nunc sīc mē amet tamquam mortuum." 4
Grātiās agere omnēs indulgentiae coeperant dominī, cum ille oblītus nūgārum ex- 5
emplar testāmentī iussit afferrī et tōtum ā prīmō ad ultimum ingemēscente familiā re- 6
citāvit. Respiciēns deinde Habinnam, "Quid dīcis," inquit, "amīce cārissime? Aedificās 7
monumentum meum, quemadmodum tē iussī? Valdē tē rogō ut secundum pedēs 8
statuae meae catellam pingās et corōnās et unguenta et Petraitis omnēs pugnās, ut mihi 9
contingat tuō beneficiō post mortem vīvere; praetereā ut sint in fronte pedēs centum, in 10
agrum pedēs dūcentī. Omne genus enim pōma volō sint circā cinerēs meōs, et 11
vīneārum largiter. Valdē enim falsum est vīvō quidem domōs cultās esse, nōn cūrārī 12
eās, ubi diūtius nōbīs habitandum est. Et ideō ante omnia adicī volō: 'Hoc monumen- 13
tum hērēdem nōn sequātur.' 14

1. What is Trimalchio's attitude toward slaves? (1–2)
2. What has Trimalchio decided to do about his slaves? (2–3)
3. Why has he decided to make this known now? (3–4)
4. What does Trimalchio do with the copy of his will? (5–7)
5. What request does he make of Habinnas? (7–8)
6. Describe the tomb Trimalchio wants built. (8–12)
7. Why does he think it is important to plan a tomb? (12–13)
8. What is the last item he wants on his tomb? (13–14)

15 **nāvēs**: Trimalchio's fortune was derived from merchant shipping.

16 **tribūnal, tribūnālis**, n., *magistrates' raised platform, tribunal.* Trimalchio was a **sēvir Augustālis**, one of the six priests in charge of the worship of the emperor in the towns. A bordered toga, gold ring, and throne were symbols of the office. Cf. line 24 below.

17 **sacculus, -ī**, m., *little sack.*
    effundō, effundere, effūdī, effūsus, *to pour out.*
    quod: *that*, introducing indirect statement.
    bīnī, -ae, -a, *two at a time, two each, two per person.* This was the cost of the dinner that Trimalchio gave.
    Faciātur: for **Fīat**, *Let there be. . . .* ; the verb is singular either because Trimalchio mistakes **trīclīnia** for a 1st declension noun, or because he is thinking in Greek, in which a neuter plural subject takes a singular verb; either way, his Latin is shaky.

18 **sibi suāviter facientem**: *enjoying themselves.*

19 **Fortūnātae**: Fortunata, Trimalchio's wife.
    columba, -ae, f., *dove.*
    cingulum, -ī, n., *belt; leash.*
    alligō, -āre, -āvī, -ātus, *to tie.*

20 **cicarōnem meum**: *my little pet*, probably his favorite slave.
    amphorās cōpiōsās gypsātās: *large wine jars sealed with gypsum.*
    effluō, effluere, efflūxī, *to flow out; to spill.*

21 **sculpō, sculpere, sculpsī, sculptus**, *to carve.*
    licet . . . sculpās: *you may carve.*
    •**super**, prep. + acc., *over, above.*
    plōrō, -āre, -āvī, -ātus, *to weep.*
    hōrologium, -ī, n., *clock, sundial.*
    in mediō: supply **sit**, *let there be.*

22 **quisquis, quisquis, quidquid**, *whoever, whatever.*
    velit nōlit: *(whether) he wishes to (or) not.*

23 **vidē . . . haec**: *consider carefully whether this (inscription). . . .*
    idōneus, -a, -um, *suitable.*

24 **requiēscō, requiēscere, requiēvī, requiētūrus**, *to rest.*
    sēvirātus: *the office of sēvir*; see note on line 16 above.
    absentī: with **huic**, *in his absence*; an additional honor, implying that he neither campaigned nor paid for the office.
    •**dēcernō, dēcernere, dēcrēvī, dēcrētus**, *to decide, decree, assign.*
    Cum: *Although.*

25 **decuriīs**: the *boards* that formed the lower ranks of the Roman civil service.
    *****pius, -a, -um**, *dutiful, conscientious.*

26 **sēstertium . . . trecentiēs**: the usual way of expressing millions of sesterces was simply to use a numerical adverb (ending in **-iēs**) with the words **centēna mīlia** understood: 300 x 100,000 = 30,000,000.
    "Valē. 'Et tū.' ": *"Farewell (to you, passerby). 'And (to) you, (Trimalchio).' "* Inscriptions on Roman tombs often take the form of a dialogue between the dead man and the passerby.

27 **fleō, flēre, flēvī, flētus**, *to weep.*
    ūbertim, adv., *copiously, abundantly.*

28 **dēnique**, adv., *finally, at last.*
    impleō, implēre, implēvī, implētus, *to fill.*

B. TRIMALCHIO'S TOMB, CONTINUED

"Tē rogō ut nāvēs etiam in monumentō meō faciās plēnīs vēlīs euntēs, et mē in 15
tribūnālī sedentem praetextātum cum ānulīs aureīs quīnque et nummōs in pūblicō dē 16
sacculō effundentem; scīs enim, quod epulum dedī bīnōs dēnāriōs. Faciātur, sī tibi 17
vidētur, et trīclīnia. Faciās et tōtum populum sibi suāviter facientem. Ad dexteram 18
meam pōnās statuam Fortūnātae meae columbam tenentem, et catellam cingulō al- 19
ligātam dūcat, et cicarōnem meum, et amphorās cōpiōsās gypsātās, nē effluant vīnum. 20
Et urnam licet frāctam sculpās, et super eam puerum plōrantem. Hōrologium in me- 21
diō, ut quisquis hōrās īnspiciet, velit nōlit, nōmen meum legat. 22

"Īnscrīptiō quoque vidē dīligenter sī haec satis idōnea tibi vidētur: C. Pompeius 23
Trimalchiō Maecēnātiānus hīc requiēscit. Huic sēvirātus absentī dēcrētus est. Cum 24
posset in omnibus decuriīs Rōmae esse, tamen nōluit. Pius, fortis, fidēlis, ex parvō crē- 25
vit, sēstertium relīquit trecentiēs, nec umquam philosophum audīvit. Valē. 'Et tū.' " 26
Haec ut dīxit Trimalchiō, flēre coepit ūbertim. Flēbat et Fortūnāta, flēbat et Habinnas, 27
tōta dēnique familia, tamquam in fūnus rogāta, lāmentātiōne trīclīnium implēvit. 28

—Petronius, *Satyricon* 71–72 (excerpts)

9. What will appear on Trimalchio's tomb that symbolizes the source of his riches? (15)
10. What will be depicted to show that Trimalchio benefited his fellow citizens? (15–18)
11. How will family members be depicted? (18–20)
12. What symbols of mourning will appear? (21)
13. How will Trimalchio ensure that people stop and look at his tomb? (21–22)
14. What honors given to Trimalchio will be mentioned in the inscription? (23–25)
15. How does Trimalchio describe himself in the rest of the inscription? (25–26)
16. How do the guests and family members react to all this? (27–28)

The tombstone of P. Gessius Romanus. On the left is one of his freedwomen, and on the right one of his freedmen. The inscription reads: **GESSIA · P(ūbliī) · L(īberta) · FAVSTA · P(ūblius) · GESSIVS · ROM(ānus) · P · GESSIVS · P(ūbliī) · L(ībertus) · PRIMVS.**
Museum of Fine Arts, Boston

BUILDING THE MEANING
Jussive and Hortatory Subjunctives

You have studied several kinds of subordinate clauses that require verbs in the subjunctive: circumstantial and causal clauses introduced by **cum**, result and purpose clauses introduced by **ut**, and indirect questions (see Chapter 57, page 38, "The Subjunctive in Subordinate Clauses"); also fear clauses (Chapter 60, page 74) and relative clauses of characteristic (Chapter 65, page 130).

The *present* subjunctive can also be used in a *main* or *independent* clause to give a command. It is found mainly in the 1st and 3rd persons; for the 2nd person, the imperative is normally used. The negative is **nē**. Several examples in the third person have occurred in the reading in this chapter:

> Hoc monumentum hērēdem nē **sequātur**. (13–14)
> ***Let** this tomb not **pass** to (my) heir.*

> **Faciātur** (more correctly, **fiant**) et trīclīnia. (17–18)
> ***Let** dining rooms **be made** also.*

> Catellam cingulō alligātam **dūcat**. (19–20)
> ***Let her lead** a puppy tied with a leash.*

When the subjunctive is used this way in the 3rd person, it is called *jussive* (from **iubeō, iubēre, iussī, iussus**, *to command*).

When this kind of subjunctive occurs in the 1st person plural, it is called *hortatory* (from **hortor, -ārī, -ātus sum**, *to urge*). Well-known examples of the hortatory subjunctive occur in the first line of Catullus' poem 5:

> **Vīvāmus**, mea Lesbia, atque **amēmus**!
> ***Let us live**, my Lesbia, and **let us love!***

and in the medieval student song:

> **Gaudeāmus** igitur, iuvenēs dum sumus.
> ***Let us rejoice** then, while we are young.*

Exercise 66a
Read aloud and translate:

1. "Testāmentum meum," inquit Trimalchiō, "afferātur."
2. Gustēmus omnēs aquam līberam!
3. Omnēs servōs manū mittant dominī.
4. Statua Fortūnātae in monumentō pōnātur.
5. Nē philosophōs audiāmus!
6. Amīcīs cārissimīs grātiās agāmus omnēs!
7. Nē iniūriam accipiat hoc monumentum.
8. Rēs gestae et nōmen Trimalchiōnis ab omnibus legantur.

9. Īnscrīptiōnem idōneam in monumentō meō habeam.
10. Requiēscat in pāce C. Pompeius Trimalchiō Maecēnātiānus.

Exercise 66b

The following is a love charm laid on a woman named Vettia by a man named Felix; it was found in Tunisia, scratched on a lead tablet. Read it aloud, translate it, and identify nine examples of the jussive subjunctive:

Faciat quodcumque dēsīderō Vettia quam peperit Optāta, amōris meī causā, nē dormiat neque cibum accipere possit. Amet mē, Fēlīcem quem peperit Frūcta; oblīvīscātur patris et mātris et propinquōrum suōrum et amīcōrum omnium et aliōrum virōrum. Sōlum mē in mente habeat, dormiēns vigilāns ūrātur frīgeat ardeat Vettia amōris et dēsīderī meī causā.

> quīcumque, quaecumque, quodcumque, *whoever, whatever*
> pariō, parere, peperī, partus, *to give birth, bear*
> quam peperit Optāta: *whom Optata bore.* The author of the charm wants to make sure that it is
>   applied to the right Vettia, so he specifies who her mother is.
> mēns, mentis, f., *mind*
> ūrō, ūrere, ūssī, ūstus, *to burn*
> frīgeō, frīgēre, *to freeze, be cold*
> dēsīderium, -ī, n., *desire*

EPITAPH FOR A SON

Lagge fīlī, bene quiēscās; māter tua rogat tē ut mē ad tē recipiās. Valē. P(edēs) q(uadrātī) XV. *Laggus my son, may you rest well; (I) your mother ask that you take me to you. Farewell. 15 square feet.*

Museum of Fine Arts, Boston

1   **Tam magnus . . . quam**: *As tall as. . . .*

2   **candēlābrum, -ī**, n., *lampstand.* Notice that Trimalchio treats this as a masculine noun.

3   **mētior, mētīrī, mēnsus sum**, *to measure.*

       rostrum, -ī, n., *beak (of a bird); chin.*

       barbātus, -a, -um, *bearded, with a beard.*

       labrum, -ī, n., *lip.*

       lucerna, -ae, f., *lamp.*

       dē lucernā unguēbam: lamps burned olive oil.

4   **cēterum**, adv., *for the rest, moreover.*

       ipsimus, -ī, m., a form derived from **ipse** and used by slaves to refer to their master, *the man himself.*

5   **cerebellum, -ī**, n., *brain.*

       Quid multa: *To put it briefly* (literally, *Why [should I say] much?*).

       cohērēs, cohērēdis, m./f., *joint heir (with)* + dat. (rich men often left something to the emperor to avoid his confiscating the whole estate).

       patrimōnium, -ī, n., *inheritance.*

       lāticlāvius, -a, -um, *with a broad purple stripe, fit for a senator.* The property qualification for the Senate was at least a million sesterces.

6   **concupīscō, concupīscere, concupīvī, concupītus**, *to long for.*

       negōtior, -ārī, -ātus sum, *to go into business.*

       Nē . . . morer: *To cut a long story short* (literally, *So that I don't delay you with many [words]*).

7   **onerō, -āre, -āvī, -ātus**, *to load.*

       contrā, prep. + acc., *opposite; equal to, worth its weight in.*

8   **Putārēs**: *You would think.*

       naufragō, -āre, -āvī, -ātus, *to be wrecked.* **naufragārunt**: = **naufragāvērunt**.

9   **trecentiēs sēstertium**: see note above on B:26.

       dēficiō, dēficere, dēfēcī, dēfectus, *to fail, falter.*

       *****mī**: = **mihi**.

10   **iactūra, -ae**, f., *loss.*

       gustus, -ūs, m., *appetizer, small portion.*

         gustī: a genitive (as if 2nd declension) expressing value, *worth a tiny bit.*

11   **fortitūdō, fortitūdinis**, f., *courage, strength.*

12   **lardum, -ī**, n., *lard.*

       faba, -ae, f., *bean.*

       sēplasium, -ī, n., *perfume.*

       manicipium, -ī, n., *slave.*

       Hōc locō: ablative of time when, *At this point.*

14   **pecūlium, -ī**, n., *small savings, nest egg.*

       fermentum, -ī, n., *yeast, leavening.*

       cursus, -ūs, m., *course, voyage, run.*

15   **centiēs sēsterium**: see note above on B:26.

       corrotundō, -āre, -āvī, -ātus, *to round off,* "clear," *make (money).*

       redimō, redimere, redēmī, redēmptus, *to buy back.* Trimalchio had perhaps sold some of this property to finance his business ventures, or perhaps his former master had sold the properties before he died.

C. THE MILLIONAIRE'S AUTOBIOGRAPHY

Having regaled his guests with a detailed account of his preparations for death, Trimalchio next treats them to the story of his life, a classic of the rags-to-riches genre.

"Sed, ut coeperam dīcere, ad hanc mē fortūnam frūgālitās mea perdūxit. Tam 1
magnus ex Asiā vēnī, quam hic candēlābrus est. Ad summam, cotīdiē mē solēbam ad 2
illum mētīrī, et ut celerius rostrum barbātum habērem, labra dē lucernā unguēbam. 3
Cēterum, quemadmodum dī volunt, dominus in domō factus sum, et ecce, cēpī ipsimī 4
cerebellum. Quid multa? Cohērēdem mē Caesarī fēcit, et accēpī patrimōnium lāti- 5
clāvium. Nēminī tamen nihil satis est. Concupīvī negōtiārī. Nē multīs vōs morer, 6
quīnque nāvēs aedificāvī, onerāvī vīnum—et tunc erat contrā aurum—et mīsī Rōmam. 7
Putārēs mē hoc iussisse; omnēs nāvēs naufragārunt, factum, nōn fābula. Ūnō diē Nep- 8
tūnus trecentiēs sēsterium dēvorāvit. Putātis mē dēfēcisse? Nōn meherculēs; mī haec 9
iactūra gustī fuit, tamquam nihil factī. Alterās fēcī maiōrēs et meliōrēs et fēlīciōrēs, ut 10
nēmō nōn mē virum fortem dīceret. Scītis, magna nāvis magnam fortitūdinem habet. 11
Onerāvī rūrsus vīnum, lardum, fabam, sēplasium, manicipia. Hōc locō Fortūnāta rem 12
piam fēcit; omne enim aurum suum, omnia vestīmenta vēndidit et mī centum aureōs in 13
manū posuit. Hoc fuit pecūliī meī fermentum. Cito fit, quod dī volunt. Ūnō cursū 14
centiēs sēstertium corrotundāvī. Statim redēmī fundōs omnēs quī patrōnī meī fuerant. 15
Aedificō domum, vēnālīcia coemō iūmenta; quicquid tangēbam, crēscēbat tamquam 16
favus. 17

—Petronius, *Satyricon* 75–76 (extracts)

1. In what two ways does the lampstand remind Trimalchio of his childhood? (1–3)
2. What happened to Trimalchio when his master died? (4–6)
3. Describe Trimalchio's first business venture. (6–7)
4. What was the outcome of this first venture? (8–9)
5. How did Trimalchio react to this? (9–10)
6. What did Trimalchio build next, and why? (10–12)
7. What did Trimalchio invest in the second time? (12)
8. Where did he get the money for this investment? (13–14)
9. How did the project turn out? (15)
10. What did Trimalchio do with the profits? (15–17)

fundus, -ī, m., *farm*
•**patrōnus, -ī**, m., *patron*. Freed slaves became **clientēs** of their former masters, and referred to them as **patrōnī**.
16 **vēnālīcia, -ōrum**, n. pl., *slaves*.
iūmentum, -ī, n., *draft animal, horse, mule*.
17 **favus, -ī**, m., *honeycomb*.

18 **patria**: Trimalchio's original home in Asia Minor.

    manum dē tābulā, *hand(s) off the tablet.* This was an expression used by teachers to tell students to stop working.

19 **negōtiātiō, negōtiātiōnis**, f., *business.*

    faenerō, -āre, -āvī, -ātus, *to lend money, finance, underwrite.*

    •**sānē**, adv., *certainly, of course, indeed.*

    *****negōtium agere**, *to do business.*

20 **exhortor, -ārī, -ātus sum**, *to encourage.* Trimalchio treats this deponent as a regular active verb, yet another example of his shaky Latin.

    mathēmaticus, -ī, m., *mathematician, astrologer.*

    colōnia, -ae, f., *colony, settlement, town.*

    Graeculiō, Graculiōnis, m., *a little Greek.*

21 **cōnsiliātor, cōnsiliātōris**, m., *adviser.*

    ab aciā et acū, *from thread and needle* (i.e., in great detail).

22 *****expōnō, expōnere, exposuī, expositus**, *to explain, reveal.*

    *****nōscō, nōscere, nōvī, nōtus**, *to become acquainted with, learn about.*

    intestīna, -ōrum, n. pl., *intestines.*

        intestīnās meās nōverat: i.e., he knew me inside out. Note again Trimalchio's confusion of genders.

    tantum: *the only thing.*

23 **Putāssēs**: = **Putāvissēs**, *You would have thought.*

    habitāsse: = **habitāvisse**.

24 *****interim**, adv., *meanwhile.*

    Mercurius: the god Mercury was the patron of merchants, and Trimalchio believed that Mercury took a special interest in him.

    •**vigilō, -āre, -āvī, -ātūrus**, *to be watchful, be vigilant.*

    casula, -ae, f., *a little house, hut.*

25 **cēnātiō, cēnātiōnis**, f., *dining room.*

    porticus, -ūs, f., *portico* (a walkway with a roof held up by columns). Trimalchio treats the noun as masculine.

    marmorātus, -a, -um, *made of marble.*

26 **sūsum** (= **sūrsum**), adv., *up, above, upstairs.*

    vipera, -ae, f., *viper* (a poisonous snake). This is a reference to Fortunata.

    sessōrium, -ī, n., *sitting-room.*

27 **ōstiārius, -ī**, m., *doorkeeper.*

    cella, -ae, f., *small room.*

    perbonus, -a, -um, *very good.*

    hospitium, -ī, n., *hospitality; lodgings, guest room.*

28 **hospitō, -āre, -āvī, -ātus**, *to entertain, lodge.*

29 **assem . . . valeās**: *(if) you have a penny, a penny is what you're worth.* An **ās**, gen., **assis**, was a Roman coin, about half an ounce of bronze.

    habēs, habēberis: *you have, you will be considered,* i.e., *you are judged by what you have.*

30 **amīcus vester**: i.e., Trimalchio.

    rāna, -ae, f., *frog;* metaphorically, *a nobody.*

D. THE MILLIONAIRE'S AUTOBIOGRAPHY, CONTINUED

"Postquam coepī plūs habēre quam tōta patria mea habet, manum dē tābulā; sustulī 18
mē dē negōtiātiōne et coepī lībertōs faenerāre. Et sānē nōlentem mē negōtium meum 19
agere exhortāvit mathēmaticus, quī vēnerat forte in colōniam nostram, Graeculiō 20
Serāpa nōmine, cōnsiliātor deōrum. Hic mihi dīxit etiam ea, quae oblītus eram; ab aciā 21
et acū mī omnia exposuit; intestīnās meās nōverat; tantum quod mihi nōn dīxerat, quid 22
prīdiē cēnāveram. Putāssēs illum semper mēcum habitāsse. 23

"Interim, dum Mercurius vigilat, aedificāvī hanc domum. Ut scītis, casula erat; 24
nunc templum est. Habet quattuor cēnātiōnēs, cubicula vīgintī, porticūs marmorātōs 25
duōs, sūsum cēnātiōnem, cubiculum in quō ipse dormiō, viperae huius sessōrium, 26
ōstiāriī cellam perbonam; hospitium hospitēs capit. Ad summam, Scaurus cum hūc 27
vēnit, nusquam māluit hospitārī, et habet ad mare paternum hospitium. Et multa alia 28
sunt, quae statim vōbīs ostendam. Crēdite mihi; assem habeās, assem valeās; habēs, 29
habēberis. Sīc amīcus vester, quī fuit rāna, nunc est rēx." 30

—Petronius, *Satyricon* 76–77 (extracts)

11. What did Trimalchio do with his money after he retired from business himself?
    (18–19)
12. Who had encouraged Trimalchio when he wanted to quit? (19–21)
13. Why did Trimalchio believe in this man and his advice? (21–23)
14. Describe the house Trimalchio built. (25–27)
15. How does Scaurus feel about the house? Why might this be surprising? (27–28)
16. How does Trimalchio sum up his feelings about life? (29–30)

The Romans developed the art of glassmaking to a high degree, and rich citizens enjoyed decorating their tables with elaborate glass pieces. This bowl dates from the first century A.D. It was made by placing a layer of white glass around the dark inner bowl and then carving the white glass away to form the design.

The Morgan Cup, gift of Arthur A. Houghton, Jr., Corning Museum of Glass, Corning

Exercise 66c

Write a character sketch of Trimalchio using Readings 67 A–D as your source of information. The following questions may help you to organize your thinking:

1. What does Trimalchio intend his guests to think about his will? His tomb? His life story?
2. Would you describe Trimalchio as hypocritical? Generous? Altruistic? Humanitarian? Self-centered? How would he describe himself?
3. Is Trimalchio afraid of death?
4. Is it true that Trimalchio "never listened to a philosopher"? What words suggest that he has somehow picked up a smattering of philosophy? Why does he make this claim? As part of an epitaph, what is the effect of the remark?
5. Explain what is humorous about the following phrases:
   ut familia . . . tamquam mortuum (A:4); **ingemēscente familiā** (A:6); **corōnās et unguenta . . . pugnās** (A:9); **nē effluant vīnum** (B:20); **velit nōlit** (B:22).
6. Does Trimalchio's story of his own life make you see him any differently than you did after reading about his tomb? If so, how? Are there ways that Trimalchio's life story reinforces the earlier impressions you had of him?
7. What qualities would be needed for a man to rise from slavery to great wealth? Does Trimalchio seem to exhibit these qualities? To what do you attribute Trimalchio's success? To what does he himself attribute it?

BUILDING THE MEANING
Commands (Consolidation)

You have now studied three ways of expressing a command or request in Latin:

A. Directly, by using the imperative (Chapter 10):
   "**Tacēte**, omnēs!" magnā vōce clāmat. "**Audīte** mē!"
   "*Be quiet*, everyone!" he cries in a loud voice. "*Listen to me!*"

The usual negative is **nōlī/nōlīte** + infinitive:

Nōlīte cistās **iacere**, servī!
Don't throw the trunks, slaves!

Nē + 2nd person of the present or perfect subjunctive can also express a negative command:

Nē discēdās! *Don't go away!*

The *passive* imperative (found mostly with deponent verbs, with an active meaning) ends in **-re** (singular) or **-minī** (plural) (Chapter 37):

"Amīcī," inquit, "**ingrediminī** domum meam!"
*"Friends," he said, "**come into** my house!"*

B. Indirectly, by using an **ut**-clause with the subjunctive (negative **nē**) (Chapter 51):

Tē rogō ut nāvēs in monumentō meō **faciās.**
*I ask you **to make** some ships on my tomb.*

C. By using the jussive or hortatory subjunctive (negative **nē**) (Chapter 66):

Catellam cingulō alligātam **dūcat.**
***Let her be leading** a puppy tied with a leash.*

Vīvāmus, mea Lesbia, atque **amēmus!**
Let us live,** my Lesbia, and **let us love!

Exercise 66d
Select, read aloud, and translate:

1. Trimalchiō praecēpit servīs ut exemplar testāmentī (afferunt / afferrent / afferant).
2. "Amīce," inquit, "(affer / afferant / afferrent) testāmentum meum!"
3. Trimalchiō dīxit, "(Afferāmus / Afferrent / Afferant) servī testāmentum meum."
4. Amīcī, (sequiminī / sequātur / sequī) mē omnēs!
5. (Adicere / Adiciātur / Adicerētur) H.M.H.N.S. monumentō meō.
6. "(Nōlīte / Nōlit / Nōlī) flēre, Fortūnāta," inquit Trimalchiō.
7. Fortūnātae autem nōn persuāsit nē (flēret / fleat / flēre).
8. Monēbat convīvās nē philosophōs (audiant / audīrentur / audīrent).
9. "Nōs," inquit, "nē philosophōs (audiant / audiāmus / audīrēmus)."
10. Tandem Habinnae, "Amīce mī," inquit, "monumentum pulcherrimum mihi (aedificētis / aedificāre / aedificēs)."

   H.M.H.N.S.: = **hoc monumentum hērēdem nē sequātur** (see note on 66A:13).

Arch of Titus overlooking the Forum Romanum. The inscription reads: **SENATVS POPVLVSQVE ROMANVS DIVO TITO DIVI VESPASIANI F(ilio) VESPASIANO AVGVSTO**. The reference to Titus as **Dīvus** indicates that he had died when the inscription was carved.

The Emperor Titus
The Vatican, Braccio Nuovo

SOME ROMAN EMPERORS OF
THE FIRST AND SECOND CENTURIES

	Claudius A.D. 41–54
End of the Julio-Claudian dynasty	Nero 54–68
Year of the 4 emperors	Galba, Otho, Vitellius, Vespasian 69
Flavian dynasty	Vespasian 69–79
	Titus 79–81
	Domitian 81–96
Five good emperors	Nerva 96–98
	Trajan 98–117
	Hadrian 117–138
	Antoninus Pius 138–161
	Marcus Aurelius 161–180

A NOBLE WOMAN

We now turn from the humorous picture of Trimalchio to a much more serious topic. In the following letter, Pliny describes to Priscus the suffering that a friend of his named Fannia has endured because of the political situation that existed under Nero and subsequent emperors (see the chart of emperors on the opposite page). For background information on Pliny, see "A Roman Senator of the Empire," page 103. In order to understand the content of the letter, it will be helpful to know something about Fannia and her family. Here is a family tree:

Caecina Paetus = Arria Maior

Thrasea Paetus = Arria Minor

Helvidius Priscus = Fannia

Fannia's grandmother, Arria Maior, was a follower of the Stoic philosophy. When her husband, Caecina Paetus, was condemned to death by the Emperor Claudius for his part in the conspiracy of Camillus Scribonianus (A.D. 42), she stabbed herself and gave Paetus the dagger, saying, **"Paete, nōn dolet."** (This story and the epigram that Martial wrote about her were presented in Chapter 53.)

Fannia's mother, Arria Minor, married Thrasea Paetus. He too was a Stoic, famous for his honesty and his opposition to autocratic rule. He wrote a biography of Cato the Younger, who opposed Julius Caesar's dictatorship; this was interpreted as a criticism of the emperor Nero. In A.D. 66, after Nero learned of a plot to assassinate him, he condemned a number of senators whom he distrusted, even if they had not taken part in the conspiracy. Among these was Thrasea Paetus; Arria wished to commit suicide with her husband but was forbidden to do so.

Helvidius Priscus, who had married Fannia, shared his father-in-law's political views. He was exiled from Rome in A.D. 66, and Fannia went with him into exile. They returned in 69 after Nero's death and the accession of the new ruler, Vespasian.

Helvidius, however, continued his opposition to imperial rule and strongly criticized the emperor Vespasian. Vespasian exiled Helvidius again and Fannia accompanied him. Helvidius was finally executed (ca. 75), and at some point later Fannia returned to Rome.

After Vespasian's death, his dynasty was continued by his sons. The younger, Domitian, became emperor in 81 after the untimely death of his elder brother Titus. Domitian was extremely distrustful of the Senate and condemned or exiled anyone whom he suspected of disloyalty. He banished Arria Minor for a third time, together with her daughter Fannia. They returned permanently to Rome in 97 after Domitian's death and the accession of Nerva. The letter that follows was written by Pliny sometime around 107.

2   **angō, angere,** *to distress, trouble.*
    •**valētūdō, valētūdinis,** f., *health, ill health, sickness.*
    contrahō, contrahere, contrāxī, contractus, *to bring about, bring on, contract.*
    assideō, assidēre, assēdī, assessūrus + dat., *to sit nearby, take care of.*
    virginī: here and in the next line **virgō** refers to the fact that Junia was one of the Vestal Virgins. (See page 108, note on 63C:7 for their duties.)
3   **adfīnis, adfīnis,** gen. pl., **adfīnium,** m./f., *relative.*
    pontifex, pontificis, m., *pontiff* (one of 15 priests in charge of the state religion).
4   **Atriō Vestae:** the building where the Vestal Virgins lived was called the **Ātrium Vestae;** its remains can still be seen in the Forum Romanum (see the photograph on page 151 and the plan on page 47).
    mandō, -āre, -āvī or **-uī, -ātus** or **-itus,** *to entrust, hand over.*
5   •**mūnus, mūneris,** n., *duty, obligation, gift.*
    sēdulō, adv., *conscientiously.*
    discrīmen, discrīminis, n., *crisis, danger.*
    implicō, -āre, -āvī or **uī, -ātus** or **-itus,** *to enfold, catch up in.*
    īnsideō, īnsidēre, īnsēdī, īnsessūrus, *to sit down, settle in.*
    •**febris, febris,** gen. pl., **febrium,** f., *fever.*
6   **tussis, tussis,** gen. pl., **tussium,** f., *cough.*
    maciēs, maciēī, f., *thinness.*
      summa maciēs: supply something like **est eī,** *she has.*
    dēfectiō, dēfectiōnis, f., *weakness, lack of strength.*
    vigeō, vigēre, viguī, *to thrive, be vigorous, flourish.*
7   **dignus, -a, -um* + abl., *worthy (of).*
    reliqua: *the other things,* i.e., Fannia's physical faculties as opposed to her spirit.
8   **oculīs:** *from the eyes.* The preposition **ex** is not used because it is already present in the compound verb **ēripī.**
    nescio an aliquid simile vīsūrīs: *(which) will see I don't know whether anything similar,* i.e., *I don't know whether they will see anyone like her.* **Vīsūrīs** is a future active participle, agreeing with **oculīs.**
9   **castitās, castitātis,** f., *devotion, loyalty.*
    illī: dative of possession; supply **est.**
    gravitās, gravitātis, f., *seriousness, nobility.*
10 **cōnstantia, -ae,** f., *steadfastness.*
    tertiō: *a third time.*
    relēgō, -āre, -āvī, -ātus, *to send away, banish.*
      relēgāta: supply **est.**

A. FANNIA'S PRESENT ILLNESS AND PAST DIFFICULTIES

C. Plīnius Prīscō suō S.   1

    Angit mē Fanniae valētūdō. Contrāxit hanc dum assidet Iūniae virginī, sponte 2
prīmum (est enim adfīnis), deinde etiam ex auctōritāte pontificum. Nam virginēs, cum 3
vī morbī ātriō Vestae cōguntur excēdere, mātrōnārum cūrae custōdiaeque mandantur. 4
Quō mūnere Fannia dum sēdulō fungitur, hōc discrīmine implicita est. Insident febrēs, 5
tussis incrēscit; summa maciēs, summa dēfectiō. Animus tantum et spīritus viget Helvi- 6
diō marītō, Thraseā patre dignissimus; reliqua lābuntur, mēque nōn metū tantum, vē- 7
rum etiam dolōre cōnficiunt. Doleō enim fēminam maximam ēripī oculīs cīvitātis, nes- 8
ciō an aliquid simile vīsūrīs. Quae castitās illī, quae sānctitās, quanta gravitās, quanta 9
cōnstantia! Bis marītum secūta in exsilium est, tertiō ipsa propter marītum relēgāta. 10

(continued)

1. What was Fannia doing when she became sick? (2–3)
2. Why was she doing this? (3–4)
3. Describe Fannia's physical condition. (5–6)
4. Why does Pliny describe her spirit as **Helvidiō marītō, Thraseā patre dignissimus**? (6–7)
5. Why is Pliny upset? (8–9)
6. What qualities does Pliny attribute to Fannia? (9–10)
7. How has Fannia suffered because of the political situation in Rome? (10)

The remains of the **Ātrium Vestae**, home of the
Vestal Virgins, in the **Forum Rōmānum**

11 **Seneciō**: Herennius Senecio was a friend of Pliny and he wrote a biography of Helvidius Priscus. He was condemned to death by Domitian.

    reus, -ī, m., *defendant, person brought to trial.*

    quod . . . composuisset: *on the grounds that he had written.*

    -que: joining the two **cum** clauses: **cum Seneciō reus esset** and **cum . . . dedisset**, *when Senecio was . . . and when he had said . . .*

    rogātum (esse) . . . dīxisset: an indirect statement, *he had said in his defense that he had been asked by Fannia.*

12 **mināciter**, adv., *threateningly.*

    Mettiō Cārō: Mettius Carus was one of Domitian's henchmen, who brought charges against many senators.

    respondet: Fannia is replying to Carus.

    *****an**, conj., *whether.*

13 **commentārius, -ī**, m., *notebook, journal, diary.*

    scrīptūrō: *to the author* (literally, *to the one going to write*), i.e., to Senecio.

14 •**postrēmō**, adv., *finally*; here, *to sum up, in short.*

    vōcem: *word.*

    cēdentem: with **perīculō** (dat.), *yielding, giving in to.*

    ēmittō, ēmittere, ēmīsī, ēmissus, *to send forth, utter.*

    nūllam . . . ēmīsit: i.e., she told the truth even though doing so would put her in danger.

    quīn, adv., *in fact.*

15 •**metus, -ūs**, m., *fear.*

    metū temporum: *the fear of the times*, a reference to the political situation during the reign of Domitian.

    aboleō, abolēre, abolēvī, abolitus, *to destroy.*

    •**cōnsultum -ī**, n., *decree.*

    pūblicō, -āre, -āvī, -ātus, *to confiscate.* Emperors often confiscated the property of aristocrats who defied them.

16 **servāvit habuit**: *she saved and kept.* Note the *asyndeton*, lack of a connecting word such as **et**.

Nam cum Seneciō reus esset quod dē vītā Helvidī librōs composuisset rogātumque 11
sē ā Fanniā in dēfēnsiōne dīxisset, quaerente mināciter Mettiō Cārō an rogāsset, re- 12
spondet: "Rogāvī": an commentāriōs scrīptūrō dedisset: "Dedī"; an sciente mātre: "Ne- 13
sciente"; postrēmō nūllam vōcem cēdentem perīculō ēmīsit.   Quīn etiam illōs ipsōs 14
librōs, quamquam ex necessitāte et metū temporum abolitōs senātūs cōnsultō, pūblicātīs 15
bonīs servāvit habuit, tulitque in exsilium, exsiliī causam. 16

8. Why was Senecio on trial? (11)
9. How did Fannia become involved in the trial? (11–12)
10. What three questions did Mettius Carus ask Fannia, and how did she answer each one? (12–14)
11. How do these answers reveal Fannia's courage? (14)
12. What orders did the Senate give regarding the biography of Helvidius? Why? (14–15)
13. What did Fannia do regarding the biography? (15–16)

A Roman Woman
The Vatican Museo Pro Clementino, Sala dei Busti

17 **quam iūcunda (erat)**: *how pleasant she was.*
   cōmis, -is, -e, *courteous, friendly.*
   *****dēnique**, adv., *finally.*
   quod: *a thing which.*
18 **amābilis, -is, -e**, *lovable.*
   quam: *than.*
   venerandus, -a, -um, *to be respected, worthy of respect.*
   Eritne quam: *Will there be (anyone) whom.*
   ostentō, -āre, -āvī, -ātus, *to show, point out.*
19 **Erit ā quā**: *Will there be (anyone) from whom.*
   virī: *we men.*
   *****cernō, cernere, crēvī, crētus**, *to see.*
20 **ut**: *as.* Remember that **ut** means *when* or *as* if the verb is indicative, *so that* or *in order that* if
   the verb is subjunctive.
   quae leguntur: *who are read about,* i.e., famous women in Roman history.
   *****nūtō, -āre, -āvī, -ātūrus**, *to nod, shake; totter.*
      nūtāre: take with **vidētur** (21).
   convellō, convellere, convellī, convulsus, *to tear away, shatter, overthrow.*
21 **sēdibus suīs**: *from its foundations.* Pliny is using the metaphor of an earthquake.
   ruō, ruere, ruī, ruitūrus, *to rush, fall, collapse.*
   suprā: *on itself* (literally, *from above*).
   licet . . . habeat: *although it may have.*
   posterī, -ōrum, m. pl., *descendants.*
   Quantīs . . . virtūtibus quantīs factīs: *With what merits (and) what deeds*; another example of
      asyndeton.
22 **adsequentur**: the subject is *they,* Fannia's descendants.
   ut . . . occiderit: result clause, *so that she has not died as the last of her line.*
   haec: = Fannia.
   novissima: *the last (of her line).* Pliny means that even if Fannia leaves descendants, they may
      not measure up to her standards; she would be the "last" of her family in this sense.
      Remember that Pliny admired not only Fannia but also both of her parents, Thrasea Paetus
      and Arria Minor, as well as her maternal grandparents, Caecina Paetus and Arria Maior.
23 •**afflīgō, afflīgere, afflixī, afflictus**, *to strike down, crush.*
   torqueō, torquēre, torsī, tortus, *to twist, torture, torment.*
   •**illūstris, -is, -e**, *notable, distinguished, honorable.*
24 •**āmittō, āmittere, āmīsī, āmissus**, *to lose.*
   haec: = Fannia.
25 **pariter**, adv., *equally.*
   rescindō, rescindere, rescīdī, rescissus, *to tear open, expose.*
   afficiō, afficere, affēcī, affectus, *to affect.* Pliny means that he will be just as much hurt by
      Fannia's death as he was by that of her mother.

B. PLINY'S ADMIRATION FOR FANNIA

Eadem quam iūcunda quam cōmis, quam dēnique (quod paucīs datum est) nōn mi- 17
nus amābilis quam veneranda!   Eritne quam posteā uxōribus nostrīs ostentāre pos- 18
sīmus?   Erit ā quā virī quoque fortitūdinis exempla sūmāmus, quam sīc cernentēs 19
audientēsque mīrēmur ut illās quae leguntur?   Ac mihi domus ipsa nūtāre, convulsaque 20
sēdibus suīs ruitūra suprā vidētur, licet adhūc posterōs habeat.   Quantīs enim virtūtibus 21
quantīs factīs adsequentur, ut haec nōn novissima occiderit?   Mē quidem illud etiam 22
afflīgit et torquet, quod mātrem eius, illam (nihil possum illūstrius dīcere) tantae fēmi- 23
nae mātrem, rūrsus videor āmittere, quam haec, ut reddit ac refert nōbīs, sīc auferet 24
sēcum, mēque et novō pariter et rescissō vulnere afficiet.   25

(continued)

14. What qualities does Pliny attribute to Fannia? (17–18)
15. For what two groups of people will a role model be lacking if Fannia dies? (18–20)
16. What are Pliny's ideas about the future of Fannia's family? (20–22)
17. If Fannia dies, why would Pliny feel a double loss? (22–25)

Nero

Domitian

26 •**colō, colere, coluī, cultus**, *to cultivate, pay attention to.*
   •**dīligō, dīligere, dīlēxī, dīlēctus**, *to prize, love.*
   uter, utra, utrum, *which, which one (of two).*
   discernō, discernere, discrēvī, discrētus, *to separate, distinguish.*
     discernī: a passive infinitive used impersonally, *a distinction to be made.*
27 •**officium, -ī**, n., *service.*
   in secundīs (rēbus): *in good times.*
   sōlācium relēgātārum: *the comfort of the exiled ones, their comforter in exile.*
28 **ultor, ultōris**, m., *avenger, champion, advocate.*
     ultor reversārum: *the champion of the returned ones*, i.e., *their champion on their return*
       (from exile).
   nōn fēcī tamen paria: *even so, I did not pay my debts* (literally, *I did not make equal things*).
   eō magis: *all the more.*
29 **solvendī tempora**: *time to pay (my debt).*
   •**supersum, superesse, superfuī**, irreg., *to be left, remain.*
   eram: the Romans often used the imperfect in letters, where we would use the present tense;
     they were writing from the point of view of the recipient when reading the letter.
30 •**gaudium, -ī**, n., *joy.*
   •**vertō, vertere, vertī, versus**, *to turn, change.*
   •**queror, querī, questus sum**, *to complain.*

C plinius·corelliae salutem·
C umpatre mtuumcrauissimmetsan
ctissimumuirumsuspexerimmacis
anamalierimdubitemteqinmemo
riameiusetinhonore mtummindice
dilicamcupiamnecesseestatquehic
quantuminmefueritenitarutfilius

Detail of manuscript on page 157

Utramque coluī utramque dīlēxī; utram magis nesciō, nec discernī volēbant. 26
Habuērunt officia mea in secundīs, habuērunt in adversīs. Ego sōlācium relēgātārum, 27
ego ultor reversārum; nōn fēcī tamen paria atque eō magis hanc cupiō servārī, ut mihi 28
solvendī tempora supersint. In hīs eram cūrīs, cum scrīberem ad tē; quās sī deus aliquis 29
in gaudium verterit, dē metū nōn querar. Valē. 30

—Pliny, *Epistulae* VII.19

18. How has Pliny felt about both mother and daughter? (26)
19. What has been Pliny's relationship with them? (27–28)
20. What is an additional reason that Pliny hopes Fannia won't die? (28–29)
21. What final comment does Pliny make about the anxiety he is feeling for Fannia? (29–30)

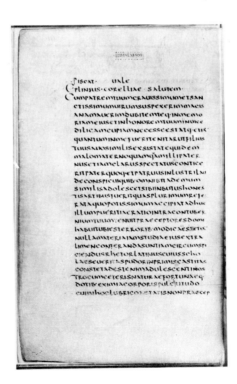

This manuscript of Pliny's *Epistulae* was written in the fifth century A.D.
It is one of the oldest and best preserved of Latin manuscripts.
The Morgan Library, New York

BUILDING THE MEANING
Conditional Sentences

A conditional sentence has two parts:

1. a subordinate clause (if-clause or *protasis*) introduced by **sī** (negative **nisi**) expressing a condition;

2. a main clause (*apodosis*) describing the situation that results if this condition is fulfilled.

You have already met many *simple* or *factual* conditions, such as the following:

Sī Fannia vult valēre, quiēscere dēbet.
If Fannia wants to get well, she ought to rest.

These conditions present no problems in translation, because they are very similar to English. You have also met some factual conditions that refer to the future. In such sentences the verb in the protasis is in either the future or the future perfect but is translated by an English present tense:

Sī Fannia nōn **valēbit**, Plīnius medicum **arcesset**.
*If Fannia **is not well** (literally, **will not be well**), Pliny **will call** the doctor.*

Sī Fannia **mortua erit**, Plīnius maximē **dolēbit**.
*If Fannia **dies** (literally, **will have died**), Pliny **will be** very sad.*

In this type of conditional sentence, when the action in the **sī**-clause takes place at the same time as that in the main clause, the future tense is used in the protasis (first example); when the action in the **sī**-clause will have been completed before the action in the main clause takes place, the future perfect is used (second example).

In addition to the simple conditions you have already met, there are *imaginary* or *unreal* conditions. In such sentences, the speaker is imagining something that might have happened in the past (but didn't), might be happening now (but isn't) or might happen in the future (but isn't likely). Such conditions always use the subjunctive mood:

a. Imaginary conditions referring to the past use the pluperfect subjunctive; translate *had . . . , would have . . .* :

Plīnius, sī Rōmae **fuisset**, Fanniam **vīsitāvisset**.
*If Pliny **had been** in Rome, he **would have visited** Fannia.*

b. Imaginary conditions referring to the present use the imperfect subjunctive; translate *were . . . , would . . .* :

Sī Fannia **valēret**, iter rūs **faceret**.
*If Fannia **were well**, she **would travel** to the country.*

c. Imaginary conditions referring to the future use the present subjunctive; translate *were to / should . . . , would . . .* :

> Sī Fannia **moriātur**, Plīnius maximē **doleat**.
> *If Fannia **were to die / should die**, Pliny **would be** very sad.*

Sometimes you will meet *mixed* conditions, which have different tenses in the protasis and apodosis:

> **Sī labōrem cōnfēcissēs, nunc discēdere possēs.**
> *If you had finished the work, you would be able to leave now.*

Conditional sentences provide a good illustration of the basic difference between the indicative and subjunctive moods. The indicative states a fact or asks a simple question; the subjunctive shows that an action is hypothetical or unreal in some way.

Exercise 67a

Read aloud, translate, and categorize each condition according to time (past, present, or future) and type (factual or imaginary):

1. Sī Plīnius Fanniam vīsitāvisset, illa laetissima fuisset.
2. Sī Plīnius Fanniam vīsitet, illa laetissima sit.
3. Sī parentēs Fanniae vīverent, fīliam suam adiuvārent.
4. Fannia, sī in exsilium ībit, librōs dē Helvidiō marītō scrīptōs sēcum feret.
5. Sī virgō Vestālis ex ātriō Vestae discēdit, cūrae mātrōnae mandātur.
6. Nisi Fannia Iūniae virginī assēdisset, hunc morbum nōn contrāxisset.
7. Plīnius gaudeat, sī Fannia convalēscat.
8. Plīnius, nisi maximē perturbātus esset, hanc epistulam Prīscō suō nōn scrīberet.
9. Sī Trimalchiō cēnam dabit, omnēs adesse volent.
10. Sī Trimalchiō monumentum inōrnātum aedificet, omnēs mīrentur.
11. Nisi Fortūnāta aurum suum vēndidisset, Trimalchiō aliās nāvēs emere nōn potuisset.
12. Sī ad cēnam ā Trimalchiōne invītātī erimus, certē aderimus.
13. Trimalchiō, sī vir modestus esset, convīvīs omnēs dīvitiās nōn ostenderet.
14. Nisi tantum vīnī bibissent, in viā nōn lāpsī essent.
15. Sī Trimalchiō dē vītā suā dīcat, attentē audiāmus.
16. Scaurus, sī ad hoc oppidum vēnerit, apud Trimalchiōnem morābitur.

assideō, assidēre, assēdī, assessūrus + dat., *to sit nearby, take care of*
inōrnātus, -a, -um, *undecorated, simple, plain*

1   **Erat**: the subject is *he* (Pliny the Elder).
    Mīsēnum, -ī, n., *Misenum* (an important Roman naval base, at the very northern end of the
        Bay of Naples; see map on page 162).
    *classis, classis, gen. pl., **classium**, f., *fleet*.
    imperiō: *with* **imperium**, *in command*.
    praesēns, praesentis, *in person*.
    •**regō, regere, rēxī, rēctus**, *to rule, govern, administer*.
    •**nōnus, -a, -um**, *ninth*.
2   •**septimus, -a, -um**, *seventh*.
    •**appāreō, appārēre, appāruī**, *to appear*.
    nūbēs, nūbis, gen. pl., **nūbium**, f., *cloud*.
    •**speciēs, speciēī**, f., *appearance*.
        inūsitātā et magnitūdine et speciē: *of unusual size and appearance*, an ablative of
            description.
3   **mīrāculum, -ī**, n., *strange sight*.
    incertus, -a, -um, *uncertain*.
    incertum: supply **erat**.
4   •**procul**, adv., *far off, from a distance*.
    intuentibus: *to those watching*.
    *orior, orīrī, ortus sum, *to arise, come up*.
5   **similitūdō, similitūdinis**, f., *likeness*.
    pīnus, -ūs, f., *pine tree*. Pliny is referring to the umbrella pine of the Mediterranean, which
        has a tall trunk with no branches until close to the top, where they spread out like an
        umbrella.
    •**exprimō, exprimere, expressī, expressus**, *to press out, express, convey*.
6   •**nōscō, nōscere, nōvī, nōtus**, *to learn, find out*.
    •**ērudītus, -a, -um**, *learned, scholarly*.
    vīsum: supply **est**.
    Magnum . . . vīsum: *To him, as a very learned man, it seemed a great thing and one that had to be
        observed at closer range*. Pliny describes his uncle as **virō ērudītissimō** because he was very
        interested in the natural world (a curiosity which many Romans did not share) and had
        written a huge encyclopedia of scientific lore called *Naturalis historia*.
    liburnica, -ae, f., *a light, fast warship*.
    aptō, -āre, -āvī, -ātus, *to fit, fit out, prepare*.
    mihi . . . facit cōpiam: *he gives me the chance*.
7   *ūnā, adv., *together*.
8   **cōdicillī, -ōrum**, m. pl., *note, short letter*.
    Rēctinae Tascī: *from Rectina, (the wife) of Tascius*.
    immineō, imminēre, imminuī, *to be imminent, hang over, threaten*.
9   **exterritus, -a, -um**, *frightened*.
    subiaceō, subiacēre, subiacuī, *to lie under, lie at the foot of* (Mt. Vesuvius).
    •**ūllus, -a, -um**, *any*.
    •**fuga, -ae**, f., *flight, escape*.
10 *discrīmen, discrīminis, n., *crisis, danger*.
    •**ēripiō, ēripere, ēripuī, ēreptus**, *to snatch away, rescue*.

THE DEATH OF PLINY THE ELDER

In this letter, written to the historian Cornelius Tacitus, Pliny the Younger describes how his uncle and adoptive father, Pliny the Elder, was killed in the eruption of the volcano Mt. Vesuvius in A.D. 79—the same eruption that destroyed the towns of Pompeii and Herculaneum. In the first paragraph of the letter (omitted here), Pliny expresses his gratitude to Tacitus for requesting information about his uncle's death and his appreciation that his uncle will be immortalized in the pages of Tacitus' work. He then continues as follows:

A. A RESCUE ATTEMPT

Erat Mīsēnī classemque imperiō praesēns regēbat. Nōnum Kal. Septembrēs hōrā 1
ferē septimā māter mea indicat eī appārēre nūbem inūsitātā et magnitūdine et speciē. 2
Ille ascendit locum ex quō maximē mīrāculum illud cōnspicī poterat. Nūbēs—incertum 3
procul intuentibus ex quō monte (Vesuvium fuisse posteā cognitum est)—oriēbātur, 4
cuius similitūdinem et fōrmam nōn alia magis arbor quam pīnus expresserit. Magnum 5
propiusque nōscendum ut ērudītissimō virō vīsum. Iubet liburnicam aptārī; mihi, sī 6
venīre ūnā vellem, facit cōpiam; respondī studēre mē mālle, et forte ipse quod 7
scrīberem dederat. Ēgrediēbātur domō; accipit cōdicillōs Rēctīnae Tascī imminentī 8
perīculō exterritae (nam vīlla eius subiacēbat, nec ūlla nisi nāvibus fuga): ut sē tantō 9
discrīminī ēriperet ōrābat. 10

(continued)

1. Why was Pliny the Elder at Misenum? (1)
2. On what day did these events take place, and at what time? (1–2)
3. What did Pliny's family see? (2)
4. What did Pliny's uncle do in response? (3)
5. Describe the cloud. Where was it coming from? (3–5)
6. Why did Pliny the Elder decide to take a closer look? (5–6)
7. Did his nephew go along? Why or why not? (6–8)
8. Why was Rectina frightened? (8–9)
9. What was the content of her message? (9–10)

11 **quod . . . maximō**: a free translation of this clause might be *what he had begun as a scholar he completed as a hero.*
   incohō, -āre, -āvī, -ātus, *to start, begin.*
   obit: *he accepts, takes on.*
   dēdūcō, dēdūcere, dēdūxī, dēductus, *to lead down, launch* (a ship).
12 **quadrirēmis, quadrirēmis**, f., *quadrireme* (a ship with four banks of oars, heavier and larger than the **liburnica** he had originally ordered).
   *frequēns, frequentis, *crowded, thickly populated.*
   amoenitās ōrae: *the pleasantness of the shore,* i.e., *the pleasant shore.* The Bay of Naples was a resort area for wealthy Romans.
13 •**properō, -āre, -āvī, -ātus**, *to hurry.*
   •**rēctus, -a, -um**, *right, straight.*
   *cursus, -ūs, m., *course, route.*
14 **gubernāculum, -ī, n.**, *a large oar used to steer a ship, steering-oar.*
   •**adeō**, adv., *so much, to such an extent.*
   solūtus, -a, -um, *free from.*
   *mōtus, -ūs, m., *motion, movement.*
15 **figūra, -ae**, f., *shape, form.*
   omnēs . . . mōtūs omnēs figūrās: another example of *asyndeton.*
   ut dēprenderat (= dēprehenderat) oculīs: *as he had caught them with his eyes,* i.e., as he had observed them.
   dictāret ēnotāretque: Pliny presumably had a slave with him who took notes as he dictated.
   ēnotō, -āre, -āvī, -ātus, *to note down.*

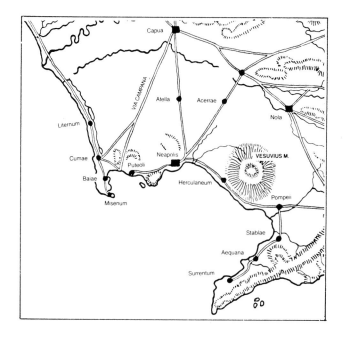

The Bay of Naples

Vertit ille cōnsilium et quod studiōsō animō incohāverat obit maximō. Dēdūcit 11
quadrirēmēs, ascendit ipse nōn Rēctinae modo sed multīs (erat enim frequēns amoeni- 12
tās ōrae) latūrus auxilium. Properat illūc unde aliī fugiunt, rēctumque cursum rēcta 13
gubernācula in perīculum tenet, adeō solūtus metū ut omnēs illīus malī mōtūs omnēs 14
figūrās ut dēprenderat oculīs dictāret ēnotāretque. 15

10. What did Pliny the Elder do in response to the message? What was his intention? (11–13)
11. What course did the ship take? (13–14)
12. What did Pliny the Elder do as he sailed along the shore? What was his state of mind? (14–15)

Mt. Vesuvius
"The Eruption of Vesuvius," by Jean Baptiste Genillon, Lille, Musée des Beaux Arts

16 **incidēbat**: deduce from **in-** + **cadō**.

 quō propius . . . calidior et dēnsior: *the nearer . . . the hotter and thicker.*

 *****accēdō, accēdere, accessī, accessūrus**, *to come near.*

17 *****pūmex, pūmicis**, m., *pumice stone.*

 •**ambustus, -a, -um**, *burned up.*

 •**lapis, lapidis**, m., *stone.*

 *****vadum, -ī**, n., *ford, shallow water.*

 subitus, -a, -um, *sudden, unexpected.*

18 •**lītus, lītoris**, n., *shore.*

 obstō, obstāre, obstitī, *to stand in the way, block.*

 (erat) vadum subitum ruīnāque montis lītora obstantia: the shape of the sea bottom
   was changed because of the eruption and the accompanying earthquake.

 cūnctor, -ārī, -ātus sum, *to delay, hesitate.*

 retrō, adv., *back, backwards.*

 *****flectō, flectere, flexī, flectus**, *to bend, turn.*

 gubernātor, gubernātōris, m., *helmsman.*

19 *****iuvō, iuvāre, iūvī, iūtus**, *to help.*

 Stabiīs: Stabiae was a town on the Bay of Naples, south of Pompeii.

 dirimō, dirimere, dirēmī, dirēmptus, *to separate, divide, cut off, isolate.*

 erat dirēmptus: the subject is Pomponianus.

20 **sinū mediō**: *by the middle of the bay (which lay in between).* The wind was blowing strongly
   from the northwest, so that the Elder Pliny was able to sail easily from Misenum down to
   Stabiae; to get away from Stabiae, however, would have meant sailing directly into the wind,
   which ancient ships could not do. By saying that Pomponianus was cut off *by the middle of
   the bay (which lay in between)*, Pliny refers to the fact that Pomponianus could not get his ship
   into the open sea without first sailing north into the Bay of Naples; the Elder Pliny could
   not escape in his ship for the same reason.

 quamquam . . . proximō: a long ablative absolute; **cōnspicuō** and **proximō** modify **perīculō**.

 cōnspicuus, -a, -um, *clear, obvious, evident.*

21 *****crēscō, crēscere, crēvī, crētūrus**, *to grow, increase.*

 sarcina, -ae, f., *pack, baggage.*

22 **resīdō, resīdere, resēdī**, *to sit down again, calm down.*

 avunculus, -ī, m., *mother's brother, uncle.*

 secundissimō: = **secundissimō ventō**.

 invehō, invehere, invexī, invectus, *to carry toward.*

 *****complector, complectī, complexus sum**, *to embrace.*

 •**trepidāns, trepidantis**, *in a panic.* This refers to Pomponianus.

23 **sēcūritās, sēcūritātis**, f., *lack of concern, freedom from anxiety.*

 lēniō, -īre, -īvī, -ītus, *to soften, soothe, calm down.*

 dēferrī: supply **sē** as the subject of this infinitive.

24 **balineum, -ī**, n., *bath.*

 •**lōtus**: perfect passive participle of **lavāre**.

 accubō, accubāre, *to recline, lie down.*

 hilaris, -is, -e, *cheerful.*

 quod (est): *(a thing) which is.*

 *****aequē**, adv., *equally.* Pliny means that it was just as admirable for his uncle to pretend not to
   be afraid as actually to be unconcerned.

B. AT POMPONIANUS' VILLA

Iam nāvibus cinis incidēbat, quō propius accēderent, calidior et dēnsior; iam 16
pūmicēs etiam nigrīque et ambustī et fractī igne lapidēs; iam vadum subitum ruīnāque 17
montis lītora obstantia. Cūnctātus paulum an retrō flecteret, mox gubernātōrī ut ita fa- 18
ceret monentī, "Fortēs," inquit, "fortūna iuvat: Pompōniānum pete." Stabiīs erat di- 19
rēmptus sinū mediō; ibi quamquam nōndum perīculō appropinquante, cōnspicuō ta- 20
men et cum crēsceret proximō, sarcinās contulerat in nāvēs, certus fugae sī contrārius 21
ventus resēdisset. Quō tunc avunculus meus secundissimō invectus, complectitur trepi- 22
dantem cōnsōlātur hortātur, utque timōrem eius suā sēcūritāte lēnīret; dēferrī in 23
balineum iubet; lōtus accubat cēnat, aut hilaris aut (quod aequē magnum) similis hilarī. 24

13. Describe what was falling from the sky. (16–17)
14. What problem did the ship encounter? (17–18)
15. What decision did Pliny the Elder have to make? (18)
16. What did he finally tell the helmsman to do? (18–19)
17. Describe the situation Pomponianus was in. (19–21)
18. What did Pomponianus intend to do if the wind changed? What action of his shows this? (21–22)
19. What did Pliny the Elder do immediately after he landed? (22–23)
20. What actions did Pliny the Elder take to reassure Pomponianus? (23–24)
21. What mood was Pliny in? (24)

Liburnica

25   **plūribus locīs**: = **in plūribus locīs.**
    ***lātus, -a, -um**, *broad, wide, widespread.*
    relūceō, relūcēre, relūxī, *to gleam, shine.*
26   **fulgor, fulgōris**, m., *brilliance, gleaming.*
    clāritās, clāritātis, f., *brightness.*
    ***tenebrae, -ārum**, f. pl., *shadows, darkness.*
    excitābātur: *was accenuated, was heightened* (literally, *was awakened*).
    Ille: Pliny the Elder. **Ille** is the subject of **dictitābat** in line 28.
    ***agrestis, -is**, gen. pl., **agrestium**, m., *farmer, peasant.*
    trepidātiō, trepidātiōnis, f., *fear.*
      agrestium trepidātiōne . . . relictōs: Pliny means that the terrified peasants fled
        without putting out their fires, which then spread as the earthquake knocked down
        the houses.
27   **sōlitūdō, sōlitūdinis**, f., *countryside, wilderness.*
    in remedium formīdinis: *as a cure for their fear.*
28   **dictitō, -āre, -āvī, -ātus**, *to keep saying, say over and over, repeat.*
    meātus, -ūs, m., *motion, movement.*
    •**anima, -ae**, f., *breath, breathing.*
29   **illī**: *in his case* (dative of reference).
    sonāns, sonantis, *making noise, loud.*
    līmen, līminis, n., *threshold, entrance.*
      līminī: *at his door, outside his door.*
30   **obversor, -ārī, -ātus sum** + dat., *to move about in front of.*
31   **diaeta, -ae**, f., *living room.*
    adībātur: *was approached.*
    oppleō, opplēre, opplēvī, opplētus, *to fill up.*
    •**surgō, surgere, surrēxī, surrēctūrus**, *to rise.* By saying that *the courtyard had risen* Pliny
    means that the level of the floor rose as the ash fell.
32   **negō, -āre, -āvī, -ātus**, *to say no, deny, refuse.*
    prōcēdit: the subject is Pliny the Elder.
    sē . . . reddit: *he rejoined*, literally, *he gave himself back to.*
33   **pervigilō, -āre, -āvī, -ātus**, *to stay awake, stay up.*
    In commūne: *Together.*
    ***tēctum, -ī**, n., *roof*; pl., *house.*
34   **subsistant an**: *(whether) they should stay . . . or.*
    apertum, -ī, n., *the open.*
    ***vagor, -ārī, -ātus sum**, *to wander.*
    ***crēber, crēbra, crēbrum**, *numerous, crowded, repeated.*
35   **ēmōta**: deduce from **ē-** + **moveō.**
    sēdibus suīs: *from its foundations.*
    Sub diō: *Under the open sky.*
36   **exēsus, -a, -um**, *eaten away, corroded, hollowed out, porous.*
    ***cāsus, -ūs**, m., *fall, chance, accident.*
    quod . . . ēlēgit: *a thing which a comparison of the dangers chose*, i.e., after comparing the dangers
    they chose the latter.

C. DISASTER COMES CLOSER

Interim ē Vesuviō monte plūribus locīs lātissimae flammae altaque incendia re- 25
lūcēbant, quōrum fulgor et clāritās tenebrīs noctis excitābātur. Ille agrestium trepidāti- 26
ōne ignēs relictōs dēsertāsque vīllās per sōlitūdinem ardēre in remedium formīdinis 27
dictitābat. Tum sē quiētī dedit et quiēvit vērissimō quidem somnō; nam meātus ani- 28
mae, quī illī propter amplitūdinem corporis gravior et sonantior erat, ab eīs quī līminī 29
obversābantur audiēbātur. 30

Sed ārea ex quā diaeta adībātur ita iam cinere mixtīsque pūmicibus opplēta sur- 31
rēxerat ut, sī longior in cubiculō mora, exitus negārētur. Excitātus prōcēdit, sēque 32
Pompōniānō cēterīsque quī pervigilāverant reddit. In commūne cōnsultant, intrā tēcta 33
subsistant an in apertō vagentur. Nam crēbrīs vastīsque tremōribus tēcta nūtābant, et 34
quasi ēmōta sēdibus suīs nunc hūc nunc illūc abīre aut referrī vidēbantur. Sub diō rūr- 35
sus quamquam levium exēsōrumque pūmicum cāsus metuēbātur, quod tamen perīcu- 36
lōrum collātiō ēlēgit; et apud illum quidem ratiō ratiōnem, apud aliōs timōrem timor 37
vīcit. Cervīcālia capitibus imposita linteīs cōnstringunt; id mūnīmentum adversus 38
incidentia fuit. 39

22. What was happening on Vesuvius? (25–26)
23. How did Pliny explain this? Why? (26–28)
24. How did the others know that Pliny was really asleep? (28–30)
25. Why could Pliny no longer remain in the bedroom? (31–32)
26. What was the subject of debate at the villa? (33–34)
27. What were the arguments on either side? (34–36)
28. What course of action was finally decided upon? (36–37)
29. According to Pliny, why did his uncle choose this course? Why did the others choose it? (37–38)
30. What precaution did the group take? (38–39)

37 **apud illum . . . ratiō ratiōnem (vīcit):** *in his case* (Pliny the Elder's) *one reason overcame the other*, i.e., he made his choice on a logical basis.

38 **cervīcal, cervīcālis,** gen. pl., **cervīcālium,** n., *pillow, cushion.*
•**caput, capitis,** n., *head.*
•**impōnō, impōnere, imposuī, impositus,** *to put on, place on.*
linteum, -ī, n., *linen cloth, piece of cloth.*
cōnstringō, cōnstringere, cōnstrīnxī, cōnstrictus, *to bind, tie up, tie on.*
mūnīmentum, -ī, n., *defense, protection.*

39 **incidentia:** *things falling,* a neuter plural substantive.

40 **diēs**: supply **erat**.
　alibī, adv., *elsewhere.*
　illīc, adv., *there* (at the villa).
　fax, facis, f., *torch.*
41 ***lūmen, lūminis**, n., *light.*
　***solvō, solvere, solvī, solūtus**, *to untie, dissolve, break up.*
　•**Placuit**: *It was decided.*
　ex proximō: *from close up.*
　adspiciō, adspicere, adspexī, adspectus, *to look at, inspect, examine.*
　ecquid iam mare admitteret: *whether the sea would now allow anything* (i.e., any escape).
42 **permanēbat**: deduce from **per-** + **maneō.**
　•**super**, prep. + acc., *over, above, on top of.*
43 **abiectus, -a, -um**, *thrown out, spread out.*
　linteum, -ī, n., *linen cloth, piece of cloth.*
　recubō, recubāre, *to lie, recline.*
　recubāns . . . hausitque: the subject of this sentence is Pliny the Elder.
　semel, adv., *once.*
　•**hauriō, haurīre, hausī, haustus**, *to drain, drink down.*
44 **praenūntius, -a, -um**, *announcing in advance, heralding, prefiguring.* Pliny means that while the villa itself was not yet on fire, the strong smell of sulphur indicated that the flames were not far away.
45 **innītor, innītī, innixus sum** + abl., *to lean on, rely on.*
　servolus, -ī, m., *little slave, young slave.*
　adsurrēxit: deduce from **ad-** + **surgō.**
　•**concidō, concidere, concidī**, *to fall down.*
　colligō, colligere, collēgī, collēctus, *to pick up, gather, infer.*
　crassus, -a, -um, *thick, dense.*
46 **cālīgō, cālīginis**, f., *darkness, murkiness* (here referring to the volcanic ash).
　spīritus, -ūs, m., *breathing.*
　crassiōre cālīgine spīritū obstructō: *with his breathing blocked by the rather thick ashes.*
　stomachus, -ī, m., *stomach: esophagus, windpipe.*
　invalidus, -a, -um, *weak, unhealthy.*
　***angustus, -a, -um**, *narrow.*
47 **aestuāns, aestuantis**, *hot; inflamed.*
　redditus: supply **est.**
　is . . . tertius: *the third from that which he had last seen*, i.e., the second day from that on which he died. Remember that the Romans counted inclusively; Pliny counts as number one the day on which his uncle died.
48 **inlaesus, -a, -um**, *unharmed.*
　opertus, -a, -um, *covered.*
　•**indūtus, -a, -um**, *clothed, dressed.*
　habitus, -ūs, m., *appearance, condition.*
49 **dēfūnctus, -a, -um**, *dead.*
　quiēscentī quam dēfūnctō: adjectives used as nouns, *a person asleep rather than a dead person.*

D. THE END

Iam diēs alibī, illīc nox omnibus noctibus nigrior dēnsiorque; quam tamen facēs 40
multae variaque lūmina solvēbant. Placuit ēgredī in lītus, et ex proximō adspicere, ec- 41
quid iam mare admitteret; quod adhūc vāstum et adversum permanēbat. Ibi super 42
abiectum linteum recubāns semel atque iterum frīgidam aquam poposcit hausitque. 43
Deinde flammae flammārumque praenūntius odor sulpuris aliōs in fugam vertunt, exci- 44
tant illum. Innītēns servolīs duōbus adsurrēxit et statim concidit, ut ego colligō, cras- 45
siōre cālīgine spīritū obstructō, clausōque stomachō quī illī nātūrā invalidus et angustus 46
et frequenter aestuāns erat. Ubi diēs redditus (is ab eō quem novissimē vīderat tertius), 47
corpus inventum integrum inlaesum opertumque ut fuerat indūtus; habitus corporis 48
quiēscentī quam dēfūnctō similior. 49

—Pliny, *Epistulae* VI.16 (extracts)

31. Why did torches and lamps need to be used during the morning? (40–41)
32. What did the Pliny the Elder and the others decide to do? (41–42)
33. What was Pliny doing at this point? (42–43)
34. What caused the group to flee and Pliny the Elder to stand up? (44–45)
35. What happened after Pliny the Elder stood with the help of slaves? (45)
36. Why does Pliny the Younger think this happened? (45–47)
37. When did daylight return? (47)
38. What condition was the body in when it was found? (48–49)

The death of Pliny

REVIEW XVII: Chapters 66-68

Exercise XVIIa: Life in the Empire

Summarize what you have learned about life during the early Empire. What was life like for members of the senatorial aristocracy? How did the institution of the Principate affect them? What was the role of freedmen such as Trimalchio in society, and how were they affected by the Principate? Base your answers on the readings in Parts IV and V as well as on any class discussion or individual research you have done.

Exercise XVIIb: Conditions and Commands

Read aloud and translate; explain the use of the subjunctive in each sentence:

1. Plīnius, nisi esset fortis vir, ad vīllam Pompōniānī nōn nāvigāret.
2. Adiuvet Plīnius eōs quī in lītore sub Vesuviō manent!
3. Plīnius, nisi ad vīllam Pompōniānī īsset, nōn mortuus esset.
4. Omnēs discēdant ē regiōne Vesuviī!
5. Nōlīte morārī! Ōrō ut properētis!
6. Nē in tēctīs maneāmus; per mare effugere cōnēmur!
7. Sī ignēs et fūmus ē monte ērumpant, omnēs mīrentur.
8. Amīcī, nisi mox ē vīllā exierint, morientur.
9. Nisi tēcta tremōribus nūtārent, Plīnius in apertum nōn īret.
10. Cornēlius Tacitus rogāvit ut Plīnius Secundus omnia dē morte avunculī sibi dīceret.

> **ērumpō, ērumpere, ērūpī, ēruptus**, *to burst forth, erupt*
> **in apertum**, *into the open*
> **avunculus, -ī**, m., *mother's brother, uncle*

Exercise XVIIc: Pliny's Estimation of His Own Work and That of Tacitus

Read aloud and translate this portion of a letter from Pliny to Tacitus:

Posterīs an aliqua cūra nostrī, nesciō; nōs certē merēmur ut sit aliqua, nōn dīcō ingeniō (id enim superbum), sed studiō et labōre et reverentiā posterōrum. Pergāmus modo itinere īnstitūtō, quod ut paucōs in lūcem fāmamque provexit, ita multōs ē tenebrīs et silentiō protulit. Valē.

—Pliny, *Epistulae* IX.14 (extract)

> **posterīs . . . cūra nostrī (sit):** dative of possession.
> **ingenium, -ī**, n., *inborn nature, talent.*
> **reverentia, -ae**, f., *concern, care.*
> **ingeniō . . . studiō . . . labōre . . . reverentiā:** ablatives of cause.
> **superbum:** supply **esset**, *would be.*
> **pergō, pergere, perrēxī, perrēctus**, *to proceed, continue on.*
> **ut . . . ita:** *although . . . nevertheless* (literally, *just as . . . so*).
> **provehō, provehere, provexī, provectus**, *to bring forward, bring out*; the subject is *it* (= **iter**).

FORMS

The following charts show the forms of typical Latin nouns, adjectives, pronouns, and verbs. As an aid in pronunciation, markings of long vowels and of word stress are included.

I. Nouns

Number Case	1st Declension	2nd Declension				3rd Declension		
	Fem.	Masc.	Masc.	Masc.	Neut.	Masc.	Fem.	Neut.
Singular								
Nominative	puéll*a*	sérv*us*	púer	áger	bácul*um*	páter	vōx	nómen
Genitive	puéll*ae*	sérv*ī*	púer*ī*	ágr*ī*	bácul*ī*	pátr*is*	vōc*is*	nómin*is*
Dative	puéll*ae*	sérv*ō*	púer*ō*	ágr*ō*	bácul*ō*	pátr*ī*	vōc*ī*	nómin*ī*
Accusative	puéll*am*	sérv*um*	púer*um*	ágr*um*	bácul*um*	pátr*em*	vōc*em*	nómen
Ablative	puéll*ā*	sérv*ō*	púer*ō*	ágr*ō*	bácul*ō*	pátr*e*	vōc*e*	nómin*e*
Vocative	puéll*a*	sérv*e*	púer	áger	bácul*um*	páter	vōx	nómen
Plural								
Nominative	puéll*ae*	sérv*ī*	púer*ī*	ágr*ī*	bácul*a*	pátr*ēs*	vōc*ēs*	nómin*a*
Genitive	puell*árum*	serv*órum*	puer*órum*	agr*órum*	bacul*órum*	pátr*um*	vōc*um*	nómin*um*
Dative	puéll*īs*	sérv*īs*	púer*īs*	ágr*īs*	bácul*īs*	pátr*ibus*	vōc*ibus*	nōmín*ibus*
Accusative	puéll*ās*	sérv*ōs*	púer*ōs*	ágr*ōs*	bácul*a*	pátr*ēs*	vōc*ēs*	nómin*a*
Ablative	puéll*īs*	sérv*īs*	púer*īs*	ágr*īs*	bácul*īs*	pátr*ibus*	vōc*ibus*	nōmín*ibus*
Vocative	puéll*ae*	sérv*ī*	púer*ī*	ágr*ī*	bácul*a*	pátr*ēs*	vōc*ēs*	nómin*a*

Number Case	4th Declension		5th Declension	
	Masc.	Neut.	Masc.	Fem.
Singular				
Nominative	árc*us*	gén*ū*	dí*ēs*	r*ēs*
Genitive	árc*ūs*	gén*ūs*	di*éī*	r*éī*
Dative	árc*uī*	gén*ū*	di*éī*	r*éī*
Accusative	árc*um*	gén*ū*	dí*em*	r*em*
Ablative	árc*ū*	gén*ū*	dí*ē*	r*ē*
Vocative	árc*us*	gén*ū*	dí*ēs*	r*ēs*
Plural				
Nominative	árc*ūs*	gén*ua*	dí*ēs*	r*ēs*
Genitive	árc*uum*	gén*uum*	di*érum*	r*érum*
Dative	árc*ibus*	gén*ibus*	di*ébus*	r*ébus*
Accusative	árc*ūs*	gén*ua*	dí*ēs*	r*ēs*
Ablative	árc*ibus*	gén*ibus*	di*ébus*	r*ébus*
Vocative	árc*ūs*	gén*ua*	dí*ēs*	r*ēs*

II. Adjectives

Number Case	1st and 2nd Declension			3rd Declension		
	Masc.	Fem.	Neut.	Masc.	Fem.	Neut.
Singular						
Nominative	mágn*us*	mágn*a*	mágn*um*	ómn*is*	ómn*is*	ómn*e*
Genitive	mágn*ī*	mágn*ae*	mágn*ī*	ómn*is*	ómn*is*	ómn*is*
Dative	mágn*ō*	mágn*ae*	mágn*ō*	ómn*ī*	ómn*ī*	ómn*ī*
Accusative	mágn*um*	mágn*am*	mágn*um*	ómn*em*	ómn*em*	ómn*e*
Ablative	mágn*ō*	mágn*ā*	mágn*ō*	ómn*ī*	ómn*ī*	ómn*ī*
Vocative	mágn*e*	mágn*a*	mágn*um*	ómn*is*	ómn*is*	ómn*e*
Plural						
Nominative	mágn*ī*	mágn*ae*	mágn*a*	ómn*ēs*	ómn*ēs*	ómn*ia*
Genitive	magn*órum*	magn*árum*	magn*órum*	ómn*ium*	ómn*ium*	ómn*ium*
Dative	mágn*īs*	mágn*īs*	mágn*īs*	ómn*ibus*	ómn*ibus*	ómn*ibus*
Accusative	mágn*ōs*	mágn*ās*	mágn*a*	ómn*ēs*	ómn*ēs*	ómn*ia*
Ablative	mágn*īs*	mágn*īs*	mágn*īs*	ómn*ibus*	ómn*ibus*	ómn*ibus*
Vocative	mágn*ī*	mágn*ae*	mágn*a*	ómn*ēs*	ómn*ēs*	ómn*ia*

III. Comparative Adjectives

Case	Masc.	Fem.	Neut.
Singular			
Nominative	púlchrior	púlchrior	púlchrius
Genitive	pulchrió*ris*	pulchrió*ris*	pulchrió*ris*
Dative	pulchrió*rī*	pulchrió*rī*	pulchrió*rī*
Accusative	pulchrió*rem*	pulchrió*rem*	púlchrius
Ablative	pulchrió*re*	pulchrió*re*	pulchrió*re*
Vocative	púlchrior	púlchrior	púlchrius
Plural			
Nominative	pulchrió*rēs*	pulchrió*rēs*	pulchrió*ra*
Genitive	pulchrió*rum*	pulchrió*rum*	pulchrió*rum*
Dative	pulchrió*ribus*	pulchrió*ribus*	pulchrió*ribus*
Accusative	pulchrió*rēs*	pulchrió*rēs*	pulchrió*ra*
Ablative	pulchrió*ribus*	pulchrió*ribus*	pulchrió*ribus*
Vocative	pulchrió*rēs*	pulchrió*rēs*	pulchrió*ra*

Adjectives have *positive*, *comparative*, and *superlative* forms. You can usually recognize the comparative by the letters **-ior(-)** and the superlative by **-issimus**, **-errimus**, or **-illimus**:

ignávus, -a, -um, *lazy*	ignávior, ignávius	ignāvíssimus, -a, -um
púlcher, púlchra, púlchrum, *beautiful*	púlchrior, púlchrius	pulchérrimus, -a, -um
fácilis, -is, -e, *easy*	facílior, facílius	facíllimus, -a, -um

Some very common adjectives are irregular in the comparative and superlative:

Positive	Comparative	Superlative
bónus, -a, -um, *good*	mélior, mélius, *better*	óptimus, -a, -um, *best*
málus, -a, -um, *bad*	péior, péius, *worse*	péssimus, -a, -um, *worst*
mágnus, -a, -um, *big*	máior, máius, *bigger*	máximus, -a, -um, *biggest*
párvus, -a, -um, *small*	mínor, mínus, *smaller*	mínimus, -a, -um, *smallest*
múltus, -a, -um, *much*	plūs,* *more*	plúrimus, -a, -um, *most, very much*
múltī, -ae, -a, *many*	plúrēs, plúra, *more*	plúrimī, -ae, -a, *most, very many*

*Note that **plūs** is not an adjective but a neuter substantive, usually found with a partitive genitive, e.g., Titus **plūs vīnī** bibit. *Titus drank **more (of the) wine**.*

IV. Present Participles

Number Case	Masc.	Fem.	Neut.
Singular			
Nominative	párāns	párāns	párāns
Genitive	parántis	parántis	parántis
Dative	parántī	parántī	parántī
Accusative	parántem	parántem	párāns
Ablative	parántī/e	parántī/e	parántī/e
Plural			
Nominative	parántēs	parántēs	parántia
Genitive	parántium	parántium	parántium
Dative	parántibus	parántibus	parántibus
Accusative	parántēs	parántēs	parántia
Ablative	parántibus	parántibus	parántibus

V. Numbers

Case	Masc.	Fem.	Neut.	Masc.	Fem.	Neut.	Masc.	Fem.	Neut.
Nom.	únus	úna	únum	dúo	dúae	dúo	trēs	trēs	tría
Gen.	ūníus	ūníus	ūníus	duórum	duárum	duórum	tríum	tríum	tríum
Dat.	únī	únī	únī	duóbus	duábus	duóbus	tríbus	tríbus	tríbus
Acc.	únum	únam	únum	dúōs	dúās	dúo	trēs	trēs	tría
Abl.	únō	únā	únō	duóbus	duábus	duóbus	tríbus	tríbus	tríbus

	Cardinal	Ordinal
I	únus, -a, -um, *one*	prímus, -a, -um, *first*
II	dúo, -ae, -o, *two*	secúndus, -a, -um, *second*
III	trēs, trēs, tría, *three*	tértius, -a, -um, *third*
IV	quáttuor, *four*	quártus, -a, -um
V	quínque, *five*	quíntus, -a, -um
VI	sex, *six*	séxtus, -a, -um
VII	séptem, *seven*	séptimus, -a, -um
VIII	óctō, *eight*	octávus, -a, -um
IX	nóvem, *nine*	nónus, -a, -um
X	décem, *ten*	décimus, -a, -um
XI	úndecim, *eleven*	ūndécimus, -a, -um
XII	duódecim, *twelve*	duodécimus, -a, -um
XIII	trédecim, *thirteen*	tértius décimus, -a, -um
XIV	quattuórdecim, *fourteen*	quártus décimus, -a, -um
XV	quíndecim, *fifteen*	quíntus décimus, -a, -um
XVI	sédecim, *sixteen*	séxtus décimus, -a, -um
XVII	septéndecim, *seventeen*	séptimus décimus, -a, -um
XVIII	duodēvīgíntī, *eighteen,*	duodēvīcésimus, -a, -um
XIX	ūndēvīgíntī, *nineteen,*	ūndēvīcésimus, -a, -um
XX	vīgíntī, *twenty*	vīcésimus, -a, -um
L	quīnquāgíntā, *fifty*	quīnquāgésimus, -a, -um
C	céntum, *a hundred*	centésimus, -a, -um
D	quīngéntī, -ae, -a, *five hundred*	quīngentésimus, -a, -um
M	mílle, *a thousand*	mīllésimus, -a, -um

N.B. The cardinal numbers from **quattuor** to **centum** do not change their form to indicate case and gender.

VI. Personal Pronouns

Number Case	1st Declension	2nd Declension	3rd Declension Masc.	Fem.	Neut.
Singular					
Nominative	égo	tū	is	éa	id
Genitive	méī	túī	éius	éius	éius
Dative	míhi	tíbi	éī	éī	éī
Accusative	mē	tē	éum	éam	id
Ablative	mē	tē	éō	éā	éō
Plural					
Nominative	nōs	vōs	éī	éae	éa
Genitive	nóstrī nóstrum	véstrī véstrum	eórum	eárum	eórum
Dative	nóbīs	vóbīs	éīs	éīs	éīs
Accusative	nōs	vōs	éōs	éās	éa
Ablative	nóbīs	vóbīs	éīs	éīs	éīs

Note: The forms of **is, ea, id** may also serve as demonstrative adjectives.

VII. Reflexive Pronoun

Singular	
Nominative	——
Genitive	súī
Dative	síbi
Accusative	sē
Ablative	sē
Plural	
Nominative	——
Genitive	súī
Dative	síbi
Accusative	sē
Ablative	sē

VIII. Relative Pronoun

	Masc.	Fem.	Neut.
Singular			
Nominative	quī	quae	quod
Genitive	cúius	cúius	cúius
Dative	cui	cui	cui
Accusative	quem	quam	quod
Ablative	quō	quā	quō
Plural			
Nominative	quī	quae	quae
Genitive	quórum	quárum	quórum
Dative	quíbus	quíbus	quíbus
Accusative	quōs	quās	quae
Ablative	quíbus	quíbus	quíbus

IX. Interrogative Pronoun

Number Case	Masc.	Fem.	Neut.
Singular			
Nominative	quis	quis	quid
Genitive	cúius	cúius	cúius
Dative	cui	cui	cui
Accusative	quem	quem	quid
Ablative	quō	quō	quō
Plural	Same as the plural of the relative pronoun on page 175.		

X. Indefinite Adjective and Pronouns

Number Case	Masc.	Fem.	Neut.	Masc.	Fem.	Neut.
Singular						
Nominative	quídam	quaédam	quóddam	áliquī	áliqua	áliquod
Genitive	cuiúsdam	cuiúsdam	cuiúsdam	álicuius	álicuius	álicuius
Dative	cúidam	cúidam	cúidam	álicui	álicui	álicui
Accusative	quéndam	quándam	quóddam	áliquem	áliquam	áliquod
Ablative	quódam	quádam	quódam	áliquō	áliqua	áliquō
Plural						
Nominative	quídam	quaédam	quaédam	áliquī	áliquae	áliqua
Genitive	quōrúndam	quārúndam	quōrúndam	aliquórum	aliquárum	aliquórum
Dative	quibúsdam	quibúsdam	quibúsdam	aliquíbus	aliquíbus	aliquíbus
Accusative	quósdam	quásdam	quaédam	áliquōs	áliquās	áliqua
Ablative	quibúsdam	quibúsdam	quibúsdam	aliquíbus	aliquíbus	aliquíbus

The indefinite pronoun **quīdam, quaedam, quiddam** has the same forms as the indefinite adjective, except for **quiddam** in the neuter nominative and accusative singular. The indefinite pronoun **aliquis, aliquis, aliquid** has the regular forms of the interrogative adjective **quis, quis, quid**, as do the indefinite pronouns **quisque, quisque, quidque** and **quisquam, quisquam, quidquam (quicquam)**. The indefinite adjective **quisque, quaeque, quodque** has the same forms as the relative pronoun **quī, quae, quod** except for **quis-** in the masculine nominative singular.

XI. Demonstrative Adjectives and Pronouns

Number Case	Masc.	Fem.	Neut.	Masc.	Fem.	Neut.
Singular						
Nominative	hic	haec	hoc	ílle	ílla	íllud
Genitive	húius	húius	húius	illíus	illíus	illíus
Dative	húic	húic	húic	íllī	íllī	íllī
Accusative	hunc	hanc	hoc	íllum	íllam	íllud
Ablative	hōc	hāc	hōc	íllō	íllā	íllō
Plural						
Nominative	hī	hae	haec	íllī	íllae	ílla
Genitive	hṓrum	hárum	hṓrum	illṓrum	illárum	illṓrum
Dative	hīs	hīs	hīs	íllīs	íllīs	íllīs
Accusative	hōs	hās	haec	íllōs	íllās	ílla
Ablative	hīs	hīs	hīs	íllīs	íllīs	íllīs

Number Case	Masculine	Feminine	Neuter
Singular			
Nominative	ípse	ípsa	ípsum
Genitive	ipsíus	ipsíus	ipsíus
Dative	ípsī	ípsī	ípsī
Accusative	ípsum	ípsam	ípsum
Ablative	ípsō	ípsā	ípsō
Plural			
Nominative	ípsī	ípsae	ípsa
Genitive	ipsṓrum	ipsárum	ipsṓrum
Dative	ípsīs	ípsīs	ípsīs
Accusative	ípsōs	ípsās	ípsa
Ablative	ípsīs	ípsīs	ípsīs

Number Case	Masc.	Fem.	Neut.	Masc.	Fem.	Neut.
Singular						
Nominative	is	éa	id	ídem	éadem	ídem
Genitive	éius	éius	éius	eiúsdem	eiúsdem	eiúsdem
Dative	éī	éī	éī	eídem	eídem	eídem
Accusative	éum	éam	id	eúndem	eándem	ídem
Ablative	éō	éā	éō	eṓdem	eádem	eṓdem
Plural						
Nominative	éī	éae	éa	eídem	eaédem	éadem
Genitive	eórum	eárum	eórum	eōrúndem	eārúndem	eōrúndem
Dative	éīs	éīs	éīs	eísdem	eísdem	eísdem
Accusative	éōs	éās	éa	eṓsdem	eásdem	éadem
Ablative	éīs	éīs	éīs	eísdem	eísdem	eísdem

XII. Adverbs

Latin adverbs may be formed from adjectives of the 1st and 2nd declensions by adding *-ē* to the base of the adjective, e.g., **strēnuē**, *strenuously*, from **strēnuus, -a, -um**. To form an adverb from a 3rd declension adjective, add *-iter* to the base of the adjective or *-er* to bases ending in **-nt-**, e.g., <u>**breviter**</u>, *briefly*, from **brevis, -is, -e**, and <u>**prūdenter**</u>, *wisely*, from **prūdēns, prūdentis**.

laétē, *happily*	**laétius**	**laetíssimē**
fēlíciter, *luckily*	**fēlícius**	**fēlīcíssimē**
celériter, *quickly*	**celérius**	**celérrimē**
prūdénter, *wisely*	**prūdéntius**	**prūdentíssimē**

Note the following as well:

díū, *for a long time*	**diútius**	**diūtíssimē**
saépe, *often*	**saépius**	**saepíssimē**
sérō, *late*	**sérius**	**seríssimē**

Some adverbs are irregular:

béne, *well*	**mélius**, *better*	**óptimē**, *best*
mále, *badly*	**péius**, *worse*	**péssimē**, *worst*
fácile, *easily*	**facílius**, *more easily*	**facíllimē**, *most easily*
magnópere, *greatly*	**mágis**, *more*	**máximē**, *most*
paúlum, *little*	**mínus**, *less*	**mínimē**, *least*
múltum, *much*	**plūs**, *more*	**plúrimum**, *most*

XIII. Regular Verbs Active: Infinitive, Imperative, Indicative

			1st Conjugation	2nd Conjugation	3rd Conjugation		4th Conjugation
Infinitive			par*áre*	hab*ére*	mítt*ere*	iác*ere* (*-iō*)	aud*íre*
Imperative			pár*ā*	háb*ē*	mítt*e*	iác*e*	aúd*ī*
			par*áte*	hab*éte*	mítt*ite*	iác*ite*	aud*íte*
Present	**Singular**	1	pár*ō*	hábe*ō*	mítt*ō*	iáci*ō*	aúdi*ō*
		2	pár*ās*	hábe*s*	mítti*s*	iáci*s*	aúdī*s*
		3	pára*t*	hábe*t*	mítti*t*	iáci*t*	aúdi*t*
	Plural	1	pará*mus*	habé*mus*	mítti*mus*	iáci*mus*	audí*mus*
		2	pará*tis*	habé*tis*	mítti*tis*	iáci*tis*	audí*tis*
		3	pára*nt*	hábe*nt*	míttu*nt*	iáciu*nt*	aúdiu*nt*
Imperfect	**Singular**	1	pará*bam*	habé*bam*	mitté*bam*	iacié*bam*	audié*bam*
		2	pará*bās*	habé*bās*	mitté*bās*	iacié*bās*	audié*bās*
		3	pará*bat*	habé*bat*	mitté*bat*	iacié*bat*	audié*bat*
	Plural	1	parā*bámus*	habē*bámus*	mittē*bámus*	iaciē*bámus*	audiē*bámus*
		2	parā*bátis*	habē*bátis*	mittē*bátis*	iaciē*bátis*	audiē*bátis*
		3	pará*bant*	habé*bant*	mitté*bant*	iacié*bant*	audié*bant*
Future	**Singular**	1	pará*bō*	habé*bō*	mítt*am*	iáci*am*	aúdi*am*
		2	pará*bis*	habé*bis*	mítt*ēs*	iáci*ēs*	aúdi*ēs*
		3	pará*bit*	habé*bit*	mítt*et*	iáci*et*	aúdi*et*
	Plural	1	pará*bimus*	habé*bimus*	mitté*mus*	iacié*mus*	audié*mus*
		2	pará*bitis*	habé*bitis*	mitté*tis*	iacié*tis*	audié*tis*
		3	pará*bunt*	habé*bunt*	mítt*ent*	iáci*ent*	aúdi*ent*
Perfect	**Singular**	1	pará*vī*	hábu*ī*	mís*ī*	iéc*ī*	audí*vī*
		2	parā*vístī*	habu*ístī*	mīs*ístī*	iēc*ístī*	audī*vístī*
		3	pará*vit*	hábu*it*	mís*it*	iéc*it*	audí*vit*
	Plural	1	pará*vimus*	habú*imus*	mís*imus*	iéc*imus*	audí*vimus*
		2	parā*vístis*	habu*ístis*	mīs*ístis*	iēc*ístis*	audī*vístis*
		3	parā*vérunt*	habu*érunt*	mīs*érunt*	iēc*érunt*	audī*vérunt*
Pluperfect	**Singular**	1	pará*veram*	habú*eram*	mís*eram*	iéc*eram*	audí*veram*
		2	pará*verās*	habú*erās*	mís*erās*	iéc*erās*	audí*verās*
		3	pará*verat*	habú*erat*	mís*erat*	iéc*erat*	audí*verat*
	Plural	1	parā*verámus*	habu*erámus*	mīs*erámus*	iēc*erámus*	audī*verámus*
		2	parā*verátis*	habu*erátis*	mīs*erátis*	iēc*erátis*	audī*verátis*
		3	pará*verant*	habú*erant*	mís*erant*	iéc*erant*	audí*verant*
Future Perfect	**Singular**	1	pará*verō*	habú*erō*	mís*erō*	iéc*erō*	audí*verō*
		2	pará*veris*	habú*eris*	mís*eris*	iéc*eris*	audí*veris*
		3	pará*verit*	habú*erit*	mís*erit*	iéc*erit*	audí*verit*
	Plural	1	parā*vérimus*	habu*érimus*	mīs*érimus*	iēc*érimus*	audī*vérimus*
		2	parā*véritis*	habu*éritis*	mīs*éritis*	iēc*éritis*	audī*véritis*
		3	pará*verint*	habú*erint*	mís*erint*	iéc*erint*	audī*verint*

XIV. Regular Verbs Passive: Infinitive, Imperative, Indicative

			1st Conjugation	2nd Conjugation	3rd Conjugation		4th Conjugation
	Infinitive	1	port**ári**	mov**éri**	mítt**i**	iác**i**	aud**íri**
	Imperative	1	port**áre**	mov**ére**	mítt**ere**	iác**ere**	aud**íre**
		2	port**ámini**	mov**émini**	mítt**imini**	iac**ímini**	aud**ímini**
Present	Singular	1	pórt**or**	móve**or**	mítt**or**	iác**ior**	aúd**ior**
		2	port**áris**	mov**éris**	mítt**eris**	iác**eris**	aud**íris**
		3	port**átur**	mov**étur**	mítt**itur**	iác**itur**	aud**ítur**
	Plural	1	port**ámur**	mov**émur**	mítt**imur**	iác**imur**	aud**ímur**
		2	port**ámini**	mov**émini**	mitt**ímini**	iac**ímini**	aud**ímini**
		3	port**ántur**	mov**éntur**	mitt**úntur**	iac**iúntur**	aud**iúntur**
Imperfect	Singular	1	port**ábar**	mov**ébar**	mitt**ébar**	iaci**ébar**	audi**ébar**
		2	port**abáris**	mov**ebáris**	mitt**ebáris**	iaci**ebáris**	audi**ebáris**
		3	port**abátur**	mov**ebátur**	mitt**ebátur**	iaci**ebátur**	audi**ebátur**
	Plural	1	port**abámur**	mov**ebámur**	mitt**ebámur**	iaci**ebámur**	audi**ebámur**
		2	port**abámini**	mov**ebámini**	mitt**ebámini**	iaci**ebámini**	audi**ebámini**
		3	port**abántur**	mov**ebántur**	mitt**ebántur**	iaci**ebántur**	audi**ebántur**
Future	Singular	1	port**ábor**	mov**ébor**	mítt**ar**	iác**iar**	aúd**iar**
		2	port**áberis**	mov**éberis**	mitt**éris**	iaci**éris**	audi**éris**
		3	port**ábitur**	mov**ébitur**	mitt**étur**	iaci**étur**	audi**étur**
	Plural	1	port**ábimur**	mov**ébimur**	mitt**émur**	iaci**émur**	audi**émur**
		2	port**abímini**	mov**ebímini**	mitt**émini**	iaci**émini**	audi**émini**
		3	port**abúntur**	mov**ebúntur**	mitt**éntur**	iaci**éntur**	audi**éntur**

			Perfect Passive		Pluperfect Passive		Future Perfect Passive	
Singular		1	portátus, -a	sum	portátus, -a	éram	portátus, -a	érō
		2	portátus, -a	es	portátus, -a	érās	portátus, -a	éris
		3	portátus, -a, -um	est	portátus, -a, -um	érat	portátus, -a, -um	érit
Plural		1	portátī, -ae	súmus	portátī, -ae	erámus	portátī, -ae	érimus
		2	portátī, -ae	éstis	portátī, -ae	erátis	portátī, -ae	éritis
		3	portátī, -ae, -a	sunt	portátī, -ae, -a	érant	portátī, -ae, -a	érunt

XV. Regular Verbs Active: Subjunctive

			1st Conjugation	2nd Conjugation	3rd Conjugation		4th Conjugation
Present	Singular	1	pórt*em*	móve*am*	mítt*am*	iáci*am*	aúdi*am*
		2	pórt*ēs*	móve*ās*	mítt*ās*	iáci*ās*	aúdi*ās*
		3	pórt*et*	móve*at*	mítt*at*	iáci*at*	aúdi*at*
	Plural	1	portḗ*mus*	movéā*mus*	mittā́*mus*	iaciā́*mus*	audiā́*mus*
		2	portḗ*tis*	moveā́*tis*	mittā́*tis*	iacā́*tis*	audiā́*tis*
		3	pórt*ent*	móve*ant*	mítt*ant*	iáci*ant*	aúdi*ant*
Imperfect	Singular	1	portā́re*m*	movḗre*m*	mítter*em*	iácer*em*	audī́r*em*
		2	portā́rē*s*	movḗrē*s*	mítter*ēs*	iácer*ēs*	audī́r*ēs*
		3	portā́re*t*	movḗre*t*	mítter*et*	iácer*et*	audī́r*et*
	Plural	1	portārḗ*mus*	movērḗ*mus*	mitterḗ*mus*	iacerḗ*mus*	audīrḗ*mus*
		2	portārḗ*tis*	movērḗ*tis*	mitterḗ*tis*	iacerḗ*tis*	audīrḗ*tis*
		3	portā́re*nt*	movḗre*nt*	mítter*ent*	iácer*ent*	audī́r*ent*
Perfect	Singular	1	portā́v*erim*	móv*erim*	mī́s*erim*	iḗc*erim*	audī́v*erim*
		2	portā́v*eris*	móv*eris*	mī́s*eris*	iḗc*eris*	audī́v*eris*
		3	portā́v*erit*	móv*erit*	mī́s*erit*	iḗc*erit*	audī́v*erit*
	Plural	1	portāvḗ*rimus*	mōvḗ*rimus*	mīsḗ*rimus*	iēcḗ*rimus*	audīvḗ*rimus*
		2	portāvḗ*ritis*	mōvḗ*ritis*	mīsḗ*ritis*	iēcḗ*ritis*	audīvḗ*ritis*
		3	portā́v*erint*	móv*erint*	mī́s*erint*	iḗc*erint*	audī́v*erint*
Pluperfect	Singular	1	portāvī́sse*m*	mōvī́sse*m*	mīsī́sse*m*	iēcī́sse*m*	audīvī́sse*m*
		2	portāvī́ssē*s*	mōvī́ssē*s*	mīsī́ssē*s*	iēcī́ssē*s*	audīvī́ssē*s*
		3	portāvī́sse*t*	mōvī́sse*t*	mīsī́sse*t*	iēcī́sse*t*	audīvī́sse*t*
	Plural	1	portāvissḗ*mus*	mōvissḗ*mus*	mīsissḗ*mus*	iēcissḗ*mus*	audīvissḗ*mus*
		2	portāvissḗ*tis*	mōvissḗ*tis*	mīsissḗ*tis*	iēcissḗ*tis*	audīvissḗ*tis*
		3	portāvī́sse*nt*	mōvī́sse*nt*	mīsī́sse*nt*	iēcī́sse*nt*	audīvī́sse*nt*

XVI. Regular Verbs Passive: Subjunctive

			1st Conjugation	2nd Conjugation	3rd Conjugation		4th Conjugation
Present	Singular	1	pórt*er*	móve*ar*	mítt*ar*	iáci*ar*	aúdi*ar*
		2	portḗ*ris*	moveā́*ris*	mittā́*ris*	iaciā́*ris*	audiā́*ris*
		3	portḗ*tur*	moveā́*tur*	mittā́*tur*	iaciā́*tur*	audiā́*tur*
	Plural	1	portḗ*mur*	moveā́*mur*	mittā́*mur*	iaciā́*mur*	audiā́*mur*
		2	portḗ*minī*	moveā́*minī*	mittā́*minī*	iaciā́*minī*	audiā́*minī*
		3	portḗ*ntur*	moveā́*ntur*	mittā́*ntur*	iaciā́*ntur*	audiā́*ntur*
Imperfect	Singular	1	portā́re*r*	movḗre*r*	mítter*er*	iácer*er*	audī́r*er*
		2	portārḗ*ris*	movērḗ*ris*	mitterḗ*ris*	iacerḗ*ris*	audīrḗ*ris*
		3	portārḗ*tur*	movērḗ*tur*	mitterḗ*tur*	iacerḗ*tur*	audīrḗ*tur*
	Plural	1	portārḗ*mur*	movērḗ*mur*	mitterḗ*mur*	iacerḗ*mur*	audīrḗ*mur*
		2	portārḗ*minī*	movērḗ*minī*	mitterḗ*minī*	iacerḗ*minī*	audīrḗ*minī*
		3	portārḗ*ntur*	movērḗ*ntur*	mitterḗ*ntur*	iacerḗ*ntur*	audīrḗ*ntur*
Perfect		1	portā́tus sim	mṓtus sim	mī́ssus sim	iáctus sim	audī́tus sim
			etc.	etc.	etc.	etc.	etc.
Pluperfect		1	portā́tus éssem	mṓtus éssem	mī́ssus éssem	iáctus éssem	audī́tus éssem
			etc.	etc.	etc.	etc.	etc.

XVII. Deponent Verbs: Infinitive, Imperative, Indicative

			1st Conjugation	2nd Conjugation	3rd Conjugation		4th Conjugation
Present Infinitive			cōn*ā́rī*	ver*ḗrī*	lóqu*ī*	régred*ī*	exper*ī́rī*
Imperative			cōn*ā́re*	ver*ḗre*	lóqu*ere*	regréd*ere*	exper*ī́re*
			cōn*ā́minī*	ver*ḗminī*	loqu*íminī*	regred*íminī*	exper*ī́minī*
Present	Singular	1	cṓn*or*	vére*or*	lóqu*or*	regrédi*or*	expér*ior*
		2	cōn*ā́ris*	ver*ḗris*	lóqu*eris*	regréd*eris*	exper*ī́ris*
		3	cōn*ā́tur*	ver*ḗtur*	lóqu*itur*	regréd*itur*	exper*ī́tur*
	Plural	1	cōn*ā́mur*	ver*ḗmur*	lóqu*imur*	regréd*imur*	exper*ī́mur*
		2	cōn*ā́minī*	ver*ḗminī*	loqu*íminī*	regred*íminī*	exper*ī́minī*
		3	cōn*ā́ntur*	ver*ḗntur*	loqu*úntur*	regredi*úntur*	experi*úntur*
Imperfect	Singular	1	cōnā́*bar*	verḗ*bar*	loqué*bar*	regrediḗ*bar*	experiḗ*bar*
		2	cōnā*bā́ris*	verē*bā́ris*	loquē*bā́ris*	regrediē*bā́ris*	experiē*bā́ris*
		3	cōnā*bā́tur*	verē*bā́tur*	loquē*bā́tur*	regrediē*bā́tur*	experiē*bā́tur*
Future	Singular	1	cōnā́*bor*	verā́*bor*	lóqu*ar*	regréd*iar*	expér*iar*
		2	cōnā́*beris*	verḗ*beris*	loqu*ḗris*	regredi*ḗris*	experi*ḗris*
		3	cōnā́*bitur*	verḗ*bitur*	loqu*ḗtur*	regredi*ḗtur*	experi*ḗtur*
Perfect		1	cōnā́tus sum	véritus sum	locū́tus sum	regréssus sum	expértus sum
Pluperfect		1	cōnā́tus éram	véritus éram	locū́tus éram	regréssus éram	expértus éram
Future Perfect		1	cōnā́tus érō	véritus érō	locū́tus érō	regréssus érō	expértus érō

XVIII. Deponent Verbs: Subjunctive

			1st Conjugation	2nd Conjugation	3rd Conjugation		4th Conjugation
Present	Singular	1	cṓn*er*	vére*ar*	lóqu*ar*	regrédi*ar*	expér*iar*
		2	cōn*ḗris*	vere*ā́ris*	loqu*ā́ris*	regredi*ā́ris*	experi*ā́ris*
		3	cōn*ḗtur*	vere*ā́tur*	loqu*ā́tur*	regredi*ā́tur*	experi*ā́tur*
	Plural	1	cōn*ḗmur*	vere*ā́mur*	loqu*ā́mur*	regredi*ā́mur*	experi*ā́mur*
		2	cōn*ḗminī*	vere*ā́minī*	loqu*ā́minī*	regredi*ā́minī*	experi*ā́minī*
		3	cōn*ḗntur*	vere*ántur*	loqu*ántur*	regredi*ántur*	experi*ántur*
Imperfect	Singular	1	cōnā́*rer*	verḗ*rer*	lóque*rer*	regréde*rer*	experī́*rer*
		2	cōnā́*rḗris*	verē*rḗris*	loque*rḗris*	regrede*rḗris*	experī*rḗris*
		3	cōnā́*rḗtur*	verē*rḗtur*	loque*rḗtur*	regrede*rḗtur*	experī*rḗtur*
	Plural	1	cōnā́*rḗmur*	verē*rḗmur*	loque*rḗmur*	regrede*rḗmur*	experī*rḗmur*
		2	cōnā́*rḗminī*	verē*rḗminī*	loque*rḗminī*	regrede*rḗminī*	experī*rḗminī*
		3	cōnā́*rḗntur*	verē*rḗntur*	loque*rḗntur*	regrede*rḗntur*	experī*rḗntur*
Perfect		1	cōnā́tus sim	véritus sim	locū́tus sim	regréssus sim	expértus sim
Pluperfect		1	cōnā́tus éssem	véritus éssem	locū́tus éssem	regréssus éssem	expértus éssem

XIX. Irregular Verbs: Infinitive, Imperative, Indicative

Infinitive			ésse	pósse	vélle	nólle	málle
Imperative			es	——	——	nólī	——
			éste	——	——	nólíte	——
Present	Singular	1	sum	póssum	vólō	nólō	málō
		2	es	pótes	vīs	nōn vīs	mávīs
		3	est	pótest	vult	nōn vult	mávult
	Plural	1	súmus	póssumus	vólumus	nólumus	málumus
		2	éstis	potéstis	vúltis	nōn vúltis	māvúltis
		3	sunt	póssunt	vólunt	nólunt	málunt
Imperfect	Singular	1	éram	póteram	volébam	nōlébam	mālébam
		2	erās	póterās	volébās	nōlébās	mālébās
		3	érat	póterat	volébat	nōlébat	mālébat
	Plural	1	erámus	poterámus	volēbámus	nōlēbámus	mālēbámus
		2	erátis	poterátis	volēbátis	nōlēbátis	mālēbátis
		3	érant	póterant	volébant	nōlébant	mālébant
Future	Singular	1	érō	póterō	vōlam	nōlam	málam
		2	éris	póteris	vólēs	nólēs	málēs
		3	érit	póterit	vólet	nólet	málet
	Plural	1	érimus	potérimus	volémus	nōlémus	mālémus
		2	éritis	potéritis	volétis	nōlétis	mālétis
		3	érunt	póterunt	vólent	nólent	málent

Infinitive			férre	férrī	fíerī	íre
Imperative			fer	férre	——	ī
			férte	ferímínī	——	íte
Present	Singular	1	férō	féror	fíō	éō
		2	fers	férris	fīs	īs
		3	fert	fértur	fit	it
	Plural	1	férimus	férimur	fímus	ímus
		2	fértis	ferímínī	fítis	ítis
		3	férunt	ferúntur	fíunt	éunt
Imperfect	Singular	1	ferébam	ferébar	fiébam	íbam
		2	ferébās	ferēbáris	fiébās	íbās
		3	ferébat	ferēbátur	fiébat	íbat
	Plural	1	ferēbámus	ferēbámur	fiēbámus	ībámus
		2	ferēbátis	ferēbámínī	fiēbátis	ībátis
		3	ferébant	ferēbántur	fiébant	íbant
Future	Singular	1	féram	férar	fíam	íbō
		2	férēs	feréris	fíēs	íbis
		3	féret	ferétur	fíet	íbit
	Plural	1	ferémus	ferémur	fiémus	íbimus
		2	ferétis	ferémínī	fiétis	íbitis
		3	férent	feréntur	fíent	íbunt

XX. Irregular Verbs: Perfect, Pluperfect, Future Perfect Indicative

Full charts are not supplied for these forms because (except for the perfect of **eō**, for which see below) they are not irregular in any way. They are made in the same way as the perfect, pluperfect, and future perfect tenses of regular verbs, by adding the perfect, pluperfect and future perfect endings to the perfect stem. The perfect stem is found by dropping the *-ī* from the third principal part. The first three principal parts of the irregular verbs are as follows:

> sum, esse, <u>fu*ī*</u>
> possum, posse, <u>potu*ī*</u>
> volō, velle, <u>volu*ī*</u>
> nōlō, nōlle, <u>nōlu*ī*</u>
> mālō, mālle, <u>mālu*ī*</u>
> ferō, ferre, <u>tul*ī*</u>
> eō, īre, <u>i*ī*</u> or <u>īv*ī*</u>

Examples:

> Perfect: fuistī, voluērunt, tulimus
> Pluperfect: fueram, potuerant, nōluerāmus
> Future Perfect: fuerō, volueris, tulerimus

The perfect forms of **eō** made from the stem **i-** are as follows:

> Singular: iī, īstī, iit
> Plural: iimus, īstis, iērunt

Note that the stem vowel (**i-**) contracts with the *-i* of the endings *-istī* and *-istis* to give **ī-** (**īstī, īstis**). Thus also the perfect infinitive: **īsse** (for **iisse**).

The perfect forms of **eō** made from the stem **īv-** are regular, as follows:

> Singular: īvī, īvistī, īvit
> Plural: īvimus, īvistis, īvērunt

XXI. Irregular Verbs: Subjunctive

Present	Singular	1	sim	póssim	vélim	nólim	málim
		2	sīs	póssīs	vélīs	nólīs	málīs
		3	sit	póssit	vélit	nólit	málit
	Plural	1	símus	possímus	velímus	nōlímus	mālímus
		2	sítis	possítis	velítis	nōlítis	mālítis
		3	sint	póssint	vélint	nólint	málint
Imperfect	Singular	1	éssem	póssem	véllem	nóllem	mállem
		2	éssēs	póssēs	véllēs	nóllēs	mállēs
		3	ésset	pósset	véllet	nóllet	mállet
	Plural	1	essémus	possémus	vellémus	nōllémus	māllémus
		2	essétis	possétis	vellétis	nōllétis	māllétis
		3	éssent	póssent	véllent	nóllent	mállent
Perfect	Singular	1	fúerim	potúerim	volúerim	nōlúerim	mālúerim
		2	fúeris	potúeris	volúeris	nōlúeris	mālúeris
		3	fúerit	potúerit	volúerit	nōlúerit	mālúerit
	Plural	1	fuérimus	potuérimus	voluérimus	nōluérimus	māluérimus
		2	fuéritis	potuéritis	voluéritis	nōluéritis	māluéritis
		3	fúerint	potúerint	volúerint	nōlúerint	māluérint
Pluperfect	Singular	1	fuíssem	potuíssem	voluíssem	nōluíssem	māluíssem
		2	fuíssēs	posuíssēs	voluíssēs	nōluíssēs	māluíssēs
		3	fuísset	potuísset	voluísset	nōluísset	māluísset
	Plural	1	fuissémus	potuissémus	voluissémus	nōluissémus	māluissémus
		2	fuissétis	potuissétis	voluissétis	nōluissétis	māluissétis
		3	fuíssent	potuíssent	voluíssent	nōluíssent	māluíssent

Present	Singular	1	féram	férar	fíam	éam
		2	férās	feráris	fíās	éās
		3	férat	ferátur	fíat	éat
	Plural	1	ferámus	ferámur	fiámus	eámus
		2	ferátis	ferámini	fiátis	eátis
		3	férant	ferántur	fíant	éant
Imperfect	Singular	1	férrem	férrer	fíerem	írem
		2	férrēs	ferréris	fíerēs	írēs
		3	férret	ferrétur	fíeret	íret
	Plural	1	ferrémus	ferrémur	fierémus	īrémus
		2	ferrétis	ferrémini	fierétis	īrétis
		3	férrent	ferréntur	fíerent	írent
Perfect	Singular	1	túlerim	látus sim	fáctus sim	íerim
		2	túleris	látus sīs	fáctus sīs	íeris
		3	túlerit	látus sit	fáctus sit	íerit
	Plural	1	tulérimus	látī símus	fáctī símus	iérimus
		2	tuléritis	látī sítis	fáctī sítis	iéritis
		3	túlerint	látī sint	fáctī sint	íerint
Pluperfect	Singular	1	tulíssem	látus éssem	fáctus éssem	íssem
		2	tulíssēs	látus éssēs	fáctus éssēs	íssēs
		3	tulísset	látus ésset	fáctus ésset	ísset
	Plural	1	tulissémus	látī essémus	fáctī essémus	īssémus
		2	tulissétis	látī essétis	fáctī essétis	īssétis
		3	tulíssent	látī éssent	fáctī éssent	íssent

Note: the perfect subjunctive of **eō** may be **ierim**, etc., as above, or **īverim**.
The pluperfect subjunctive of **eō** may be **īssem**, etc., as above, or **īvissem**.

XXII. Participles of Non-deponent Verbs

		Active	Passive
Present	1	párāns, parántis	
	2	hábēns, habéntis	
	3	míttēns, mitténtis	
	-iō	iáciēns, iaciéntis	
	4	aúdiēns, audiéntis	
Perfect	1		parắtus, -a, -um
	2		hábitus, -a, -um
	3		míssus, -a, -um
	-iō		iáctus, -a, -um
	4		audītus, -a, -um
Future	1	parātū́rus, -a, -um	parándus, -a, -um
	2	habitū́rus, -a, -um	habéndus, -a, -um
	3	missū́rus, -a, -um	mitténdus, -a, -um
	-iō	iactū́rus, -a, -um	iaciéndus, -a, -um
	4	audītū́rus, -a, -um	audiéndus, -a, -um

Note: the future passive participle is also known as the gerundive.

XXIII. Participles of Deponent Verbs

		Active	Passive
Present	1	cṓnāns, cōnántis	
	2	vérēns, veréntis	
	3	lóquēns, loquéntis	
	-iō	ēgrédiēns, ēgrediéntis	
	4	expériēns, experiéntis	
Perfect	1	cōnắtus, -a, -um	
	2	véritus, -a, -um	
	3	locū́tus, -a, -um	
	-iō	ēgréssus, -a, -um	
	4	expértus, -a, -um	
Future	1	cōnātū́rus, -a, -um	cōnándus, -a, -um
	2	veritū́rus, -a, -um	veréndus, -a, -um
	3	locūtū́rus, -a, -um	loquéndus, -a, -um
	-iō	ēgressū́rus, -a, -um	ēgrediéndus, -a, -um
	4	expertū́rus, -a, -um	experiéndus, -a, -um

XXIV. Infinitives of Non-deponent Verbs

		Active	Passive
Present	1	paráre	parári
	2	habére	habéri
	3	míttere	mítti
	-iō	iácere	iáci
	4	audíre	audíri
Perfect	1	parāvísse	parátus, -a, -um ésse
	2	habuísse	hábitus, -a, -um ésse
	3	mīsísse	míssus, -a, -um ésse
	-iō	iēcísse	iáctus, -a, -um ésse
	4	audīvísse	audítus, -a, -um ésse
Future	1	parātúrus, -a, -um ésse	
	2	habitúrus, -a, -um ésse	
	3	missúrus, -a, -um ésse	
	-iō	iactúrus, -a, -um ésse	
	4	audītúrus, -a, -um ésse	

XXV. Infinitives of Deponent Verbs

Present	1	cōnári
	2	veréri
	3	lóqui
	-iō	égredi
	4	experíri
Perfect	1	cōnátus, -a, -um ésse
	2	véritus, -a, -um ésse
	3	locútus, -a, -um ésse
	-iō	ēgréssus, -a, -um ésse
	4	expértus, -a, -um ésse
Future	1	cōnātúrus, -a, -um ésse
	2	veritúrus, -a, -um ésse
	3	locūtúrus, -a, -um ésse
	-iō	ēgressúrus, -a, -um ésse
	4	expertúrus, -a, -um ésse

XXVI. Gerunds of Non-deponent Verbs

Case	1st Conjugation	2nd Conjugation	3rd Conjugation	3rd -*iō* Conjugation	4th Conjugation
Genitive	pará*ndī*	habé*ndī*	mitté*ndī*	iacié*ndī*	audié*ndī*
Dative	pará*ndō*	habé*ndō*	mitté*ndō*	iacié*ndō*	audié*ndō*
Accusative	pará*ndum*	habé*ndum*	mitté*ndum*	iacié*ndum*	audié*ndum*
Ablative	pará*ndō*	habé*ndō*	mitté*ndō*	iacié*ndō*	audié*ndō*

XXVII. Gerunds of Deponent Verbs

Case	1st Conjugation	2nd Conjugation	3rd Conjugation	3rd -*iō* Conjugation	4th Conjugation
Genitive	cōná*ndī*	veré*ndī*	loqué*ndī*	ēgredié*ndī*	experié*ndī*
Dative	cōná*ndō*	veré*ndō*	loqué*ndō*	ēgredié*ndō*	experié*ndō*
Accusative	cōná*ndum*	veré*ndum*	loqué*ndum*	ēgredié*ndum*	experié*ndum*
Ablative	cōná*ndō*	veré*ndō*	loqué*ndō*	ēgredié*ndō*	experié*ndō*

REFERENCE GRAMMAR

This section reviews all structures introduced or discussed in Book III. For a complete list of the structures found in Books I and II, see the Reference Grammar at the end of Book II.

I. NOUNS

A. Genitive Case

1. Special Verbs with the Genitive

    Some verbs are used with the genitive case (see page 93):

    . . . potītus **rērum omnium.** (63B:2)
    . . . *having gotten control **of all affairs.***
    . . . oblītus **nūgārum,** . . . (66A:5)
    . . . *forgetting **trifles,** . . .*

2. Genitive with impersonal verbs

    The genitive is used with some impersonal verbs to show the cause of the feeling (see page 118):

    Mē <u>taedet</u> **sermōnis.**
    *I <u>am tired</u> **of conversation.***

3. Genitive of Characteristic

    A word or phrase in the genitive may show what something is typical or characteristic of:

    Nam et **pessimī exemplī** nec **nostrī saeculī** est. (65B:8)
    *For it (to accept charges made anonymously) is **(characteristic) of the worst sort of precedent** and is not **(characteristic) of our age.***

B. Dative Case

1. Dative of Possession

    When used with a form of the verb **esse,** the dative case may indicate possession; the thing possessed is the subject of the clause and the person who possesses it is in the dative (see pages 94–95):

    Interim cum scīret Clōdius . . . iter . . . **Milōnī** <u>esse</u>. . . . (59A:1–2)
    *Meanwhile, since Clodius knew that there <u>was a journey</u> **to / for Milo** . . .*
    . . . *that **Milo** <u>was having / was making</u> a journey. . . .*

2. Dative of Agent

    With the passive periphrastic construction, consisting of a gerundive and a form of the verb **esse,** the person by whom the thing is to be done is regularly shown by a dative, not by **ab** with the ablative (see page 64):

    . . . quid <u>sit</u> **vōbīs** <u>faciendum.</u> (60A:3–4)
    . . . *what <u>must be done</u> **by you.***

3. Dative with Special Intransitive Verbs
   The dative case is used with special intransitive verbs (see pages 93–94):
   >   . . . quī **competītōribus** Milōnis <u>studēbant</u> . . . (58B:26–27)
   >   *. . . who <u>supported</u> Milo's **political rivals** . . .*

4. Dative with Intransitive Compound Verbs
   Many intransitive compound verbs are used with the dative case (see page 94):
   >   . . . cum <u>īnstārent</u> Parthī **fugientī** . . . (56B:7–8)
   >   *. . . when the Parthians <u>were pursuing</u> (him) **as he fled** . . .*

5. Dative with Transitive Compound Verbs
   Some transitive compound verbs are used with a dative in addition to an accusative object (see page 94):
   >   Octāviānus C. Cornēlium Gallum **Aegyptō** <u>praeposuit</u>. (cf. 56B:13–14)
   >   *Octavian <u>placed</u> C. Cornelius Gallus <u>in charge of</u> Egypt.*

6. Dative with Compounds of **Esse**
   Some compounds of **esse** are used with a dative (see page 94):
   >   . . . (exercitus) **cui** semper omnia . . . <u>dēfuissent</u>. (61C:9–10)
   >   *. . . (the army) **which** <u>had</u> always <u>lacked</u> everything (literally, **to which** everything <u>had</u> always <u>been lacking</u>).*

7. Dative of Purpose
   The dative may be used to show the purpose for which something is done or exists:
   >   . . . mē . . . triumvirum **reī pūblicae cōnstituendae** creāvit. (63A:7)
   >   *. . . chose me triumvir **for the reorganization of the state**.*

8. Dative with Adjectives
   The dative is used with certain adjectives:
   >   Haec īnscrīptiō **mihi** <u>idōnea</u> est. (cf. 66B:23)
   >   *This inscription is <u>suitable</u> **for me**.*

D. Ablative case

1. Ablative of Price
   The ablative case is used to refer to the specific price of something:
   >   Bona eius . . . **sēmiunciā** vēniērunt. (59E:5–6)
   >   *His goods . . . were sold **for 1/24th** (their value).*

2. Ablative of Separation
   Verbs or adjectives implying separation are often accompanied by words in the ablative, sometimes with **ab** or **ex** and sometimes without a preposition, to express the thing from which something is separated or free:
   >   . . . neque rem pūblicam **alterutrō exercitū** <u>prīvāre</u> voluisse. (61A:3–4)
   >   *. . . that he did not wish <u>to deprive</u> the state **of either army**.*

3. Ablative of Description
   A noun and adjective in the ablative may be used without a preposition to describe another noun:
   >   . . . vir **singulārī virtūte**. (61A:7)
   >   *. . . a man **of outstanding courage**.*

4. Ablative with Special Verbs
The verbs **fruor, fungor, potior, ūtor,** and **vēscor** are used with the ablative case (see pages 84–85):

> . . . omnēs **ducibus ūsī centuriōnibus tribūnīs**que mīlitum in altissimōs montēs . . . cōnfūgērunt. (62B:10–11)
> . . . *they all fled to the very high mountains, <u>using</u> **the centurions** and military **tribunes as leaders.***

II. ADJECTIVES

A. Adjectives as Substantives
Adjectives may be used as substantives, i.e., as nouns:

> Ita cum **recentēs** atque **integrī dēfessīs** successissent, . . . (62A:2)
> *So when **fresh** and **unhurt** (troops) came to the aid of the **tired** (men), . . .*

III. VERBS

A. Impersonal Passive
Verbs may be used impersonally in the passive to place emphasis on the action itself rather than on any of the participants (see page 92):

> **Pugnātum** tum **est** ingentī contentiōne, . . . (55C:9)
> *Then **fighting took place** with great strife, . . .*
> *Then **the battle was fought**. . . .*
> *Then **they fought**. . . .*

B. Passive Periphrastic or Gerundive of Obligation
The gerundive (future passive participle) can be used with any form of the verb **esse** to form a passive periphrastic; the meaning is *am to be, should be,* or *must be,* expressing obligation or necessity (see page 63):

> Iānum Quirīnum . . . ter mē prīncipe senātus **claudendum esse** cēnsuit. (63C:9–12)
> *The Senate ordered that the shrine of Janus Quirinus **should be shut** three times during my principate.*

The construction is often impersonal:

> . . . ubi diūtius nōbīs **habitandum est.** (66A:13)
> . . . *where **living must take place** by us for a longer time,* better English, *where we **must live**. . . .*

C. Hortatory and Jussive Subjunctive
   The present subjunctive may be used in a main clause to issue a command. When such commands are in the first person, they are called hortatory (see page 140):
   Vīvāmus, mea Lesbia, atque **amēmus**. (Catullus 5)
   Let us live, *my Lesbia, and **let us love**.*
   When they are in the third person, they are called jussive (see page 140):
   . . . catellam cingulō alligātam **dūcat**. (66B:19–20)
   . . . ***let her be leading*** *a puppy tied with a leash.*
D. Deliberative Subjunctive
   The subjunctive may be used in the first person to show deliberation:
   Ego quid **agam**? (60B:2)
   *What **should I do**?*

IV. VERBAL NOUNS AND VERBAL ADJECTIVES

A. Gerund
   The gerund is a neuter verbal noun that appears in the genitive, dative, accusative, and ablative singular only. Gerunds are often translated as verbal nouns in English (see pages 48–49):
   . . . deinde **vincendō** . . . usque ad Ōceanum Britannicum prōcessit. (55A:8–9)
   . . . *then he advanced **by conquering** . . . as far as the English Channel.*
   They can also be used with ad, grātiā, or causā to show purpose (see page 48):
   Cōnsul creātus est **gubernandī** <u>causā</u>.
   *The consul was elected <u>for the sake</u> **of governing** (**to govern**).*
B. Gerundive or Future Passive Participle
   The gerundive is a verbal adjective that appears in all genders, numbers, and cases. It is future and passive in meaning and is often called a future passive participle (see page 61).
   . . . in **excutiendīs** causīs. . . . (65B:2)
   (literally) . . . *in cases **to be investigated** . . .*
   (better English) . . . *in **investigating** the cases. . . .*
   The following constructions are particularly common with gerundives:
   1. To express purpose, with the prepositions **ad, grātiā,** or **causā** (see pages 61–62):
      Catilīna . . . **ad dēlendam patriam** coniūrāvit. (55A:3)
      *Catiline . . . made a conspiracy **to destroy his country**.*
      . . . dīcam enim apertē nōn **dērīvandī crīminis causā**, . . . (59D:25)
      . . . *I will say this openly not **in order to turn away the accusation**, . . .*
   2. To show obligation or necessity, when combined with some form of the verb **esse**. This is called the passive periphrastic or gerundive of obligation (see page 63 and III.B page 191):
      Conquīrendī nōn **sunt**, . . . (65B:4)
      *They **are** not **to be sought out**, . . .*

V. SENTENCES

A. Subordinate Clauses with the Subjunctive

1. **Clauses of Fearing**

   After the verbs **timēre, metuere,** and **verērī** or after expressions such as **est perī-culum,** a subordinate clause with the subjunctive is used to show what is feared. In fear clauses, **nē** introduces a positive clause and **ut** a negative one (see page 74):

   Etiam illud verendum est, **nē** . . . famēs in urbe **sit.** (60A:10–11)

   That also is to be feared, **that** *there* **may be famine** *in the city.*

   . . . vereor **ut** Dolabella ipse satis nōbīs prōdesse **possit.** (60A:5–6)

   . . . *I fear* **that** *Dolabella himself* **may not be** *of sufficient help to us.*

2. **Relative Clauses of Characteristic**

   A relative clause whose verb is in the subjunctive identifies the person or thing described as one of a general group or class (see page 130):

   Iste est vir quem omnēs **timeant.**

   He is the **type of man** *whom everyone* **fears.**

3. **Clauses introduced by quīn**

   After a negative main verb, the conjunction **quīn,** *that,* may introduce a clause with the subjunctive. This is particularly common with phrases that express doubt, hinderance, or objection:

   . . . nōn dubitāvī quīn et **scrīberem** ad tē et grātiās tibi **agerem,** . . . (60D:2–3)

   . . . *I did <u>not</u> doubt <u>that</u>* **I should write** *to you and* **thank** *you,* . . .

   <u>Neque</u> vērō Caesarem fefellit, <u>quīn</u> ab eīs cohortibus . . . initium victōriae **orīrētur.** (62A:4–5)

   <u>*Nor was Caesar wrong in thinking <u>that</u> the beginning of his victory*</u> **arose** *from those cohorts.*

4. **Substantive clauses of result**

   A noun clause introduced by **ut** with its verb in the subjunctive may function as the object of the verb. The verb **faciō** is translated *to see to it* or *to bring it about* when it introduces such a clause:

   Faciam . . . **ut** aut vīvō mihi aut mortuō grātiās **agās.**

   I will see to it ***that you will give*** *thanks to me either dead or alive.* (61A:10–11)

B. Subjunctive with Impersonal Verbs

Several impersonal verbs are used with a subjunctive (see page 118):

Et urnam <u>licet</u> frāctam **sculpās** . . . (66B:20)

And you <u>*may*</u> **carve** *a broken urn* . . .

C. Conditional Sentences

1. A conditional sentence consists of two parts: a protasis or if-clause and an apodosis or conclusion (see pages 158–159).

2. Simple or factual conditions use the indicative:

   Sī Rōmae **erātis,** saepe ad Forum **ībātis.** (referring to the past)

   If you **were** *in Rome, you often* **went** *to the Forum.*

   Sī vōs **valētis,** nōs **valēmus.** (60A:3) (referring to the present)

   If you **are well,** *we* **are well.**

Nisi in nāvem sē **contulerit, excipiētur.** (Cf. 60B:3) (referring to the future)
*Unless he **boards** (literally, **will have boarded**) a ship, he **will be captured.***

Factual conditions that refer to the future use either the future or the future perfect in the protasis, and the future in the apodosis. If the action in the **sī-clause** will have been completed before that in the main clause, the future perfect is used (see example above); if the two actions will occur simultaneously, the future is used. These are called future more vivid conditions.

3. Imaginary conditions present a supposition or hypothesis and always use the subjunctive:

> . . . contiōnem . . . quam, nisi obīre facinoris locum tempusque **voluisset,** numquam **relīquisset.** (59A:5–7) (referring to the past)
> *. . . a meeting which he never **would have left, unless he had wanted** to go to a place and time for crime.*

> Contiōnem, nisi obīre facinoris locum tempusque **vellet,** nōn **relinqueret.** (referring to the present)
> *He **would** not **be leaving** the meeting, unless he **wanted** to go to a place and time for crime.*

> Sī Fannia **moriātur,** Plīnius maximē **doleat.** (referring to the future)
> *If Fannia **were to die / should die,** Pliny **would be** very **sad.***

The pluperfect subjunctive is used in both halves to refer to past time, and the imperfect subjunctive to refer to present time; such conditions are called contrary-to-fact conditions. The present subjunctive is used to refer to the future, and these conditions are known as future less vivid conditions.

D. Potential Subjunctive

The imperfect or pluperfect subjunctive may be used in a main clause that stands by itself but implies a conditional sentence with the subjunctive:

> **Putārēs** mē hoc iussisse. (66C:8)
> *You **would think** (if you thought about it) that I had ordered this.*
> **Putāssēs** (= **putāvissēs**) illum semper mēcum habitāsse. (66D:23)
> *You **would have thought** that he had always lived with me.*

E. Infinitive with Impersonal Verbs

The impersonal verbal phrase **necesse est** and several impersonal verbs are found with the infinitive (see page 118):

> Nōbīs <u>necesse est</u> statim **discēdere.** (9:15)
> ***To leave** immediately <u>is necessary</u> for us.*
> *It <u>is necessary</u> for us **to leave** immediately.*
> Vōbīs <u>licet</u> hīc **cēnāre.** (20:7)
> ***To dine** here <u>is allowed</u> for you.*
> *It <u>is allowed</u> for you **to dine** here.*
> *You are <u>allowed</u> **to dine** here.*
> *You <u>may</u> **dine** here.*

Technically speaking, the infinitive is the subject of the impersonal verb, as the literal translation shows. However, we often supply *it* as the subject in translation or use other alternatives to produce good English.

LATIN TO ENGLISH VOCABULARY

This list includes all basic words that do not appear in the running vocabularies. It also includes all words that appear in the running vocabularies with asterisks, since these words are usually not repeated in the running vocabularies when they reappear in the readings. Numbers in parentheses at the end of entries refer to the chapters in all the ECCE ROMANI student books in which the words appear in the running vocabulary or in a Building the Meaning section. However, this list includes only words used in Book III; for a cumulative list of words introduced in Books I and II, see the Latin to English Vocabulary at the end of Book II.

A

ā, ab, prep. + abl., *from, away from, by* (13, 29, 31)

abeō, abīre, abiī or **abīvī, abitūrus**, irreg., *to go away* (3, 9)

abnegō, -āre, -āvī, -ātus, *to refuse, deny* (65A)

absēns, absentis, *absent*

absolvō, absolvere, absolvī, absolūtus, *to set free, acquit* (59E)

absum, abesse, āfuī, āfutūrus, irreg., *to be away, be absent, be distant* (11, 25)

ac, conj., *and* (30)

accēdō, accēdere, accessī, accessūrus, *to approach, come toward* (68B)

accidit, accidere, accidit, *it happens* (14, 26)

accipiō, accipere, accēpī, acceptus, *to receive, get* (31)

accurrō, accurrere, accurrī, accursūrus, *to run toward, run up to* (29)

ācer, ācris, ācre, *fierce, sharp, keen* (59C)
  ācriter, adv., *fiercely* (48)

aciēs, -ēī, f., *battle line* (55C)

ad, prep. + acc., *to, toward, at, near* (2, 9); + gerund(ive), *to, in order to* (58)

adeō, adīre, adiī, aditus, irreg., *to come to, approach*

adferō, see **afferō**

adhūc, adv., *still, as yet* (5, 13)

adiciō, adicere, adiēcī, adiectus, *to add* (56B)

adimō, adimere, adēmī, adēmptus + dat., *to take away (from)* (35)

adiuvō, adiuvāre, adiūvī, adiūtus, *to help* (6, 21)

administrō, -āre, -āvī, -ātus, *to administer, govern* (57B)

admittō, admittere, admīsī, admissus, *to let in, allow* (56B)

admoveō, admovēre, admōvī, admōtus, *to move toward, bring to* (22, 64A)

adoptō, -āre, -āvī, -ātus, *to adopt* (56A)

adorior, adorīrī, adortus sum, *to attack* (42)

adsequor, adsequī, adsecūtus sum, *to follow* (67B)

adsum, adesse, adfuī, adfutūrus, irreg., *to be present* (26)

adsurgō, adsurgere, adsurrēxī, adsurrēctūrus, *to stand up* (68D)

adulēscēns, adulēscentis, m., *young man, youth* (36)

adulterium, -ī, n., *adultery* (65A)

adversus, prep. + acc., *against* (68C)

adversus, -a, -um, *opposite, turned toward, facing; unfavorable, bad* (59C)

aedēs, aedis, gen. pl., **aedium**, f., *building, temple*; pl., *house* (63B)

aedificō, -āre, -āvī, -ātus, *to build* (24)

aegrōtō, -āre, -āvī, -ātūrus, *to be ill* (39)

aestus, -ūs, m., *heat* (24, 25)

aequus, -a, -um, *fair, equal*

aequō, -āre, -āvī, -ātus, *to make equal* (57A)

aetās, aetātis, f., *age, time of life* (55C)

afferō, afferre, attulī, allātus, irreg., *to bring in, carry to* (29, 32, 65A)

afflīgō, afflīgere, afflīxī, afflictus, *to strike down* (60C)

ager, agrī, m., *field, territory, land* (2)

aggredior, aggredī, aggressus sum, *to attack* (55A)

agmen, agminis, n., *column, line* (58A)

agrestis, -is, gen. pl., **agrestium**, m., *farmer, peasant* (68C)

agō, agere, ēgī, āctus, *to do, drive* (8, 14, 23, 52)
  grātiās agere + dat., *to thank* (26, 51)

aliquī, aliqua, aliquod, *some (or other), any* (38, 63)

aliquis, aliquis, aliquid, *someone, something, anyone, anything* (25, 51, 63)

nē quis (**quis = aliquis**), *that no one* (52, 63)

sī quis (quis = aliquis), *if anyone* (51, 63)

aliter, adv., *otherwise* (26, 64B)

alius, alia, aliud, *another, other* (10)

  aliī . . . aliī, *some . . . others* (9)

alter, altera, alterum, *the other, the other (of two), the second* (1)

altitūdō, altitūdinis, f., *height* (64B)

altus, -a, -um, *high, deep* (38)

ambūrō, ambūrere, ambussī, ambustus, *to burn up* (58C)

ambō, ambae, ambō, *both* (46)

āmēns, āmentis, *mad, insane, mindless* (60A)

amīcus, -ī, m., *friend* (3)

āmittō, āmittere, āmīsī, āmissus, *to lose* (56A)

amō, -āre, -āvī, -ātus, *to like, love* (4)

amor, amōris, m., *love* (34, 57B)

ampliō, -āre, -āvī, -ātus, *to enlarge, increase* (63D)

amplitūdō, amplitūdinis, f., *size* (68C)

amplius, adv., *more* (55D)

an, conj., *whether, or* (51, 67A)

ancilla, -ae, f., *slave-woman* (6)

angō, angere, *to distress, trouble* (67A)

angustus, -a, -um, *narrow* (68D)

anima, -ae, f., *breath of life, soul; darling* (33, 60A)

animadvertō, animadvertere, animadvertī, animadversus, *to notice* (39)

animus, -ī, m., *mind, spirit, heart* (16)

annus, -ī, m., *year* (38)

ante, prep. + acc., *before, in front of* (36, 39)

anteā, adv., *before, previously* (20)

ānulus, -ī, m., *ring* (50)

appāreō, -ēre, -uī, -itūrus, *to appear* (15, 18)

apparō, -āre, -āvī, -ātus, *to prepare, make ready* (59B)

appellō, -āre, -āvī, -ātus, *to call by name, name* (21, 55A)

appropinquō, -āre, -āvī, -ātūrus + dat., *to approach, draw near to* (4, 62)

apud, prep. + acc., *at the house of, near, at, with, among* (16)

aqua, -ae, f., *water, aqueduct* (6)

āra, -ae, f., *altar* (53)

arbor, arboris, f., *tree* (1)

ardeō, ardēre, arsī, *to burn, blaze* (53)

ārea, -ae, f., *open space, courtyard* (11)

argentum, -ī, n., *silver* (62C)

arma, -ōrum, n. pl., *arms, weapons* (39)

ascendō, ascendere, ascendī, ascēnsus, *to climb up* (4, 22)

Asia, -ae, f., *Asia* (Roman province in western Asia Minor) (38)

a(d)spiciō, a(d)spicere, a(d)spexī, a(d)spectus, *to look at, see, examine* (68D)

atque, conj., *and, also* (22)

ātrium, -ī, n., *atrium* (main room of a Roman house) (26)

  ātrium Vestae, *the residence of the Vestal Virgins* (67A)

attentē, adv., *attentively, closely* (20)

auctor, auctōris, m., *author, authority* (65A)

auctōritās, auctōritātis, f., *influence, prestige; authority* (63B, 67A)

audāx, audācis, *bold, daring, reckless* (36)

audiō, -īre, -īvī, -ītus, *to hear, listen to* (4)

auferō, auferre, abstulī, ablātus, irreg., *to carry away, take away* (29, 32)

augeō, augēre, auxī, auctus, *to increase, enlarge*

aureus, -a, -um, *golden, of gold* (25)

  aureus, -ī, m., *aureus (gold coin)* (66C)

aurum, -ī, n., *gold* (21)

aut, conj., *or* (26)

  aut . . . aut, conj., *either . . . or* (26)

autem, conj., *however, moreover* (31)

auxilium, -ī, n., *help, aid* (5, 15)

  auxilia, -ōrum, n. pl., *auxiliary troops; reinforcements* (55C)

B

barbaricus, -a, -um, *barbarian, foreign* (57B)

barbarus, -a, -um, *barbarian, foreign* (55C)

basilica, -ae, f., *courthouse, basilica* (58C)

bellum, -ī, n., *war* (39)

  bellum commovēre, *to begin war, undertake war*

  bellum gerere, *to wage war* (56A)

  bellum īnferre + dat., *to make war upon* (55A)

bellus, -a, -um, *pretty, elegant, comfortable* (60A)

bēstia, -ae, f., *beast, animal* (49)

bibō, bibere, bibī, *to drink* (31)

bis, adv., *twice* (55A)

bonus, -a, -um, *good* (12, 34)

  bona, -ōrum, n. pl., *goods, possessions* (26, 59E)

brevis, -is, -e, *short, brief* (2, 34)

C

cadō, cadere, cecidī, cāsūrus, *to fall* (3, 22)

caedēs, caedis, gen. pl., **caedium**, f., *murder, killing* (59B)

caedō, caedere, cecīdī, caesus, *to cut, beat, cut down, kill* (57B)

calamitās, calamitātis, f., *disaster* (55B)

campus, -ī, m., *field, plain* (41)

candidātus, -ī, m., *candidate*

capiō, capere, cēpī, captus, *to take, capture* (21)

captīvus, -a, -um, *captive, captured* (26)

caput, capitis, n., *head* (25)

carcer, carceris, m., *prison* (55A)

carmen, carminis, n., *song, verse, poem* (65A)

cārus, -a, -um, *dear, beloved* (53)

castra, -ōrum, n. pl., *camp* (55C)

cāsus, -ūs, m., *falling; chance, misfortune, accident*
cāsū, *by chance, accidentally* (32)

catella, -ae, f., *pupppy* (66A)

causa, -ae, f., *cause; case* (52, 65B)
causā + gen., *for the sake of* (52, 58)

caveō, cavēre, cāvī, cautus, *to be careful, watch out
for, beware* (4, 13, 23)

cēdō, cēdere, cessī, cessūrus + dat., *to yield to,
retreat* (62)

celer, celeris, celere, *swift, quick* (34)
celeriter, adv., *quickly* (8, 13, 35)

celeritās, celeritātis, f., *speed* (29)

cēna, -ae, f., *dinner* (19)

cēnō, -āre, -āvī, -ātus, *to dine, eat dinner, eat* (19)

cēnseō, cēnsēre, cēnsuī, cēnsus, *to be of the
opinion, think* (60C)

centēnī, -ae, -a, *a hundred each* (55A)

centiēs, adv., *a hundred times* (66C)

centuriō, centuriōnis, m., *centurion, commander
of a century (unit of about 80 men)* (61)

centum, *a hundred* (15, 38)

cernō, cernere, crēvī, crētus, *to discern, see,
understand* (67B)

certus, -a, -um, *certain* (35)
certē, adv., *certainly, surely, at least* (19, 35)

cēterī, -ae, -a, *the rest, the others, the remainder*
(33)

cibus, -ī, m., *food* (6)

cingō, cingere, cīnxī, cīnctus, *to surround; to
equip, strap on* (58A)

cinis, cineris, m., *ash* (66A)

circiter, adv., *around, about* (61A)

circuitus, -ūs, m., *circuit, circumference, perimeter*
(55A)

circumeō, circumīre, circumiī, circumitus,
irreg., *to go around, surround* (24, 61B)

cīvicus, -a, -um, *civic, civil* (63B)

cito, adv., *quickly, soon* (66A)

cīvīlis, -is, -e, *civil* (55B)

cīvis, cīvis, gen. pl., **cīvium,** m./f., *citizen* (13)

cīvitās, cīvitātis, f., *state; city* (56A)

clārus, -a, -um, *bright; well-known, distinguished*
(53, 55A)

classis, classis, gen. pl., **classium,** f., *fleet* (68A)

claudō, claudere, clausī, clausus, *to shut, close* (26)

cōdex, cōdicis, m., *ledger* (58C)

coemō, coemere, coēmī, coēmptus, *to buy up*
(66C)

coepī, coepisse, coeptus (perfect system only),
to begin (38, 55B)

cōgitō, -āre, -āvī, -ātus, *to think, consider* (21)

cognōscō, cognōscere, cognōvī, cognitus, *to
find out, learn, hear of* (43)

cōgō, cōgere, coēgī, coāctus, *to compel, force* (49)

cohors, cohortis, f., *cohort (one-tenth of a legion)*
(61C)

cohortor, -ārī, -ātus sum, *to encourage, exhort*
(61A)

collēga, -ae, m., *colleague, partner* (63B)

collis, collis, gen. pl., **collium,** m., *hill* (35)

collocō, -āre, -āvī, -ātus, *to locate, set up* (59A)

columna, -ae, f., *column* (64B)

comes, comitis, m., *companion, comrade* (39)

comitātus, -ūs, m., *company, retinue* (59B)

comitia, -ōrum, n. pl., *comitia (assembly of the
people)* (59)

commemorō, -āre, -āvī, -ātus, *to remember,
recall* (54)

committō, committere, commīsī, commissus,
to bring together, entrust (48, 55D)

**commoveō, commovēre, commōvī,
commōtus,** *to move, upset* (29, 30, 56A)
bellum commovēre, *to begin war, undertake war*

commūnis, -is, -e, *common, joint* (45)

comparō, -āre, -āvī, -ātus, *to prepare* (32)

competītor, competītōris, m., *political rival* (58B)

complector, complectī, complexus sum, *to
embrace* (68B)

complūrēs, -ēs, -a, *several* (32)

compōnō, compōnere, composuī, compositus,
to compose, arrange (53)

concēdō, concēdere, concessī, concessus, *to
admit, grant* (64)

concurrō, concurrere, concurrī, concursūrus,
to run together, rush up, charge (34)

condemnō, -āre, -āvī, -ātus, *to condemn, find
guilty* (49)

condō, condere, condidī, conditus, *to establish,
found* (36, 55A)

cōnferō, cōnferre, contulī, collātus, irreg., *to
bring together, collect; to confer, bestow* (54, 64B)
sē cōnferre, *to take oneself, go, flee* (60B)

cōnficiō, cōnficere, cōnfēcī, cōnfectus, *to accomplish, finish, finish off; overwhelm* (30)

cōnfīdō, cōnfīdere, cōnfīsus sum + dat., *to give trust (to), trust completely, believe in* (26, 60D, 62)

cōnfīrmō, -āre, -āvī, -ātus, *to strengthen, support, assert, encourage* (62A)

cōnfodiō, cōnfodere, cōnfōdī, cōnfossus, *to dig up; stab*

cōnfugiō, cōnfugere, cōnfūgī, *to flee, run away* (44)

congregō, -āre, -āvī, -ātus, *to bring together, assemble, flock* (55B)

coniūrō, -āre, -āvī, -ātūrus, *to plot, make a conspiracy* (55A)

cōnor, -ārī, -ātus sum, *to try* (36, 37)

conquīrō, conquīrere, conquīsīvī, conquīsītus, *to procure, obtain, seek out* (62C, 65B)

cōnscrībō, cōnscrībere, cōnscrīpsī, cōnscrīptus, *to enlist, recruit* (55)

cōnsēnsus, -ūs, m., *agreement* (49, 63B)

cōnservō, -āre, -āvī, -ātus, *to protect, guard, save*

cōnsīderō, -āre, -āvī, -ātus, *to consider, think about, make plans* (60A)

cōnsilium, -ī, n., *plan, counsel, advice* (45)
  cōnsilium capere, *to adopt a plan* (45)

cōnsistō, cōnsistere, cōnstitī, *to halt, stop; to stand fast, make a stand* (48)

cōnsōlor, -ārī, -ātus sum, *to console, comfort*

cōnspiciō, cōnspicere, cōnspexī, cōnspectus, *to catch sight of, notice* (4, 21)

cōnstat, cōnstāre, *it is agreed* (47)

cōnstituō, cōnstituere, cōnstituī, cōnstitūtus, *to decide, determine* (23)

cōnsuētūdō, cōnsuētūdinis, f., *custom, habit, practice* (55D)

cōnsul, cōnsulis, m., *consul (one of two chief officials in Roman government)* (36, 55A)

cōnsulāris, -is, -e, *belonging to a consul, consular; as noun, ex-consul* (55C)

cōnsulātus, -ūs, m., *consulship, office of consul* (55B)

cōnsultō, -āre, -āvī, -ātus, *to consult* (68C)

cōnsultum, -ī, n., *decree, decision, edict* (52)
  Senātūs cōnsultum, *decree of the Senate*

cōnsūmō, cōnsūmere, cōnsūmpsī, cōnsūmptus, *to drain, use up, destroy* (61B, 63D)

contendō, contendere, contendī, contentus, *to hurry, exert, gallop* (62C)

contineō, continēre, continuī, contentus, *to hold together, contain, enclose* (47)

contingō, contingere, contigī, contactus, *to befall, happen to* (64A)

contiō, contiōnis, f., *public meeting, assembly* (58C)

contrā, prep. + acc., *opposite, facing, against* (34, 55B)

contrādīcō, contrādīcere, contrādīxī, contrādictus, *to speak out against, oppose* (55B)

contrahō, contrahere, contrāxī, contractus, *to contract, get* (67A)

contrārius, -a, -um, *opposing, contrary* (68)

contrōversia, -ae, f., *strife, controversy* (60e)

convalēscō, convalēscere, convaluī, *to grow stronger, get well* (42)

conveniō, convenīre, convēnī, conventūrus, *to come together, meeet, assemble, gather* (43)

convīva, -ae, m., *guest (at a banquet)* (31)

convīvium, -ī, n., *feast, banquet* (34)

convocō, -āre, -āvī, -ātus, *to call together, assemble* (12)

cōpia, -ae, f., *abundance, supply; pl., troops* (55C)

cornū, -ūs, n., *horn, wing of an army, end of a battle line* (55C)

corōna, -ae, f., *garland, wreath, crown* (34)

corpus, corporis, n., *body* (21)

cotīdiē, adv., *daily, every day* (37)

crēber, crēbra, crēbrum, *thick, crowded, frequent* (68C)

crēdō, crēdere, crēdidī, crēditus + dat., *to trust, believe* (35, 62)

creō, -āre, -āvī, -ātus, *to appoint, create, elect, choose* (34, 54)

crēscō, crēscere, crēvī, crētūrus, *to increase, grow, enlarge* (68B)

crīmen, crīminis, n., *charge, accusation* (59D)

crūdēlitās, crūdēlitātis, f., *cruelty*

cubiculum, -ī, n., *room, bedroom* (8, 15)

culpa, -ae, f., *fault, blame* (14)

cum, prep. + abl., *with* (12)

cum, conj., *when, whenever, after, since, because, although* (22, 40)

cūnctī, -ae, -a, *all* (14)

cupidus, -a, -um + gen., *desirous of, wanting, greedy for* (58)

cupiō, cupere, cupīvī, cupītus, *to desire, want* (40)

cūr, adv., *why* (1)

cūra, -ae, f., *care, anxiety, concern* (34, 48)

Cūria, -ae, f., *Senate House* (23)

cūrō, -āre, -āvī, -ātus, *to look after, take care of, attend to* (6)

currō, currere, cucurrī, cursūrus, *to run* (2, 23)

cursus, -ūs, m., *a running, course, voyage* (61B)

custōdia, -ae, f., *guard, protection, custody*

D

dē, prep. + abl., *down from; concerning, about* (16, 53)

dēbeō, -ēre, -uī, -itus, *to owe;* + infin., *ought, should* (26)

decem, *ten* (15, 38)

dēcernō, dēcernere, dēcrēvī, dēcrētus, *to decide, assign* (55A)

decumānus, -a, -um, *related to the tenth* (62C)

decuriō, decuriōnis, m., *town councilman* (58A)

dēdō, dēdere, dēdidī, dēditus, *to give up, surrender*

dēfendō, dēfendere, dēfendī, dēfēnsus, *to defend* (35)

dēferō, dēferre, dētulī, dēlātus, irreg., *to carry down, offer, confer; to inform against* (55B, 65A)

dēfessus, -a, -um, *tired, weary* (2)

deinde, also spelled dein, adv., *then, next* (8, 13, 59B)

dēleō, dēlēre, dēlēvī, dēlētus, *to destroy* (38)

dēnārius, -ī, m., *denarius (silver coin)* (31)

dēnique, adv., *finally, at last*

dēnsus, -a, -um, *dense, thick* (68D)

dēpositum, -ī, n., *deposit* (of money or valuables for safekeeping) (65A)

dēserō, dēserere, dēseruī, dēsertus, *to desert, abandon* (68C)

dēsīderō, -āre, -āvī, -ātus, *to long for, miss* (26)

dēsignō, -āre, -āvī, -ātus, *to mark, indicate* (62C)

dēsinō, dēsinere, dēsiī, dēsitus, *to stop, cease from* (65A)

dēsum, dēesse, dēfuī, dēfutūrus + dat., irreg., *to be lacking, wanting* (61B, 62)

dētrīmentum, -ī, n., *damage, harm* (63A)

deus, -ī, nom. pl., dī, m., *god* (35, 39)

dēvorō, -āre, -āvī, -ātus, *to devour, swallow* (20)

dexter, dextra, dextrum, *right* (the direction) (61A)

dextra, -ae, f., *right hand* (53)

dīcō, dīcere, dīxī, dictus, *to say, tell* (20, 21)

diēs, diēī, m., *day* (5, 13, 25)

difficilis, -is, -e, *difficult* (34)

diffīdō, diffīdere, diffīsus sum + dat., *not to trust* (62)

diffundō, diffundere, diffūdī, diffūsus, *to spread out, extend* (64B)

dignitās, dignitātis, f., *good name, reputation* (60D)

dignus, -a, -um + abl., *worthy (of), deserving* (64A)

dīligenter, adv., *carefully, attentively* (19)

dīligō, dīligere, dīlēxī, dīlēctus, *to love, have special regard for* (54, 67B)

dīmicō, -āre, -āvī, -ātūrus, *to fight, struggle* (55B)

dīmittō, dīmittere, dīmīsī, dīmissus, *to send away, let go* (51)

dīripiō, dīripere, dīripuī, dīreptus, *to lay waste, plunder, ransack* (55C)

discēdō, discēdere, discessī, discessūrus, *to go away, depart, leave* (9, 22)

discrīmen, discrīminis, n., *crisis, danger* (68A)

diū, adv., *for a long time* (15, 35)

diūtius, adv., *longer*

dīvidō, dīvidere, dīvīsī, dīvīsus, *to divide, separate* (56A)

dīvitiae, -ārum, f. pl., *wealth, riches* (48)

dīvus, -a, -um, *divine, deified* (57B)

dō, dare, dedī, datus, *to give* (21)

doceō, docēre, docuī, doctus, *to teach* (6, 21)

doleō, -ēre, -uī, -itūrus, *to be sad, grieve* (18, 49)

dolor, dolōris, m., *pain, grief, sadness* (38)

dominātiō, dominātiōnis, f., *control, power, mastery* (63A)

dominus, -ī, m., *master, overlord* (11)

domus, -ūs, f., *home* (23, 25, 39)

dōnum, -ī, n., *gift* (46)

dormiō, -īre, -īvī, -ītūrus, *to sleep* (4)

dubitō, -āre, -āvī, -ātus, *to doubt, hesitate* (60D)

dūcō, dūcere, dūxī, ductus, *to lead* (7, 19, 20)

dum, conj., *while, as long as* (1)

duo, duae, duo, *two* (15, 38)

dūrus, -a, -um, *hard, tough, cruel* (62A)

dux, ducis, m., *leader, general* (55B)

E

ē, ex, prep. + abl., *from, out of* (2, 5, 9)

ecce, interj., *look, look at* (1)

ēdūcō, ēdūcere, ēdūxī, ēductus, *to lead out, withdraw* (46)

effugiō, effugere, effūgī, *to flee, run away, escape* (11, 21, 29)

ego, *I* (5, 27)

ēgredior, ēgredī, ēgressus sum, *to go out* (37, 39)

ēiciō, ēicere, ēiēcī, ēiectus, *to throw out* (30)

emō, emere, ēmī, ēmptus, *to buy* (21, 31)

ēmoveō, ēmovēre, ēmōvī, ēmōtus, *to move (from)* (68C)

enim, conj., *for, because* (20)

eō, adv., *there, to that place* (23)

eō, īre, iī or **īvī, itūrus,** irreg., *to go* (7, 17, 19, 20, 21)

epistula, -ae, f., *letter* (7)

epulum, -ī, n., *banquet, feast* (66B)

eques, equitis, m., *knight, horseman, member of the equestrian order* (55C)

equidem, adv., *certainly, surely* (60B)

equitātus, -ūs, m., *cavalry* (61B)

equus, -ī, m., *horse* (10)

ergō, conj., *therefore, so* (55D)

ēripiō, ēripere, ēripuī, ēreptus, *to snatch away, rescue* (29)

error, errōris, m., *mistake, crime* (65A)

ērudītus, -a, -um, *learned, scholarly* (37)

et, conj., *and, also, too* (1)

etiam, adv., *also, even* (1, 6, 13)

    etiam sī, *even if, although* (37, 58)

etsī, conj., *even if, although* (60D)

ēvenit, ēvenīre, ēvēnit, *it happens, it turns out* (55D)

ēventus, -ūs, m., *outcome, result* (62A)

exaudiō, -īre, -īvī, -ītus, *to hear* (62A)

excēdō, excēdere, excessī, excessūrus, *to withdraw, depart* (54, 61C)

excīdō, excīdere, excīdī, excīsus, *to cut out, exterminate* (63C)

excipiō, excipere, excēpī, exceptus, *to take away, receive, withstand* (5, 16, 22)

excitō, -āre, -āvī, -ātus, *to rouse, wake up* (8)

exemplar, exemplāris, n., *copy* (66A)

exemplum, -ī, n., *example, precedent* (65B)

exeō, exīre, exiī or **exīvī, exitūrus,** irreg., *to go out, leave* (5, 23, 44)

exercitus, -ūs, m., *army* (55B)

exīstimō -āre, -āvī, -ātus, *to think, judge* (62B)

exitus, -ūs, m., *exit* (68C)

expellō, expellere, expulī, expulsus, *to drive out, expel* (39)

explicō, -āre, -āvī, -ātus, *to explain* (19)

exsilium, -ī, n., *exile* (59E)

exspectō, -āre, -āvī, -ātus, *to look out for, wait for* (15)

exstinguō, exstinguere, exstīnxī, exstīnctus, *to put out, exstinguish* (30)

externus, -a, -um, *foreign, outside* (63C)

extrahō, extrahere, extrāxī, extractus, *to drag out, drag away* (14, 21)

F

fābula, -ae, f., *story* (20)

facile, adv., *easily* (35)

facinus, facinoris, n., *villainy, crime, foul deed* (59A)

faciō, facere, fēcī, factus, *to make, do* (1, 23)

    iter facere, *to make a journey, travel* (13)

factiō, factiōnis, f., *gang, political faction* (27, 63A)

factum, -ī, n., *deed, act* (58C)

fallō, fallere, fefellī, falsus, *to deceive, mislead, betray* (62A)

fāma, -ae, f., *fame* (X)

famēs, famis, f., *hunger, starvation, famine* (56B)

familia, -ae, f., *family, household* (51)

familiāris, familiāris, gen. pl., **familiārium,** m./f., *close friend* (54)

fateor, fatērī, fassus sum, *to admit, confess* (65A)

faveō, favēre, fāvī, fautūrus + dat., *to give favor (to), favor, support* (27, 62)

fēlīx, fēlīcis, *lucky, happy, fortunate* (34)

    fēlīciter, adv., *happily* (35)

fēmina, -ae, f., *woman* (3)

ferē, adv., *almost, approximately* (46)

ferō, ferre, tulī, lātus, irreg., *to bring, carry, bear* (5, 12, 17, 21)

festīnō, -āre, -āvī, -ātūrus, *to hurry* (9)

fēstus, -a, -um, *pertaining to a holiday, festive* (61)

fidēlis, -is, -e, *faithful, loyal* (31, 34)

fidēs, fideī, f., *faith, reliability, trust, loyalty* (52)

fidūcia, -ae, f., *confidence* (62C)

fīgō, fīgere, fīxī, fīxus, *to fasten, attach* (63B)

fīlia, -ae, f., *daughter* (11)

fīlius, -ī, m., *son* (11)

fīniō, -īre, -īvī, -ītus, *to finish* (21)

fīnis, fīnis, gen pl., **fīnium,** m., *end, limit, boundary,* pl., *territory* (29)

fīnitimus, -a, -um, *neighboring, having the same boundary* (63C)

fīō, fierī, factus sum, irreg., *to become, be made, happen* (34)

flagrō, -āre, -āvī, -ātus, *to burn, blaze* (58C)

flāmen, flāminis, m., *priest* (58A)

flamma, -ae, f., *flame, fire* (29)

flectō, flectere, flexī, flexus *to bend, change* (68B)

fleō, flēre, flēvī, flētus, *to weep, cry* (53)

flūmen, flūminis, n., *river*

fore, = **futūrus esse** (see **sum**) (55)

flōreō, flōrēre, flōruī, *to flourish, prosper* (57A)

fōrma, -ae, f., *shape, form; rule, formula* (65B)

forte, adv., *by chance* (33)

fortis, -is, -e, *brave, strong* (18)

    fortiter, adv., *bravely* (35)

fortitūdō, fortitūdinis, f., *courage* (64B)

fortūna, -ae, f., *fortune, good luck, prosperity* (54, 55B)

forum, -ī, n., *forum* (center of a Roman town) (25)

frangō, frangere, frēgī, frāctus, *to break, shatter, wreck* (a ship) (54)

frāter, frātris, m., *brother* (11)

frequēns, frequentis, *closely packed, crowded, thronged* (68A)

    frequenter, adv., *frequently*

frīgidus, -a, -um, *cool, cold* (5)

frūgālitās, frūgālitātis, f., *frugality, economy* (66C)

frūmentārius, -a, -um, *pertaining to grain* (62C)

fruor, fruī, frūctus sum + abl., *to enjoy, have benefit of* (61)

fuga, -ae, f., *flight, escape* (61C)

fugiō, fugere, fūgī, fugitūrus, *to flee, run away* (18, 25)

fugitīvus, -ī, m., *fugitive, deserter*

fugō, -āre, -āvī, -ātus, *to put to flight* (55B)

fūmus, -ī, m., *smoke* (29)

funditor, funditōris, m., *slinger*

fundō, fundere, fūdī, fūsus, *to pour out, shed* (55C)

fundus, -ī, m., *farm, estate* (39)

fungor, fungī, fūnctus sum + abl., *to perform, discharge* (61)

fūnus, fūneris, n., *funeral* (53)

furor, furōris, m., *frenzy, madness* (48)

fūrtum, -ī, n., *theft, fraud* (65A)

G

Gallia, -ae, f., *Gaul* (modern France and Belgium) (55A)

gaudeō, gaudēre, gāvīsus sum, *to be glad, rejoice* (14, 40)

gēns, gentis, gen. pl., **gentium,** f., *family, clan, race* (50, 54)

genus, generis, n., *type, class, race, family* (39, 55A)

gerō, gerere, gessī, gestus, *to carry on, perform, do; to wear* (clothing) (10, 63C)

    rēs gestae, *deeds, accomplishments* (63)

gladiātor, gladiātōris, m., *gladiator, sword-fighter* (47)

gladius, -ī, m., *sword* (21, 26)

glōria, -ae, f., *fame, glory* (27)

grandis, -is, -e, *great, huge, considerable* (56A)

grātia, -ae, f., *favor, influence* (26, 60D)

    grātiā + gen., *for the sake of* (58)

    grātiās agere + dat., *to thank* (26, 51)

grātulor, -ārī, -ātus sum + dat., *to congratulate* (50)

gravis, -is, -e, *heavy, serious* (35)

gubernō, -āre, -āvī, -ātus, *to govern, rule* (58)

gustō, -āre, *to taste, enjoy* (66A)

H

habeō, -ēre, -uī, -itus, *to have, hold* (10, 20, 26)

habitō, -āre, -āvī, -ātus, *to live, dwell* (1)

hērēs, hērēdis, m., *heir* (55D)

hetaeria, -ae, f., *political club, association* (65A)

hīc, adv., *here* (9, 13, 54)

hic, haec, hoc, *this,* pl., *these* (18, 19, 20, 25, 26, 31)

hilaris, -is, -e, *cheerful* (54)

hodiē, adv., *today* (2, 13)

homō, hominis, m., *man, fellow* (18)

honor, honōris, m., *honor, political office* (IX, 55D)

honōrō, -āre, -āvī, -ātus, *to honor* (55D)

hōra, -ae, f., *hour* (9)

hortor, -ārī, -ātus sum, *to encourage, urge* (51, 53)

hospes, hospitis, m., *guest, host* (16)

hospitium, -ī, n., *lodging, accomodation* (66A)

hostis, hostis, gen. pl., **hostium,** m., *enemy*

hūc, adv., *here, to this place* (36)

    hūc illūc, adv., *here and there, this way and that* (23)

hūmānus, -a, -um, *human* (48)

I

iam, adv., *now, already* (1, 8, 13)

iānua, -ae, f., *door* (9)

ibi, adv., *there, in that place* (5, 13)

īdem, eadem, idem, *the same* (3, 31)

ideō, adv., *for this reason, therefore* (66A)

idōneus, -a, -um + dat., *fit, suitable* (58)

igitur, conj., *therefore* (4)

ignis, ignis, gen. pl., **ignium,** m., *fire* (32)

ignōrō, -āre, -āvī, -ātus, *to be ignorant of, be unaware of* (40)

ignōscō, ignōscere, ignōvī, ignōtus + dat., *to pardon, forgive, excuse* (60D, 62)

ille, illa, illud, *that,* pl., *those* (11, 15, 16, 20, 22, 25, 26, 31)

illūc, adv., *there, to that place* (23)

imāgō, imāginis, f., *likeness, image* (54)

immānis, -is, -e, *huge, immense, extensive* (49)

immittō, immittere, immīsī, immissus, *to send in, attack* (49)

immortālis, -is, -e, *immortal* (27)

impēnsa, -ae, f., *expense, cost* (63A)

imperātor, imperātōris, m., *commander; emperor* (49, 60C)

imperium, -ī, n., *power, right to command soldiers; empire* (56B)

imperō, -āre, -āvī, -ātus + dat., *to order; to impose, levy something* (acc.) *upon someone* (dat.) (51, 62)

impetrō, -āre, -āvī, -ātus, *to obtain, secure by request* (65B)

impetus, -ūs, m., *attack* (49)

impōnō, impōnere, imposuī, impositus, *to place something* (acc.) *upon something* (dat.) (54, 62)

in, prep. + abl., *in, on, among* (1, 9, 28)

in, prep. + acc., *into, toward, against* (3, 9)

incendium, -ī, n., *fire* (30)

incendō, incendere, incendī, incēnsus, *to burn, set on fire* (38)

incidō, incidere, incidī, incāsūrus, *to fall, fall into, occur, turn up* (54, 65A, 68B)

incipiō, incipere, incēpī, inceptus, *to begin, undertake* (49)

incitō, -āre, -āvī, -ātus, *to spur on, arouse, stir up* (10)

incrēscō, incrēscere, incrēvī, incrētūrus, *to grow, increase* (67A)

inde, adv., *from there, then, in consequence of that* (38, 40)

index, indicis, m., *sign, proof; informer, spy* (65A)

indicō, -āre, -āvī, -ātus, *to point out, make known* (68)

indulgentia, -ae, f., *indulgence, kindness* (66A)

inermis, -is, -e, *unarmed* (61C)

īnferō, īnferre, intulī, illātus, irreg., *to bring in, carry on, inflict on* (39, 55A)

īnfestus, -a, -um, *hostile, prepared for attack* (61B)

īnfīnītus, -a, -um, *countless* (56A)

īnflexibilis, -is, -e, *inflexible, stubborn* (65A)

ingēns, ingentis, *huge, big, long* (22)

ingredior, ingredī, ingressus sum, *to go in, go against, attack* (37)

initium -ī, n., *beginning* (57A)

iniūria, -ae, f., *injury, injustice, wrong* (55B)

inquit, *(he / she) says, said* (7)

īnscius, -a, -um, *not knowing, ignorant* (45)

īnscrīptiō, īnscrīptiōnis, f., *inscription* (63B)

īnsidiae, -ārum, f. pl., *ambush, treachery* (59A)

īnsidiātor, īnsidiātōris, m., *someone in ambush, waylayer* (59B)

īnsigne, īnsignis, gen. pl., **īnsignium**, n., *badge, insignia* (62C)

īnsolenter, adv., *arrogantly* (55D)

īnspiciō, īnspicere, īnspexī, īnspectus, *to look at, examine* (21)

īnstituō, īnstituere, īnstituī, īnstitūtus, *to establish, set up, organize* (61C)

īnstō, īnstāre, īnstitī, *to press on, attack* (61B)

integer, integra, integrum, *vigorous, sound, intact* (62A)

intellegō, intellegere, intellēxī, intellēctus, *to understand, realize* (49)

inter, prep. + acc., *between, among* (33)

interclūdō, interclūdere, interclūsī, interclūsus, *to shut off, cut off* (60A)

intereā, adv., *meanwhile* (10, 13)

interficiō, interficere, interfēcī, interfectus, *to kill* (55A)

interim, adv., *meanwhile* (59A)

intermittō, intermittere, intermīsī, intermissus, *to separate, interrupt* (61B)

interrogō, -āre, -āvī, -ātus, *to ask, question* (53)

intrā, prep. + acc., *inside, within* (22)

intueor, intuērī, intuitus sum, *to gaze at, look at, contemplate* (55C)

inveniō, invenīre, invēnī, inventus, *to come upon, find, discover* (12, 21)

invicem, adv., *back and forth, in turn* (65A)

invictus, -a, -um, *unconquered* (57A)

invidia, -ae, f., *hatred, ill-will* (58C)

invītō, -āre, -āvī, -ātus, *to invite* (28, 32, 51)

ipse, ipsa, ipsum, *himself, herself, itself*, pl., *themselves* (6, 10, 29, 31)

irrumpō, irrumpere, irrūpī, irruptus, *to break in*

is, ea, id, *he, she it; this, that* (27, 31)

iste, ista, istud, *that* (used to show contempt) (60B)

ita, adv., *thus, so, in this way, in such a way* (3, 13, 21, 50)

itaque, adv., *and so, therefore* (16)

item, adv., *likewise, also* (58C)

iter, itineris, n., *journey, route, road* (10, 13, 15)
    iter facere, *to make a journey, travel* (13)

iterum, adv., *again, a second time* (8, 13)

iubeō, iubēre, iussī, iussus, *to order* (10, 19, 21)

iūcundus, -a, -um, *pleasant* (54)

iūdex, iūdicis, m., *judge, juror; governor* (56B)

iūdicium, -ī, n., *judgment* (63A)

iūdicō, -āre, -āvī, -ātus, *to judge, ascertain* (55D)
iungō, iungere, iūnxī, iūnctus, *to join, attach*
iūrō, -āre, -āvī, -ātus, *to swear an oath* (63A)
iussū, *by the order* (59E)
iūstitia, -ae, f., *justice* (63B)
iūstus, -a, -um, *fair, just, well-deserved* (56B)
iuvō, iuvāre, iūvī, iūtus, *to help* (68B)
    iuvat, impersonal idiom, *it is helpful, it is pleasant* (64)

K

Kalendae, -ārum, f. pl., *the Kalends* (first day in the month) (36)

L

lābor, lābī, lāpsus sum, *to slip, fall; fall away, fail* (44, 53)
labor, labōris, m., *work, labor, struggle* (24, 48)
labōrō, -āre, -āvī, -ātus, *to work; suffer, be in distress* (3)
lacrima, -ae, f., *tear, weeping* (45)
lacrimō, -āre, -āvī, -ātus, *to weep, cry* (9)
laedō, laedere, laesī, laesus, *to harm, injure* (46)
laetus, -a, -um, *happy, glad* (1)
lamentātiō, lamentātiōnis, f., *lamentation, weeping* (58C)
lapis, lapidis, m., *stone, rock* (25)
lateō, -ēre, -uī, *to lie in hiding, hide* (49)
latrōcinium, -ī, n., *robbery* (65A)
lātus, see **ferō**
lātus, -a, -um, *wide, broad, extensive* (68C)
latus, lateris, n., *side, flank* (61B)
laudō, -āre, -āvī, -ātus, *to praise* (18)
lavō, lavāre, lāvī, lautus or **lōtus,** *to wash, bathe* (20, 54)
lectīca, -ae, f., *litter* (23)
lectus, -ī, m., *bed, couch, litter, bier* (19)
lēgātus, -ī, m., *envoy, ambassador; second-in-command of an army* (18)
legiō, legiōnis, f., *legion* (a military unit) (55A)
legō, legere, lēgī, lēctus, *to read* (1, 24)
levis, -is, -e, *light* (54)
lēx, lēgis, f., *law*
libenter, adv., *gladly* (36)
liber, librī, m., *book* (24)
līber, lībera, līberum, *free* (66A)
līberō, -āre, -āvī, -ātus, *to set free* (49)
lībertās, lībertātis, f., *freedom* (21, 55D)

lībertus, -ī, m., *freedman, ex-slave* (29)
librārius, -ī, m., *secretary, clerk* (58C)
licet, licēre, licuit + dat., *it is allowed* (20, 24, 62, 64)
litterae, -ārum, f. pl., *letter, epistle; literature* (39)
lītus, lītoris, n., *shore* (39)
locus, -ī, m., n. in pl., *place* (33)
longus, -a, -um, *long* (15)
    longē, adv., *far, far away* (35)
    longē lātēque, adv., *far and wide*
lūmen, lūminis, n., *light, lamp* (68D)
lūx, lūcis, f., *light, daylight* (21)
lūxuria, -ae, f., *luxury* (62C)

M

magis, adv., *more, rather* (34, 35)
magistrātus, -ūs, m., *official, magistrate; office, magistracy* (46)
magnitūdō, magnitūdinis, f., *size, large size*
magnopere, adv., *greatly, seriously* (31, 35)
magnus, -a, -um, *big, great, large* (4, 34)
maior, maior, maius, gen., **maiōris,** *bigger* (34)
    maiōrēs, maiōrum, m. pl., *ancestors* (54, 63C)
mālō, mālle, māluī, *to prefer* (47)
malus, -a, -um, *bad, evil* (21, 34)
    malum, -ī, n., *bad thing, evil, disaster* (68A)
mandātum, -ī, n., *order, instruction* (22)
mandō, -āre, -āvī, -ātus, *to entrust, hand over* (67A)
maneō, manēre, mānsī, mānsūrus, *to remain, stay, wait* (9, 20, 23)
manifestus, -a, -um, *clear, evident* (65B)
manus, -ūs., f., *hand* (18, 25)
    manū mittere, *to send from one's power, set free, manumit* (66A)
mare, maris, gen. pl., **marium,** n., *sea* (38)
marītus, -ī, m., *husband* (53)
māter, mātris, f., *mother* (6, 11)
mātrōna, -ae, f., *married woman* (52)
maximus, -a, -um, *biggest, greatest, largest* (23, 24)
    maximē, adv., *most, very much, very* (35, 35)
medius, -a, -um, *mid-, middle of* (20)
mehercule or **meherculēs,** *by Hercules* (18)
melior, melior, melius, gen. **meliōris,** *better* (19, 34)
meminī, meminisse (perfect system only) + gen., *to be mindful of, remember* (61)
memoria, -ae, f., *memory* (30)
mēnsa, -ae, f., *table* (29)

mēnsis, mēnsis, m., *month* (38)

mereō, merēre, meruī, meritus, sometimes deponent, *to deserve, earn* (60D)

merīdiēs, -ēī, m., *noon, midday* (46)

meritō, adv., *deservedly* (64B)

meritum, -ī, n., *good deed, merit, honor* (54, 63B)

metuō, metuere, metuī, metūtus, *to fear, be afraid of* (60A)

metus, -ūs, m., *fear* (26, 60)

meus, -a, -um, *my, mine* (7)

mī, masc. vocative sing. of **meus**

mī, = **mihi** (see **ego**)

mīles, mīlitis, m., *soldier* (20)

mīlitāris, -is, -e, *military* (61A)

mīlle, *a thousand* (15, 38)

　mīlia, mīlium, n. pl., *thousands* (48)

　mīlle passūs, *a thousand paces, a mile*

　mīlia passuum, *miles* (55A)

Milōniānus, -ī, m., *follower of Milo* (58B)

ministra, -ae, f., *attendant* (65A)

minor, -ārī, -ātus sum, *to threaten* (65A)

minor, minor, minus, gen., **minōris**, *smaller, lesser* (34)

mīror, -ārī, -ātus sum, *to wonder, be amazed at* (49)

misceō, miscēre, miscuī, mixtus, *to mix* (34)

miser, misera, miserum, *unhappy, miserable, wretched* (9)

misereor, -ērī, -itus sum + gen., *to pity, feel sorry for* (61)

　miseret, miserēre, miseruit, *it makes one* (acc.) *feel sorry for something* (gen.) (64)

mittō, mittere, mīsī, missus, *to send, let go* (9, 20)

　manū mittere, *to send from one's power, set free, manumit* (66A)

moderātus, -a, -um, *restrained, controlled* (57A)

modestus, -a, -um, *modest* (66d)

modo, adv., *only; provided that* (18, 60A)

modus, -ī, m., *way, method* (34)

molestus, -a, -um, *troublesome, annoying* (4)

moneō, -ēre, -uī, -itus, *to advise, warn* (39, 51)

mōns, montis, gen. pl., **montium**, m., *mountain, hill* (24)

monumentum -ī, n., *monument, tomb* (54)

mora, -ae, f., *delay* (68C)

morbus, -ī, m., *disease, illness* (54)

morior, morī, mortuus sum, *to die* (39, 45)

moror, morārī, morātus sum, *to delay, remain, stay* (36, 37)

mors, mortis, gen. pl., **mortium**, f., *death* (21)

mortuus, -a, -um, *dead* (16)

mōs, mōris, m., *custom, habit* (52)

moveō, movēre, mōvī, mōtus, *to move, remove* (14, 24)

mox, adv., *soon* (6, 13)

multitūdō, multitūdinis, f., *crowd, mob* (23)

multus, -a, -um, *much*; pl., *many* (31, 34)

　multō, adv., *greatly, by much, very* (47)

mūnicipium, -ī, n., *town* (58A)

mūnus, mūneris, n., *gift; duty, obligation; gladiatorial show* (47, 54, 57B)

mūrus, -ī, m, *wall* (23)

mūtō, -āre, -āvī, -ātus, *to change, transform* (55B)

N

nam, conj., *for* (8)

nancīscor, nancīscī, nactus sum, *to find, gain possession of, acquire, get* (62C)

nāscor, nāscī, nātus sum, *to be born* (39)

nātūra, -ae, f., *nature* (IX)

　nātūrā, *by nature, naturally* (68D)

nāvālis, -is, -e, *naval* (56B)

nāvigō, -āre, -āvī, -ātus, *to sail* (38)

nāvis, nāvis, gen. pl., **nāvium**, f., *ship* (38)

-ne (indicates a question) (3)

nē, conj. + subjunctive, *not to, so that . . . not, to prevent, to avoid* (51, 53, 57, 66); introducing clause of fearing, *that* (60)

nē . . . quidem, adv., *not even* (34)

nec, conj., *and . . . not, but . . . not, nor* (45)

necessārius, -a, -um, *necessary* (59A)

necesse, adv. or indecl. adj., *necessary* (6, 13, 52, 64)

necessitās, necessitātis, f., *necessity* (67A)

necō, -āre, -āvī, -ātus, *to kill* (20)

negō, -āre, -āvī, -ātus, *to say no, deny, refuse* (59)

nēmō, nēminis, m./f., *no one* (9)

nepōs, nepōtis, m., *grandson, nephew* (55D)

Neptūnus, -ī, m., *Neptune* (god of the sea) (66C)

neque, conj., *and . . . not* (6)

　neque . . . neque, *neither . . . nor* (5)

nesciō, -īre, -īvī, -ītus, *to be ignorant, not to know* (9)

niger, nigra, nigrum, *black* (33)

nihil, *nothing* (3)

nihilō amplius, adv., *nothing more* (63B)

nisi, conj., *unless, if . . not, except* (18, 26, 67)

nōbilis, -is, -e, *of noble birth, known* (50)

noceō, -ēre, -uī, -itūrus + dat., *to do harm (to), harm* (26, 62)

nocturnus, -a, -um, *occurring at night* (22)

nōlō, nōlle, nōluī, irreg., *to be unwilling, not to wish, refuse* (5, 17, 21)

    nōlī / nōlīte + infin., *don't . . . !* (9, 66)

nōmen, nōminis, n., *name* (1, 15)

nōminō, -āre, -āvī, -ātus, *to name, call by name, speak of* (54)

nōn, adv., *not, no* (2, 13)

nōndum, adv., *not yet* (6, 13)

nōnnūllī, -ae, -a, *some, several* (51)

nōnus, -a, -um, *ninth* (16, 38, 58A)

nōs, *we, us* (8, 27)

nōscō, nōscere, nōvī, nōtus, *to find out, get to know, ascertain* (66D)

noster, nostra, nostrum, *our* (14, 27)

    nostrī, nostrōrum, m. pl., *our (men), our (soldiers)*

nōtus, -a, -um, *known, well-known* (31)

novem, *nine* (15, 38)

novus, -a, -um, *new* (16)

nox, noctis, gen. pl., **noctium**, f., *night* (11)

nūbō, nūbere, nūpsī, nūptūrus + dat., *to marry* (62)

nūdus, -a, -um, *naked, bare* (58C)

nūllus, -a, -um, *no, none* (9)

num, adv., *surely . . . not . . . ?* (introduces a question that expects the answer "no") (46)

nūmen, nūminis, n., *divine power, divinity, god* (65A)

nummus, -ī, m., *coin* (66B)

numquam, adv., *never* (20)

nunc, adv., *now* (6, 13)

nusquam, adv., *nowhere* (39)

nūtō, -āre, -āvī, -ātūrus, *to nod, shake, totter* (67B)

O

ob, prep. + acc., *on account of, because of* (39, 64B)

obeō, obīre, obiī or **obīvī, obitūrus**, irreg., *to go to, appear at; to die* (59A, 64B)

obiciō, obicere, obiēcī, obiectus, *to throw in one's face, taunt* (62C)

oblīvīscor, oblīvīscī, oblītus sum + gen., *to forget* (60, 62)

obsecrō, -āre, -āvī, -ātus, *to beseech, beg* (40, 51)

observō, -āre, -āvī, -ātus, *to watch, pay attention to, obey* (6, 50)

obses, obsidis, m., *hostage* (55A)

obtineō, obtinēre, obtinuī, obtentus, *to hold, possess* (57A)

obviam, adv., *in the way, on the way* (59B)

occīdō, occīdere, occīdī, occīsus, *to kill* (45)

occupō, -āre, -āvī, -ātus, *to seize, take over* (56A)

occurrō, occurrere, occurrī, occursūrus + dat., *to meet* (24, 62)

octō, *eight* (15, 38)

oculus, -ī, m., *eye* (26)

odor, odōris, m., *smell, odor* (68D)

officium, -ī, n., *duty, job* (51)

ōlim, adv., *once (upon a time)* (18)

omnīnō, adv., *altogether* (63C)

omnis, -is, -e, *all, the whole, every, each* (6, 18)

opera, -ae, f., *work, task, undertaking*

    operam dare, *to make effort, pay attention*

operō, -āre, -āvī, -ātus, *to operate*

opīniō, opīniōnis, f., *opinion, supposition* (62C)

oportet, oportēre, oportuit, *it is fitting; ought* (50, 52, 64)

oppidum, -ī, n., *town, stronghold* (39)

opprimō, opprimere, oppressī, oppressus, *to overwhelm* (30)

oppugnō, -āre, -āvī, -ātus, *to attack, storm* (62B)

ops, opis, f., *power, aid, help* (60C)

optō, -āre, -āvī, -ātus, *to wish* (54)

opus, operis, n., *work, effort* (63D)

ōrātiō, ōrātiōnis, f., *oration, speech* (26, 59)

    ōrātiōnem habēre, idiom, *to deliver a speech* (26)

ōrātor, ōrātōris, m., *orator, speaker* (22)

orbis, orbis, gen. pl., **orbium**, m., *circle*

    orbis terrārum, idiom, *the world* (55C)

ōrdō, ōrdinis, m., *order, rank, class* (61B)

orior, orīrī, ortus sum, *to rise, arise, come or derive from* (45, 68A)

ōrō, -āre, -āvī, -ātus, *to beg, ask* (51)

os, ossis, n., *bone* (54)

ostendō, ostendere, ostendī, ostentus, *to show, point out* (48)

P

paene, adv., *almost* (30)

paenitet, paenitēre, paenituit, *it causes one (acc.) to regret something (gen.), it makes one (acc.) be sorry for something (gen.)* (64)

parcō, parcere, pepercī + dat., *to spare* (49, 62)

parēns, parentis, m./f., *parent* (11)

pāreō, pārēre, pāruī, pāritūrus + dat., *to obey* (39, 62)

pariō, parere, peperī, partus, *to bear, give birth to* (63C)

parō, -āre, -āvī, -ātus, *to prepare* (5, 20)

pars, partis, gen. pl., **partium**, f., *part, direction;* pl., *faction* (13)

partim, adv., *partly, some* (59C)

parvus, -a, -um, *small, little* (30, 34)

pateō, patēre, patuī, *to be open, accessible* (55A)

pater, patris, m., *father* (6, 11)

paternus, -a, -um, *inherited from one's father, belonging to one's family, ancestral* (66A)

patria, -ae, f., *country, native land* (55A)

paucī, -ae, -a, *few* (34)

paulātim, adv., *gradually, little by little* (34)

paulisper, adv., *for a short time* (20)

paulum, adv., *a little* (35)

pāx, pācis, f., *peace* (63C)

pedes, peditis, m., *foot-soldier, infantryman* (55C)

pellō, pellere, pepulī, pulsus, *to drive away, dislodge* (62A)

penitus, adv., *thoroughly, completely* (57A)

per, prep. + acc., *through, along* (6, 9)

perdūcō, perdūcere, perdūxī, perductus, *to bring through, bring to* (66C)

pereō, perīre, periī, peritūrus, irreg., *to die, perish* (61)

perfungor, perfungī, perfūnctus sum + abl., *to carry out, complete* (61)

perīculōsus, -a, -um, *dangerous* (17)

perīculum, -ī, n., *danger* (14, 15)

perītus, -a, -um + gen., *skilled, experienced (in)* (61B)

permaneō, permanēre, permansī, permansūrus, *to remain, stay* (68D)

perpetuus, -a, -um, *continuous, complete, entire* (60C)

persequor, persequī, persecūtus sum, *to follow, pursue* (55D)

persuādeō, persuādēre, persuāsī, persuāsus, *to make something* (acc.) *agreeable to someone* (dat.), *to persuade someone of something; to persuade someone* (dat.) (36, 51, 62)

perterritus, -a, -um, *frightened* (5)

pertineō, -ēre, -uī, *to extend to, reach* (62B)

perturbātus, -a, -um, *confused, upset* (50)

perveniō, pervenīre, pervēnī, perventūrus, *to come through to, arrive at, reach* (25)

pervigilō, -āre, -āvī, -ātūrus, *to stay awake all night* (68C)

pēs, pedis, m., *foot* (13)

petō, petere, petīvī, petītus, *to look for, seek, head for, aim at, attack* (5, 21)

philosophus, -ī, m., *philosopher* (66B)

pietās, pietātis, f., *devotion* (to duty) (63B)

pīlum, -ī, n., *spear, javelin* (61B)

pius, -a, -um, *dutiful* (66B)

placeō, -ēre, -uī + dat., *to please* (34, 52, 62, 64)

    placuit, *it was decided* (52, 64)

plēbs, plēbis, f., *plebeians, common people* (58A)

plēnus, -a, -um, *full* (11)

plērīque, plēraeque, plēraque, *very many* (62B)

plūs, plūris, n., *more* (34)

poena, -ae, f., *punishment, penalty* (40)

pōnō, pōnere, posuī, positus, *to put, place* (10, 21)

pōns, pontis, gen. pl., **pontium**, m., *bridge* (23)

populus, -ī, m., *people* (47)

porta, -ae, f., *gateway* (11)

poscō, poscere, poposcī, *to demand, ask for* (34)

possessiō, possessiōnis, f., *possession*

possum, posse, potuī, irreg., *to be able; can* (5, 14, 21)

post, prep. + acc., *after* (20)

posteā, adv., *afterward* (33)

posterus, -a, -um, *next, following* (52)

    posterī, -ōrum, m. pl., *posterity, future generations*

postis, postis, gen. pl., **postium**, m., *door-post* (25)

postquam, conj., *after* (20)

postrēmus, -a, -um, *last*

    postrēmō, adv., *finally, at last, in the end* (46)

potēns, potentis, *powerful*

potestās, potestātis, f., *power, opportunity, ability* (59)

potior, potīrī, potītus sum + gen. or abl., *to get possession of, get control of, obtain* (55D, 61, 62)

praecipiō, praecipere, praecēpī, praeceptus + dat., *to instruct, order* (51, 62)

praecipuus, -a, -um, *notable, outstanding, remarkable* (55D)

praedīcō, praedīcere, praedīxī, praedictus, *to set forth, relate* (61A)

praedō, praedōnis, m., *robber, thief* (26)

praeeō, praeīre, praeiī, irreg., *to go before, lead the way* (65A)

praeferō, praeferre, praetulī, praelātus, irreg., *to carry in front, give precedence to, prefer* (37)

praeficiō, praeficere, praefēcī, praefectus, *to place someone* (acc.) *in charge of something* (dat.) (62)

praemittō, praemittere, praemīsī, praemissus, *to send ahead* (60D)

praepōnō, praepōnere, praeposuī, praepositus, *to put someone* (acc.) *in charge of something* (dat.) (62)

praesēns, praesentis, *present* (59D)

praesentia, -ae, f., *presence* (60A)

praesidium, -ī, n., *defense, protection* (61C)

praestō, praestāre, praestitī, praestitus, *to stand out, surpass; to bestow* (55D)

praesum, praeesse, praefuī, praefutūrus, irreg., *to be in charge of something* (dat.) (62)

praeter, prep. + acc., *except* (21, 63D)

praetereā, adv., *besides, too, moreover* (15)

praeteritus, -a, -um, *past, bygone*
  in praeteritum, *in the past, formerly* (65B)

praetermittō, praetermittere, praetermīsī, praetermissus, *to pass over, neglect, omit* (63D)

praetextātus, -a, -um, *wearing the* **toga praetexta** (52)

praetor, praetōris, m., *praetor, judge*

prīdiē, adv., *on the day before* (36)

prīmus, -a, -um, *first* (21, 38)
  prīmō, adv., *first, at first* (40)
  prīmum, adv., *first, at first* (23)
  in prīmīs, *in particular* (60D)

prīmus pīlus, *foremost centurion of a legion* (61A)

prīnceps, prīncipis, m., *leader, leading citizen; emperor* (7)

prīncipātus, -ūs, m., *principate, imperial rule* (57A)

prīstinus, -a, -um, *previous, former* (60C)

priusquam, conj., *before* (63C)

prīvātim, adv., *privately, in private* (64A)

prīvātus, -a, -um, *private, personal* (63A)

prīvignus, -ī, m., *stepson* (57B)

prīvō, -āre, -āvī, -ātus + abl., *to deprive of* (61A)

prō, prep. + abl., *before, on behalf of* (60C)

prōcēdō, prōcēdere, prōcessī, prōcessūrus, *to go forward, come forth* (33)

prōcōnsul, prōcōnsulis, m., *official acting on behalf of a consul, proconsul, governor* (60C)

procul, adv., *in the distance, far off* (15)

prōcurrō, procurrere, pro(cu)currī, procursūrus, *to run forth, rush out* (61A)

prōdō, prōdere, prōdidī, prōditus, *to hand over, betray; to nominate, appoint* (58A)

proelium, -ī, n., *battle* (55A)

proferō, proferre, protulī, prolātus, irreg., *to carry forward, continue* (52)

proficīscor, proficīscī, profectus sum, *to set out* (36, 37)

prohibeō, -ēre, -uī, -itus, *to prohibit, forbid, prevent* (59D)

prōnūntiō, -āre, -āvī, -ātus, *to declare, state* (62A)

prope, adv., *near, nearby* (45)

prope, prep. + acc., *near* (5, 9)

properō, -āre, -āvī, -ātus, *to hurry, hasten* (60D)

propinquus, -ī, m., *relative* (50)

prōpraetor, prōpraetōris, m., *official acting for a praetor, propraetor, governor* (57B)

propter, prep. + acc., *because of* (26)

prosperus, -a, -um, *prosperous, successful, favorable* (64A)

prōsum, prōdesse, prōfuī, irreg. + dat., *to be useful, benefit, help* (60A, 62)

prōtinus, adv., *immediately* (54, 61C)

prōvideō, prōvidēre, prōvīdī, prōvīsus, *to foresee, expect* (63A)

prōvincia, -ae, f., *conquered territory, province* (57B)

proximus, -a, -um, *nearby, nearest, next* (33, 58B)

prūdēns, prūdentis, *wise, sensible* (34)

prūdentia, -ae, f., *good sense, wisdom, discretion, skill* (52)

pūblicē, adv., *publicly* (63B)

pudet, pudēre, puduit, *it causes one* (acc.) *to be ashamed of something* (gen.) (64)

puer, -ī, m., *boy, youth, slave* (3)

pugna, -ae, f., *fight, battle* (48)

pugnō, -āre, -āvī, -ātūrus, *to fight* (48)

pulcher, pulchra, pulchrum, *beautiful, handsome* (28)

pūmex, pūmicis, m., *pumice stone* (68B)

pūniō, -īre, -īvī, -ītus, *to punish* (21)

putō, -āre, -āvī, -ātus, *to think* (46)

Q

quādrāgintā, *forty* (55D)

quaerō, quaerere, quaesīvī, quaesītus, *to seek, look for, ask for* (30)

quam . . . ! adv., *how . . . !, what a . . . !* (13, 29, 36)

quam . . . ? adv., *how . . . ?* (36)

quam, adv., *than, as* (34, 36)
  quam, adv. + superlative adj. or adv., *as . . . as possible* (35, 36)

quamquam, conj., *although* (11)

quamvīs, conj., *although* (65B)

quantus, -a, -um, *how big, how much* (41, 61A)

quārē, adv., *why, for what reason, wherefore, thus* (55D)

quārtus, -a, -um, *fourth* (38)

quasi, adv., *as if, just as, as* (49)

quattuor, *four* (15, 38)

-que, enclitic conj., *and* (36)

quemadmodum, *in what way, as* (66A)

queror, querī, questus sum, *to moan, whine, complain* (62C)

quī, quae, quod, *who, which, that* (1, 3, 14, 28, 29, 36, 65); *after a period or semicolon,* he, she, it, this (44)

quia, conj., *because, since, that* (55B)

quīdam, quaedam, quoddam, *a certain,* pl., *some* (10, 29, 63)

quidem, adv., *indeed* (31)

quiēs, quiētis, f., *rest, sleep* (23)

quiēscō, quiēscere, quiēvī, quiētūrus, *to rest, sleep* (13, 23)

quiētus, -a, -um, *at rest, inactive, peaceful* (62A)

quīn, conj., *(but) that, who . . . not* (60D)

quīnquāgintā, *fifty* (57A)

quīnque, *five* (15, 38)

quis . . . ? quid . . . ? *who . . . ? what . . . ?* (1, 4, 29)

quis, nē (see **aliquis**) (52, 63)

quis, sī (see **aliquis**) (51, 63)

quisquam, quisquam, quidquam (or **quicquam**), *anyone, anything* (63)

quisque, quaeque, quidque or **quicque,** *each, every* (63)

quō . . . ? adv., *where . . . to?* (4)

quō, adv., *there, to that place* (43)

quoad, conj., *until* (59B)

quod, conj., *because;* with verbs of feeling, *that* (1, 11, 13, 29)

quōmodo, adv., *in what way, how* (12)

quondam, adv., *once, formerly* (55C)

quoniam, conj., *since, because* (42)

quoque, adv., *also* (2, 13)

quot, indecl. adj., *as many, how many* (15, 38)

R

raeda, -ae, f., *carriage* (10)

raedārius, -ī, m., *coachman, driver* (10)

recēns, recentis, *fresh* (62A)

recipiō, recipere, recēpī, receptus, *to receive, accept* (54)

recitō, -āre, -āvī, -ātus, *to read aloud, recite* (29)

recognōscō, recognōscere, recognōvī, recognitus, *to recognize* (60C)

rēctus, -a, -um, *right, proper, correct, straight* (35)
  rēctē, adv., *rightly, properly, correctly* (31, 35)

recuperō, -āre, -āvī, -ātus, *to recover, regain* (21, 61A)

recurrō, recurrere, recurrī, recursūrus, *to run back, return* (59C)

reditus, -ūs, m., *return*

reddō, reddere, reddidī, redditus, *to give back, return* (29)

redeō, redīre, rediī or **redīvī, reditūrus,** irreg., *to return, go back* (7, 23)

referō, referre, retulī, relātus, irreg., *to bring back, bring back again* (46, XI)

reficiō, reficere, refēcī, refectus, *to remake, repair, rebuild* (32, 63D)

refugiō, refugere, refūgī, *to turn and run away, flee for safety* (62B)

rēgīna, -ae, f., *queen* (38)

regiō, regiōnis, f., *region* (XVII)

rēgnō, -āre, -āvī, -ātus, *to rule, reign over* (56B)

rēgnum, -ī, n., *kingdom, realm* (32)

regō, regere, rēxī, rēctus, *to rule* (36)

regredior, regredī, regressus sum, *to go back, return* (36)

reiciō, reicere, reiēcī, reiectus, *to throw back, throw off* (59C)

relinquō, relinquere, relīquī, relictus, *to leave behind, abandon* (16, 21)

reliquus, -a, -um, *the rest, the remaining, other* (60A)

remaneō, remanēre, remānsī, *to remain* (56A)

remittō, remittere, remīsī, remissus, *to send back* (65A)

renovō, -āre, -āvī, -ātus, *to renew* (38)

reparō, -āre, -āvī, -ātus, *to restore, renew, make good* (55D)

repellō, repellere, reppulī, repulsus, *to drive off, drive back* (5, 40)

repudiō, -āre, -āvī, -ātus, *to reject, divorce* (56B)

requiēscō, requiēscere, requiēvī, requiētūrus, *to rest*

rēs, reī, f., *thing, event, matter, situation, affair* (19, 25)
  rēs gestae, *deeds, accomplishments* (63)
  rēs pūblica, *state, government*
  rē vērā, adv., *really, actually* (49, 59D)

resistō, resistere, restitī + dat., *to resist, stand up to* (42, 62)

respiciō, respicere, respexī, respectus, *to look back at* (58B)

respondeō, respondēre, respondī, respōnsūrus, *to answer, reply* (5, 21)

revertor, revertī, reversus sum, *to turn back, return* (58B)

rēx, rēgis, m., *king* (36)

Rhēnus, -ī, m., *the Rhine River* (57A)

rīpa, -ae, f., *river bank* (57B)

rīvus, -ī, m., *stream, river; channel of aqueduct* (5, 63D)

rogō, -āre, -āvī, -ātus, *to ask* (12, 51)

Rōma, -ae, f., *Rome* (7)

Rōmānus, -a, -um, *Roman* (1)

rōstrum, -ī, n., *beak* (of a ship); n. pl., *speaker's platform* (58C)

ruīna, -ae, f., *collapse, ruin, destruction* (38)

rūrsus, adv., *again* (36)

rūs, rūris, n., *country* (as opposed to city) (39, 58B)

S

sacerdōs, sacerdōtis, m., *priest* (63C)

sacrificium, -ī, n., *sacrifice* (63C)

saepe, adv., *often* (2, 13, 35)

salūs, salūtis, f., *good health, safety; greetings* (36)

salūtō, -āre, -āvī, -ātus, *to greet, welcome* (7)

sānctitās, sānctitātis, f., *purity, virtue*

sānctus, -a, -um, *hallowed, sacred, august* (64A)

sanguis, sanguinis, m., *blood* (33)

satis, adv., *enough* (23)

scelestus, -a, -um, *wicked* (10)

scelus, sceleris, n., *crime* (41)

scīlicet, adv., *obviously, of course, no doubt* (sometimes ironic) (57B)

sciō, scīre, scīvī, scītus, *to know* (16, 49)

scrībō, scrībere, scrīpsī, scrīptus, *to write* (1, 24)

sē, *himself, herself, itself, themselves* (11)

secundus, -a, -um, *second, next, following; favorable* (9, 38)

secus, adv., *otherwise, not so* (59C)

sed, conj., *but* (2)

sedeō, sedēre, sēdī, sessūrus, *to sit* (1, 21)

sēmis, sēmissis, m., *one-half*

semper, adv., *always* (4, 13)

senātor, senātōris, m., *senator* (7)

senātus, -ūs, m., *Senate* (25, 55B)

sententia, -ae, f., *feeling, opinion, motion* (63A)

sepeliō, sepelīre, sepelīvī, sepultus, *to bury* (39)

September, Septembris, Septembre, *September* (36)

septimus, -a, -um, *seventh* (13, 38, 68A)

septingentēsimus, -a, -um, *700th* (55D)

septuāgēsimus, -a, -um, *70th* (57A)

sequor, sequī, secūtus sum, *to follow* (36, 37)

servō, -āre, -āvī, -ātus, *to save, preserve, protect, keep, guard* (26, 30)

servus, -ī, m., *slave* (3)

sēstertius, -ī, gen. pl., **sēstertium,** *sesterce* (small silver coin, worth one-quarter of a denarius) (66B)

sex, *six* (15, 38)

sexāgintā, *sixty*

sextus, -a, -um, *sixth* (37, 38)

sī, conj., *if* (5, 67)

sīc, adv., *thus, in this way, so* (38, 39, 50)

sīcut, adv., *just as* (57B)

signum, -ī, n., *sign, signal, military standard or insignia* (27, 57B)

silentium, -ī, n., *silence* (15)

similis, -is, -e + dat., *similar (to), like* (34, 50)

simul, adv., *together, at the same time* (9, 13)

sīn (sī + nē), conj., *but if, on the other hand* (60A)

sine, prep. + abl., *without* (26)

sinister, sinistra, sinistrum, *left, on the left* (50)

socius, -ī, m., *companion, friend, ally* (55A)

sōlācium, -ī, n., *comfort, consolation, relief* (58B)

soleō, solēre, solitus sum + infin., *to be accustomed (to), be in the habit of* (10, 40)

sōlus, -a, -um, *alone* (3)
  sōlum, adv., *alone, only* (60A)

solvō, solvere, solvī, solūtus, *to release, untie; pay* (a debt) (54, 68D)

somnus, -ī, m., *sleep* (21)

soror, sorōris, f., *sister* (11)

spatium, -ī, n., *space, distance* (61B)

speciēs, -ēī, f., *appearance, kind, type* (65A)

spērō, -āre, -āvī, -ātus, *to hope* (47)

spīritus, -ūs, m., *breathing; spirit* (67A, 68D)

sponte, *of one's own accord, voluntarily* (61B, 63A)

statim, adv., *immediately* (5, 13)

statiō, statiōnis, f., *post, station, duty* (62A)

statua, -ae, f., *statue* (3)

stīpendium, -ī, n., *tax, tribute* (55A)

strangulō, -āre, -āvī, -ātus, *to strangle, choke*

stringō, stringere, strīnxī, strictus, *to draw* (a sword) (26)

studeō, studēre, studuī + dat., *to be eager, be enthusiastic, favor, support; to study* (39)

studium, -ī, n., *enthusiasm, zeal, support; study* (41)

stultitia, -ae, f., *foolishness*

suāvis, -is, -e, *sweet* (34, 60A)

sub, prep. + abl., *under, beneath, at the foot of* (1, 9)

subeō, subīre, subiī, subitus, irreg., *to go under, undergo, endure, occur* (58B)

subitō, adv., *suddenly* (3, 13)

succēdō, succēdere, successī, successūrus + dat., *to follow, succeed* (55B, 62A)

succurrō, succurrere, succurrī, succursūrus + dat., *to come to the aid of* (62)

sulpur, sulpuris, n., *sulphur* (68D)

sum, esse, fuī, futūrus, irreg., *to be* (1, 14, 20, 21)

summoveō, summovēre, summōvī, summōtus, *to drive off, remove* (57B)

summus, -a, -um, *greatest, very great; highest; the top of . . .* (35)

    ad summam, *on the whole; in short*

sūmō, sūmere, sūmpsī, sūmptus, *to take, take up* (22, 51)

super, prep. + acc., *over, above* (53, 63B)

superbus, -a, -um, *proud, arrogant* (48)

superior, superior, superius, gen., **superiōris,** *higher, previous, earlier* (59C)

superō, -āre, -āvī, -ātus, *to overcome, defeat* (42)

superstitiō, superstitiōnis, f., *superstition*

supersum, superesse, superfuī, irreg., *to be left, remain, survive*

supplicium, -ī, n., *punishment* (65A)

supplicō, -āre, -āvī, -ātus, *to worship* (65B)

suprā, prep. + acc., *above, over* (23)

suscipiō, suscipere, suscēpī, susceptus, *to undertake, support, receive under one's protection* (56A)

suspicor, -ārī, -ātus sum, *to suspect* (65C)

sustineō, sustinēre, sustinuī, sustentus, *to withstand, hold out* (62A)

sustulī, see **tollō**

suus, -a, -um, *his, her, one's, its, their (own)* (9, 27)

T

taberna, -ae, f., *shop, inn* (25)

tabernāculum, -ī, n., *tent* (62C)

taedet, taedēre, taesum est, *it bores, makes one* (acc.) *tired of something* (gen.) (16, 50, 52, 64)

tālis, -is, -e, *such, of this kind* (23, 50)

tamen, adv., *however, nevertheless* (6, 13)

tamquam, conj., *just as if, as* (33, 65A)

tangō, tangere, tetigī, tāctus, *to touch* (54)

tantus, -a, -um, *so great, such a big, so much* (24, 50)

    tantum adv., *only; so much, to such an extent* (15, 50)

tardus, -a, -um, *slow* (15)

    tardē, adv., *slowly*

tēlum, -ī, n., *weapon* (59C)

templum, -ī, n., *temple* (40)

tempus, temporis, n., *time* (2, 8, 12, 15)

tēctum, -ī, n., *roof;* pl., *house* (68C)

tenebrae, -ārum, f. pl., *darkness, shadows* (68C)

teneō, tenēre, tenuī, tentus, *to hold* (9, 25)

tergum, -ī, n., *back* (35)

terra, -ae, f., *earth, land* (26, 38)

tertius, -a, -um, *third* (25, 36, 38)

testāmentum, -ī, n., *will, testament* (IX, 55D)

testor, -ārī, -ātus sum, *to bear witness to, give evidence of* (63B)

theātrum, -ī, n., *theater* (63D)

timeō, -ēre, -uī, *to fear, be afraid* (5)

timor, timōris, m., *fear, anxiety* (35)

tollō, tollere, sustulī, sublātus, irreg., *to lift, raise, pick up* (48)

tormentum, -ī, n., *torment, torture* (65A)

tot, indecl. adj., *so many* (48)

tōtus, -a, -um, *all, the whole, the entire* (21)

trādō, trādere, trādidī, trāditus, *to hand over, surrender; pass on (information), report* (7, 22)

trādūcō, trādūcere, trādūxī, trāductus, *to lead across*

tranquillus, -a, -um, *tranquil, peaceful, calm* (64B)

trāns, prep. + acc., *across* (39)

trānseō, trānsīre, trānsiī, trānsitus, irreg., *to go across, go over; to desert* (56B)

trānsferō, trānsferre, trānstulī, trānslātus, irreg., *to carry over, carry across, transport* (63B)

trecentiēs, adv., *three hundred times* (66B)

tremor, tremōris, m., *tremor* (68C)

trepidāns, trepidantis, *in a panic, frightened* (52)

trēs, trēs, tria, *three* (13, 15, 38)

tribūnus, -ī, m., *tribune*

    tribūnus aerārius, *treasury official* (59E)

    tribūnus mīlitum, *one of six senior officers in a Roman legion* (62B)

tribuō, tribuere, tribuī, tribūtus, *to allot, grant* (63A)

tribus, -ūs, f., *tribe* (62)

triciēs, *30 times* (55A)

trīclīnium, -ī, n., *dining room* (31)

trīgintā, *thirty* (62C)

triumphālis, -is, -e, *of victory, triumphal*

triumphus, -ī, m., *victory parade* (56B)

tū, *you* (sing.) (4, 27)

tueor, tuērī, tuitus sum, *to watch over, guard* (62A)

tulī, see **ferō**

tum, adv., *at that moment, then* (4, 13)

tumultus, -ūs, m., *uproar, din, commotion* (25)

tunc, adv., *then, at that moment*

turbō, -āre, -āvī, -ātus, *to upset*

tūtus, -a, -um, *safe*
tuus, -a, -um, *your* (sing.) (9, 27)
tyrannicus, -a, -um, *pertaining to a tyrant, tyrannical* (55D)
tyrannus, -ī, m., *tyrant*

U

ubi, adv., conj., *where, when* (1, 5, 13)
ulcīscor, ulcīscī, ultus sum, *to take revenge on, punish* (63A)
ūllus, -a, -um, *any* (57A)
ultimus, -a, -um, *last, least, farthest* (36)
umquam, adv., *ever* (31)
ūnā, adv., *together, along with* (33, 68A)
unde . . . ?, adv., *from where . . . ?* (12)
ūndecimus, -a, -um, *eleventh* (17, 38)
ūndēvīgintī, *nineteen* (38, 63A)
unguentum, -ī, n., *ointment, oil, perfume* (34, 43)
unguō, unguere, ūnxī, ūnctus, *to anoint, smear (with oil)* (43)
ūniversus, -a, -um, *the whole of, the entire* (48, 55B)
ūnus, -a, -um, *one, single* (15, 38)
urbs, urbis, gen. pl., **urbium**, f., *city* (7)
urna, -ae, f., *pot, vessel, urn, vase* (64B)
usque ad + acc., *up to, as far as* (55A)
ūsus, -ūs, m., *use, need, requirement* (62C)
ut, conj. + indicative, *as, how, when; whether;* + subjunctive, *so that, that, in order to;* introducing clause of fearing, *that . . . not* (16, 50, 53, 54, 55, 60, 66)
uterque, utraque, utrumque, *each* (of two), *both* (45)
ūtor, ūtī, ūsus sum + abl., *to use, take advantage of* (60D, 61)
uxor, uxōris, f., *wife* (11)

V

vacuus, -a, -um, *empty* (55B)
vadum, -ī, n., *shallow water*
vagor, -ārī, -ātus sum, *to wander* (68C)
valdē, adv., *very, very much, exceedingly* (19)
valeō, valēre, valuī, valitūrus, *to be strong, be well, fare well* (40)
  valē / valēte, *goodbye* (9)
valētūdō, valētūdinis, f., *health, good health, sickness* (39)
vāllum, -ī, n., *rampart* (62B)

varius, -a, -um, *different, varied, diverse* (43, 53)
vastus, -a, -um, *huge, immense, vast*
vehementer, adv., *very much, violently, greatly* (19)
vehiculum, -ī, n., *vehicle* (13, 15)
vehō, vehere, vexī, vectus, *to carry, convey;* pass., *to ride* (54, 58A)
vel, conj., *or* (37)
vēlum, -ī, n., *sail* (66B)
vēndō, vēndere, vēndidī, vēnditus, *to sell* (28)
venēnum, -ī, n., *poison, venom* (56B)
venia, -ae, f., *pardon, forgiveness* (63C)
veniō, venīre, vēnī, ventūrus, *to come* (7, 20)
ventus, -ī, m., *wind* (42)
verbum, -ī, n., *word* (39)
vereor, -ērī, -itus sum, *to be afraid, fear* (37)
versor, -ārī, -ātus sum, *to stay, be situated* (62C)
vertō, vertere, vertī, versus, *to turn; to change* (16, 62A)
vērum, -ī, n., *truth*
vērus, -a, -um, *true, real* (40)
  vērō, adv., *truly, really, indeed* (31)
  vērum, adv., *truly* (67A)
vēscor, vēscī + abl., *to feed (on)* (49, 61)
vester, vestra, vestrum, *your* (pl.) (22, 27)
vestīmenta, -ōrum, n. pl., *clothes* (33)
Vesuvius, -ī, m., *Vesuvius* (volcano near the Bay of Naples)
vetō, vetāre, vetuī, vetitus, *to forbid, prohibit* (26)
vexō, -āre, -āvī, -ātus, *to annoy, bother* (4)
via, -ae, f., *road, way* (10)
victor, victōris, m., *conqueror, victor* (27)
victōria, -ae, f., *victory*
videō, vidēre, vīdī, vīsus, *to see* (4, 21, 49)
  videor, vidērī, vīsus sum, *to seem* (21)
  vidētur, idiom, *it seems (good), it seems (best)* (64)
vigilō, -āre, -āvī, -ātūrus, *to stay awake, be watchful* (19)
vīgintī, *twenty* (36, 38)
vīlla, -ae, f., *country house, estate* (1)
vincō, vincere, vīcī, victus, *to conquer, overcome, defeat* (27)
vindicō, -āre, -āvī, -ātus, *to claim as free, liberate; to avenge, get revenge for* (56A, 63A)
vīnum, -ī, n., *wine* (25)
vir, virī, m., *man* (3, 11)
virgō, virginis, f., *maiden, young girl* (45)
  Virgō Vestālis, *Vestal Virgin* (one of six priestesses of Vesta) (63, 67)
virtūs, virtūtis, f., *courage, determination, virtue* (60C)

vīs, acc., **vim**, abl., **vī**, f., *force, violence; amount;* pl. **vīrēs**, *strength, violence* (30, 61B)

vīsitō, -āre, -āvī, -ātus, *to visit* (23)

vīta, -ae, f., *life* (54)

vītō, -āre, -āvī, -ātus, *to avoid* (13)

vīvō, vīvere, vīxī, vīctūrus, *to live, be alive* (39)

vīvus, -a, -um, *alive, living* (58B)

volō, velle, voluī, irreg., *to wish, want* (5, 17, 20, 21)

voluntārius, -a, -um, *voluntary, willing* (61A)

voluntās, voluntātis, f., *will, willingness, consent* (55D)

voluptās, voluptātis, f., *pleasure, comfort* (62C)

vōs, *you* (pl.) (8, 27)

vulgus, -ī, n., *common people, mob, rabble* (58C)

vulnerō, -āre, -āvī, -ātus, *to wound* (33)

vulnus, vulneris, n., *wound* (35)

INDEX OF GRAMMAR

INDEX OF CULTURAL INFORMATION

Page numbers in **boldface** refer to illustrations.

▪▪▪▪▪ CREDITS ▪▪▪▪▪

The authors and publisher are grateful to the following for permission to reproduce photographs:

▪▪▪▪▪ TIMELINE ▪▪▪▪▪

ca. 1184 B.C.   The Fall of Troy and the Wanderings of Aeneas

THE REGAL PERIOD

753 B.C.   The Founding of Rome by Romulus

753–509 B.C.   The Kings of Rome
Romulus ▪ Numa Pompilius ▪ Tullus Hostilius ▪ Ancus Marcius ▪
Tarquinius Priscus ▪ Servius Tullius ▪ Tarquinius Superbus

THE REPUBLIC

509–264 B.C.   The Early Republic
Legendary Heroes of Early Rome
Horatius ▪ Mucius Scaevola ▪ Cloelia ▪ Cincinnatus
Invasion of the Gauls
War with Pyrrhus

264–241 B.C.   The First Punic War

218–201 B.C.   The Second Punic War

201–146 B.C.   Rome Becomes a World Leader
The Third Punic War

146–63 B.C.   Deadly Struggles within the Roman Republic
The Gracchi ▪ Gaius Marius ▪ Lucius Cornelius Sulla ▪ Gnaeus
Pompeius

63–44 B.C.   The Collapse of the Republic
Marcus Tullius Cicero ▪ Gaius Julius Caesar ▪ Mark Antony ▪
Cleopatra ▪ Octavian

THE EMPIRE

31 B.C. – A.D. 14   The Augustan Age

A.D. 14–180   The Early Empire

The Julio-Claudians: Tiberius ▪ Caligula ▪ Claudius ▪ Nero
The Flavians: Vespasian ▪ Titus **OUR STORY: A.D. 80–81** ▪ Domitian
The Five Good Emperors: Nerva ▪ Trajan ▪ Hadrian ▪ Antoninus Pius ▪
Marcus Aurelius

A.D. 211–476   The Late Empire
Caracalla ▪ Diocletian ▪ Constantine

A.D. 330   Founding of Constantinople

A.D. 403   Legiō XX defeats Alaric the Visigoth

A.D. 476   Romulus Augustulus, last of the Roman emperors, overthrown by
Odoacer the German